D1460346

IN THE NAME OF

ALLAH

THE ALL-COMPASSIONATE, ALL-MERCIFUL

The True Secret

- Title: The True Secret
- Author: Dr. Amira Ayad
- English Edition 1 (2011)
- Layout Design: IIPH, Riyadh, Saudi Arabia
- Filming and Cover Design: Samo Press Group

The True Secret

السّر الحقيقي

Dr. Amira Ayad

الدار العالمية للكتاب الإسلامي

INTERNATIONAL ISLAMIC PUBLISHING HOUSE

King Fahd National Library Cataloging-in-Publication Data

Ayad, Amira

The True Secret / Amira Ayad .- Riyadh, 2011

304 p ; 21 cm

ISBN Hardcover: 978-603-501-107-5

1- Islam and self-improvement I- Title

214.61 dc 1432/5703

Legal Deposit no. **1432/5703**
ISBN Hardcover: **978-603-501-107-5**

International Islamic Publishing House (IIPH)
P.O. Box 55195 Riyadh 11534, Saudi Arabia
Tel: 966 1 4650818 / 4647213 — Fax: 966 1 4633489
E-mail: iiph@iiph.com.sa — iiphsa@gmail.com
www.iiph.com.sa

﴿رَبَّنَا لَا تُؤَاخِذْنَآ إِن نَّسِينَآ أَوْ أَخْطَأْنَاۚ ﴿٢٨٦﴾﴾

[البَقَرَة: ٢٨٦]

﴿O Allah! Do not condemn us if we forget or fall into error.﴾ *(Qur'an 2: 286)*

Contents

To my True Secret teachers:
my dearest grandmother,
my mother, my husband
& my friend Hala

Arabic honorific symbols used in this book

(سبحانه وتعالى): *Subḥânahu wa ta'âlâ — 'The Exalted'*

(صلى الله عليه وسلم): *Ṣalla-Allâhu 'alayhi wa sallam — 'Blessings and peace be upon him'*

(عليه السلام): *'Alayhis-salâm — 'Peace be upon him'*

(رضي الله عنه): *Raḍiya Allâhu 'anhu — 'May Allah be pleased with him'*

(رضي الله عنها): *Raḍiya Allâhu 'anhâ — 'May Allah be pleased with her'*

Pronunciation and Transliteration Chart

Arabic script	Pronunciation	Transliterated as:
أ	short ‘a’, as in *cat*	a
آ – ى	longer ‘a’, as in *cab (not as in cake)*	â
ب	/b/ as in *bell, rubber and tab*	b
ت	/t/ as in *tap, mustard and sit*	t
ة	takes the sound of the preceding diactrical mark sometimes ending in h (when in pausal form): ah, ih, or ooh; or atu(n), ati(n) or ata(n) when in uninterrupted speech	h or t (when followed by another Arabic word)
ث	/th/ as in *thing, maths and wealth*	th
ج	/j/ as in *jam, ajar and age*	j
ح	a ‘harsher’ sound than the English initial /h/, and may occur medially and in word-final position as well	ḥ
خ	as in *Bach (in German); may occur initially and medially as well*	kh
د	/d/ as in *do, muddy and red*	d
ذ	as in *this, father, and with*	dh
ر	/r/ as in *raw, art and war; may also be a rolled r, as with Spanish words*	r

Arabic script	Pronunciation	Transliterated as:
ز	/z/ as in *zoo, easy and gaze*	z
س	/s/ as in *so, messy and grass*	s
ش	as in *ship, ashes and rush*	sh
ص	no close equivalent in English, but mạy be approximated by pronouncing it as /sw/ or /s/ farther back in the mouth	ṣ
ض	no close equivalent in English, but may be approximated by pronouncing /d/ farther back in the mouth	ḍ
ط	no close equivalent in English, but may be approximated by pronouncing /t/ farther back in the mouth	ṭ
ظ	no close equivalent in English, but may be approximated by pronouncing 'the' farther back in the mouth	<u>dh</u>
ع	no close equivalent in English: a guttural sound in the back of the throat	'
غ	no close equivalent in English, but may be closely approximated by pronouncing it like the French /r/ in 'rouge'	gh
ف	/f/ as in *fill, effort and muff*	f

Arabic script	Pronunciation	Transliterated as:
ق	no close equivalent in English, but may be approximated by pronouncing /k/ farther back in the mouth	q
ك	/k/ as in *king, buckle and tack*	k
ل	/l/ as in *lap, halo; in the word Allah, it becomes velarized as in ball*	l
م	/m/ as in *men, simple and ram*	m
ن	/n/ as in *net, ant and can*	n
هـ – ه – ـه	/h/ as in hat; unlike /h/ in English, in Arabic /h/ is pronounced in medial and word-final positions as well	h
و	as in *wet and away*	w
و (as a vowel)	long u, as in *boot and too*	oo
ي	as in *yet and yard*	y
ي (as a vowel)	long e, as in *eat, beef and see*	ee
ء	glottal stop: may be closely approximated by pronouncing it like 't' in the Cockney English pronunciation of *butter: bu'er, or the stop sound in uh — oh!*	' (Omitted in initial position)

Diphthongs:

Arabic script	Pronunciation	Transliterated as:
أَو ، و	Long o, as in *owe, boat and go*	au, aw, ow
أَي ، يَ	Long 'a', as in *able, rain and say*	ay, ai, ei

Diacritical marks (*tashkeel*):

Name of mark	Pronunciation	Transliterated as:
َ fatḥah	very short 'a' or schwa (unstressed vowel)	a
ِ kasrah	shorter version of ee or schwa (unstressed vowel)	i
ُ Dammah	shorter version of oo	u
ّ shaddah	a doubled consonant is stressed in the word, and the length of the sound is also doubled	Double letter
ْ sukoon	no vowel sound between consonants or at the end of a word	Absence of vowel

About the word 'Lord'

The word *lord* in English has several related meanings. The original meaning is 'master' or 'ruler', and in this sense it is often used to refer to human beings: 'the lord of the mansion' or 'Lord So-and-So' (in the United Kingdom, for example). The word *Lord* with a capital L is used in the lexicon of Islam to refer to the One and Only God — Allah. In Islam, there is no ambiguity about the meaning of this word. While it is true that one may occasionally use the word *lord* (whether capitalized or not) to refer to a human being, in Islamic discourse the reference of this term is always clear from the context.

The Editor

Publisher's Note

All praise and thanks belong to Allah alone, the One, the Almighty and All-Merciful. Blessings and peace be upon Prophet Muhammad, the last of His Messengers and Prophets, and upon his family, his Companions and all those who follow in his footsteps until the end of time.

As Muslims, we know that our purpose in life is to worship Allah and that our goal is to reach paradise. However, when we find ourselves busy with work, family and various other responsibilities and activities, it is easy to lose sight of what is really important.

In *The True Secret*, Dr. Ayad explains what she considers to be the key to happiness and success. She offers practical steps for evaluating our current situation, identifying improvements we should make, setting goals, planning, organizing our time, and implementing and monitoring changes. As we strive to do the best we can, we also gain peace of mind by accepting that whatever happens to us is by the will of Allah, and that He is All-Powerful and All-Knowing.

We hope that the suggestions in this book will enable the reader to clearly assess his or her lifestyle and then use the guidelines given here to steadily improve his or her position, both in this life and in the hereafter.

May Allah accept the efforts of all those who contributed to the production of this book, and may it be acceptable to Him, *âmeen.*

Muhammad Abdul Mohsin Al-Tuwaijri
Managing Director
International Islamic Publishing House
Riyadh, Saudi Arabia

The True Secret

Happiness, health and peace of mind: those are the basic hopes and ultimate endeavours of every human being. Naturally, we are in continuous pursuit of happiness, health and peace of mind, but unfortunately for many of us, life often seems a constant struggle. Meanwhile, people tend to be in an unremitting quest for material possessions, making that the focus of their lives, while health and happiness seem ever elusive.

When a certain idea is repeated frequently enough, it gradually becomes engraved in our minds. Whether this idea is true or false, if we allow it, it soon takes root in our beliefs and becomes a mindset, or part of what we think of as 'common sense'. Through the media, school curricula and workplaces, all day long we are fed a diet of the 'virtues' of consumerism. The value of a human being has been reduced to what he or she owns — money, car, house, fame, position — or even worse, to the way he or she looks; a man should be handsome and attractive, while a woman should be beautiful, with a nice, slim figure.

Blindly copying the opinions, customs and manners of others can be very dangerous. It can cause us to hold false beliefs and to submit to erroneous modes of thinking. For us as Muslims, besides striving for success in this world, we also seek the eternal happiness and bliss of paradise:

﴿وَمِنْهُم مَّن يَقُولُ رَبَّنَآ ءَاتِنَا فِى ٱلدُّنْيَا حَسَنَةً وَفِى ٱلْءَاخِرَةِ حَسَنَةً وَقِنَا عَذَابَ ٱلنَّارِ ﴿٢٠١﴾﴾ [البقرة: ٢٠١]

﴾And of them there are some who say: Our Lord, give us in this world that which is good and in the hereafter that which is good, and save us from the torment of the fire!﴿[1]

(Qur'an 2: 201)

The question is: How can we reach worldly success along with eternal satisfaction? What is our own Islamic way, the 'True Secret' to temporal as well as everlasting happiness?

Before revealing the 'True Secret', let me tell you about something that happened to me a few years ago. In a local newspaper, I read an article written by a middle class employee who had barely been earning his living. At the beginning of his story, he had no money to marry and start a family. Years passed, and he lost all hope of making his dream of a family life become a reality.

One day, returning home from work, he passed by an orphanage. Seeing the poor orphans, he thought about how fortunate he was compared to those little ones. He suddenly felt grateful for his situation and decided to help those children. "*I*

---

[1] The translations of the meanings of the verses of the Qur'an have been adapted from Dr. Muhammad Muhsin Khan and Dr. Muhammad Taqi-ud-Din Al-Hilali, *Interpretation of the Meaning of The Noble Quran,* Dar-us-Salam Publications; A. Yusuf Ali, *The Meaning of the Holy Qur'an* (revised edition), Amana Publications; and Saḥeeḥ International Translations, *The Qur'an: Arabic Text with Corresponding English Meanings*, Abul Qasim Publishing House.

cannot afford to build a home in this life, so let me seek one in paradise, inshallah (God willing)," he thought. Acting with total faith, altruism and dedication, the man started setting aside five percent of his monthly salary to help the orphans. His life went on as usual, and he did not regret his decision for a single moment, even though he occasionally became penniless before the end of the month.

Sometime later, a job opened up in his company's branch in one of the Arab Gulf countries. Usually an opportunity like this was only available to someone with connections or was given as a way of showing favouritism, but to his surprise, his boss nominated him for the post, and he got the job. His life changed completely, as he reported in his story in the newspaper. He is now happily married, living in a nice, big house, and earning a decent living. Most importantly, he added, he never forgot to deduct the five percent of his salary to give to the little children in the orphanage.

I was so very touched by this tale of total faith, altruism and honesty that I suggested that my husband and I do as the man did. "*We should deduct part of our salary to give to the less fortunate,*" I said excitedly. My husband's reaction was an eye-opener. He said: "*If you think this is a magic prescription for wealth, then you have the wrong intention. If you want to do it, you should do it only to seek the pleasure of Allah.*"

His words made me reconsider my motives for a moment, and then I responded that I really was seeking the pleasure of Allah (*Subḥânahu wa Ta'âlâ* — Glorified and Exalted is He). I thought that I already had so many blessings for which I was truly grateful, and I wanted to help others as a sign of gratitude. Clarifying my intention helped me to honestly mean it. So my husband and I participated in an orphanage construction project, giving part of our monthly earnings to help the orphans. We went on with our daily lives, not forgetting to pay our share every month.

Two years went by, and my husband was offered a job in another country. We were packing up when I found a folded piece of paper that I had kept in one of my drawers. It was the article I read two years back. Only when I saw it did I start to reflect on my life, and I realized how dramatically it had changed within those past two years. We had our own house instead of an apartment; my old, difficult to start car had been replaced by a brand new one with automatic transmission; and we could now afford an expensive international education for our children. *Subḥân Allâh* (All glory be to God)! It was truly an unexplainable phenomenon, a divine prescription that asked only for pure faith and honest intention!

Our Prophet (*ṣalla Allâhu 'alayhi wa sallam* — blessings and peace be upon him) used a very touching story to teach us the same concept, to assist us in the difficult situations we face. He (ﷺ) said: «Three men, from among those who were before you, set out together until they reached a cave by night and entered it. A big rock rolled down the mountain and closed the mouth of the cave. They said to each other: Nothing can save us from this rock except invoking Allah (ﷻ) by mentioning the righteous deeds that we have done for the sake of Allah (ﷻ) only.

One of them said: O Allah! I had old parents to whom I used to provide milk, and I never gave that milk to my wife and children until I had offered it to my parents first. One day, I happened to be delayed and I came home late at night. I milked the sheep and took the milk to my parents, but I found them sleeping. I disliked offering it to my family before them, so I waited for them with the bowl of milk in my hands, and I kept on waiting for them to get up until it was dawn; then they got up and drank the milk. O

Allah! If I did that for Your sake only, I invoke You to relieve us from our critical situation caused by this rock. The rock moved a little, but they still could not get out.

The second man said: O Allah! I had a cousin who was the dearest of all people to me, and I wanted to have sexual intercourse with her, but she refused. Later, she had a hard time in a year of famine, and she came to me. I gave her one hundred and twenty dinars on the condition that she would not resist my desire, and she agreed. When I was about to fulfil my desire, she said: It is illegal for you to violate my chastity except through legitimate marriage. So I recognized that indeed it was a sin to have sexual intercourse with her. I left her, although she was the dearest of all people to me, and I left her the gold I had given her. O Allah! If I did that for Your sake only, please relieve us from this present calamity. The rock moved a little more, but still they could not get out.

The third man said: O Allah! I employed a few labourers, and I paid all of them their wages, with the exception of one man who had gone away before taking his money. I invested his wages, and through that investment I greatly increased my property. After some time, he came and said to me: O servant of Allah, pay me the money you owe me. I said: All the camels, cows, sheep and slaves you see are yours. He said: O servant of Allah, do not mock me. I said: I am not mocking you. He took the herd and drove them away, leaving nothing. O Allah! If I did that for Your sake only, please relieve us from our present suffering. The rock moved completely, and they walked out of the cave.» (Bukhari)

Did you realize what the 'True Secret' to success is? It is **sincerity** to Allah (ﷻ)![2]

---

2 Please note here that this is a personal opinion based on my own practical experience. There is no one lesson in Islamic teachings that you can regard=

Allah (ﷻ) says:

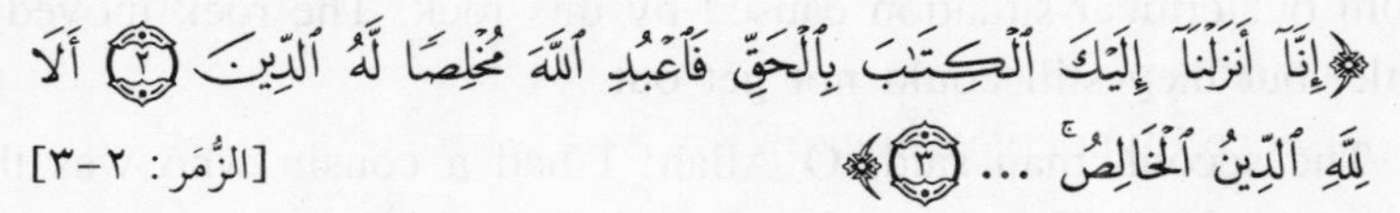

﴿Verily, We have sent down the Book to you [O Muhammad] in truth, so worship Allah [alone] by doing religious deeds sincerely for Allah's sake only. Surely, the religion [the worship and the obedience] is for Allah only.﴾ *(Qur'an 39: 2-3)*

The previous stories clearly showed how acting out of pure intention and sincere devotion to Allah (ﷻ) can totally change one's life. Allah (ﷻ) saved the three men in the cave because of a sincere deed that each of them had once performed. Their sincerity was the key to their salvation. Allah (ﷻ) grants assistance, comfort, guidance and support according to a person's level of sincerity.[3] Pure hearts, righteous intentions and true faith are always rewarded by Allah (ﷻ).

Sincerity is the essence of our faith. Sincerity is our complete wholesome way of living. It is the rule upon which all our life is built, the truth that should be settled in our hearts and souls and reflected in each and every deed we perform, be it a worldly matter or an act of worship.

The fruits of sincerity are not restricted to the hereafter, since a person's sincerity affects his or her current life as well as the life

---

=solely as the True Secret while ignoring the others. Your True Secret could be any number of things: God-consciousness, faith, the love of Allah, remembrance of Allah, a clear and vivid awareness of the hereafter, contentment, surrender to the divine will, and so on. In the end, these are all tightly interconnected, as we will see in the course of this book, leading to one and only one truth: true love and devotion to Allah and following His straight path.

[3] Al-Qaraḍâwi, *Intention and Sincerity*

after death. Sincerity and integrity are required to straighten out worldly matters. Sincerity is a prerequisite for justice to prevail and for corruption to end. Life decays without sincerity because in its absence, hypocrisy, materialism and selfishness will flourish.[4]

Sincerity is a result of true faith and submissiveness to Allah (ﷻ), and this is so clear in the first chapter of Qur'an:[5]

﴿إِيَّاكَ نَعْبُدُ وَإِيَّاكَ نَسْتَعِينُ ۝٥﴾ [الفَاتِحَة : ٥]

﴿You [Allah, alone] we worship, and You [alone] we ask for help [for each and every thing].﴾ *(Qur'an 1: 5)*

We are ordered to repeat this chapter at least seventeen times each day in our five obligatory prayers.

Your sincerity is between you and Allah (ﷻ). No one else can see it, and no one can check it. It is not a mere word that you utter with your tongue; it is a deep feeling rooted inside your heart. Just like a seed that has to be buried before it can grow and flourish, sincerity has to be kept deep within your heart, unseen by others. This is your own seed that you should care for and water daily with love, devotion, prayers, supplication and detachment from worldly attractions and material possessions. Allah (ﷻ) says:

﴿قُلْ إِنِّيٓ أُمِرْتُ أَنْ أَعْبُدَ ٱللَّهَ مُخْلِصًا لَّهُ ٱلدِّينَ ۝١١﴾ [الزُّمَر : ١١]

﴿Say [O Muhammad]: Verily, I am commanded to worship Allah [alone] by obeying Him and doing religious deeds sincerely for Allah's sake only.﴾ *(Qur'an 39: 11)*

Being able to be sincere and devoted to Allah (ﷻ), the One and Only God, is in itself a blessing that we must be grateful for:

---

4 Ibid.

5 Ibid.

﴿ضَرَبَ ٱللَّهُ مَثَلًا رَّجُلًا فِيهِ شُرَكَآءُ مُتَشَٰكِسُونَ وَرَجُلًا سَلَمًا لِّرَجُلٍ هَلۡ يَسۡتَوِيَانِ مَثَلًاۚ ٱلۡحَمۡدُ لِلَّهِۚ بَلۡ أَكۡثَرُهُمۡ لَا يَعۡلَمُونَ ﴿٢٩﴾﴾ [الزُّمَر: ٢٩]

﴿Allah puts forth the parable: a slave belonging to many partners disputing with one another and a slave belonging entirely to one master. Are those two equal in comparison? All praise and thanks be to Allah! But most of them know not.﴾ *(Qur'an 39: 29)*

Worshipping one God, Allah (ﷻ), adds a sense of relief and stability to our lives. Being devoted to one way of living, one perfectly ordered system for sustenance and support, gives us strength and reliability.[6] Allah (ﷻ) says:

﴿أَلَيۡسَ ٱللَّهُ بِكَافٍ عَبۡدَهُۥۖ وَيُخَوِّفُونَكَ بِٱلَّذِينَ مِن دُونِهِۦۚ وَمَن يُضۡلِلِ ٱللَّهُ فَمَا لَهُۥ مِنۡ هَادٍ ﴿٣٦﴾ وَمَن يَهۡدِ ٱللَّهُ فَمَا لَهُۥ مِن مُّضِلٍّۗ ... ﴿٣٧﴾﴾ [الزُّمَر: ٣٦-٣٧]

﴿Is not Allah Sufficient for His slave? Yet they try to frighten you with those [whom they worship] besides Him! And whomever Allah sends astray, for him there will be no guide. And whomever Allah guides, for him there will be no one to mislead him.﴾ *(Qur'an 39: 36-37)*

Sincerity to our One and Only God gives us tranquillity, peace of mind, reassurance, confidence and security. Allah (ﷻ) gives us a firm and decisive declaration:

﴿قُلۡ حَسۡبِيَ ٱللَّهُۖ عَلَيۡهِ يَتَوَكَّلُ ٱلۡمُتَوَكِّلُونَ ﴿٣٨﴾﴾ [الزُّمَر: ٣٨]

﴿Say: Sufficient for me is Allah; in Him those [believers] who trust must put their trust.﴾ *(Qur'an 39: 38)*

---

6 Quṭb

There is a chapter in the Qur'an called *al-Ikhlâṣ* (Sincerity):

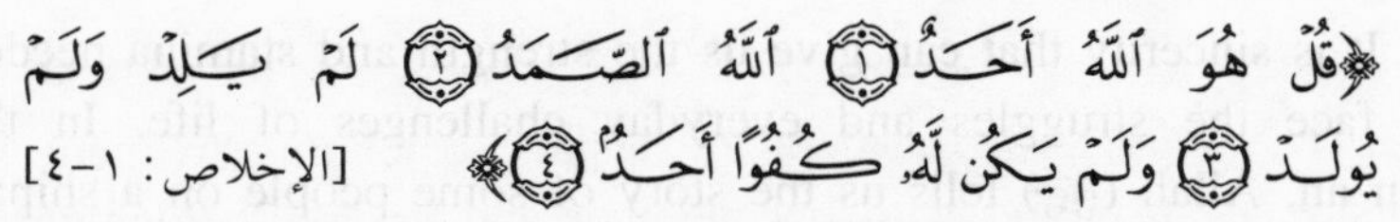

﴾Say [O Muhammad]: He is Allah, the One, the *Samad* [the Self-Sufficient Master, Whom all creatures need, and Who Himself is in need of nothing]. He begets not, nor was He begotten; and there is none co-equal or comparable unto Him.﴿ *(Qur'an 112: 1-4)*

This chapter is equivalent to one-third of the Qur'an, according to the following *hadith*, which is a statement or action of Prophet Muhammad (ﷺ) that was remembered and recorded by his Companions and followers: «By the One in Whose Hand is my soul, it [the Qur'anic chapter *al-Ikhlâṣ*] is equivalent to a third of the Qur'an.» (Bukhari)

There is no wonder that this chapter has such weight and importance, since it holds the meaning of existence and the key to the only truly successful way of living.[7]

- Try to think of a deed that you performed sincerely, only for the sake of Allah (ﷻ).
- You can always ask for Allah's help directly or through your sincere deeds. Never ask through prophets, saints, righteous people or angels, as this idolatry is a major sin that is contrary to the belief in Allah (ﷻ) as the One and Only God.

---

[7] Quṭb

Sincerity, a behaviour for all times

It is sincerity that can give us the strength and stamina needed to face the struggles and everyday challenges of life. In the Qur'an, Allah (سبحانه وتعالى) tells us the story of some people on a ship:

﴿هُوَ ٱلَّذِى يُسَيِّرُكُمْ فِى ٱلْبَرِّ وَٱلْبَحْرِ حَتَّىٰٓ إِذَا كُنتُمْ فِى ٱلْفُلْكِ وَجَرَيْنَ بِهِم
بِرِيحٍ طَيِّبَةٍ وَفَرِحُوا۟ بِهَا جَآءَتْهَا رِيحٌ عَاصِفٌ وَجَآءَهُمُ ٱلْمَوْجُ مِن كُلِّ مَكَانٍ
وَظَنُّوٓا۟ أَنَّهُمْ أُحِيطَ بِهِمْ دَعَوُا۟ ٱللَّهَ مُخْلِصِينَ لَهُ ٱلدِّينَ لَئِنْ أَنجَيْتَنَا مِنْ هَـٰذِهِۦ
لَنَكُونَنَّ مِنَ ٱلشَّـٰكِرِينَ ﴿٢٢﴾ فَلَمَّآ أَنجَىٰهُمْ إِذَا هُمْ يَبْغُونَ فِى ٱلْأَرْضِ بِغَيْرِ
ٱلْحَقِّ يَـٰٓأَيُّهَا ٱلنَّاسُ إِنَّمَا بَغْيُكُمْ عَلَىٰٓ أَنفُسِكُم مَّتَـٰعَ ٱلْحَيَوٰةِ ٱلدُّنْيَا ثُمَّ إِلَيْنَا
مَرْجِعُكُمْ فَنُنَبِّئُكُم بِمَا كُنتُمْ تَعْمَلُونَ ﴿٢٣﴾﴾ [يونس: ٢٢-٢٣]

﴿He [Allah] it is Who enables you to travel through land and sea, until when you are in the ships and they sail on with them with a favourable wind, and they are glad therein, then comes a stormy wind, and the waves come to them from all sides, and they think that they are encircled. They invoke Allah, making their faith pure for Him alone, saying: If You [Allah] deliver us from this, we shall truly be of the grateful. But when He delivers them, behold! They rebel [and disobey Allah] in the earth wrongfully. O humankind! Your rebellion [and disobedience to Allah] is only against your own selves — a brief enjoyment of this worldly life, then [in the end] unto Us is your return, and We shall inform you of that which you used to do.﴾ *(Qur'an 10: 22-23)*

Allah (سبحانه وتعالى) saved them from their ordeal when they supplicated to Him sincerely. At that moment of hardship, they reached their basic instinct, the natural inclination of humans that is instilled by Allah (سبحانه وتعالى). They felt the real need for Allah's help, the need for His might as well as His mercy. However, we should act with true sincerity at all times, making it our way of life in times of happiness as well as in calamities, in health and in sickness, in prosperity and in poverty. Do we remember to be sincere in difficult situations? Do we remember to be sincere during times of ease? Allah (ﷻ) describes human beings, saying:

﴿لَّا يَسْـَٔمُ ٱلْإِنسَـٰنُ مِن دُعَآءِ ٱلْخَيْرِ وَإِن مَّسَّهُ ٱلشَّرُّ فَيَـُٔوسٌ قَنُوطٌ ﴿٤٩﴾﴾

[فُصِّلَت: ٤٩]

﴿Man does not get tired of asking for good things, but if an evil touches him, then he gives up all hope and is lost in despair.﴾
(Qur'an 41: 49)

﴿وَإِذَآ أَنْعَمْنَا عَلَى ٱلْإِنسَـٰنِ أَعْرَضَ وَنَـَٔا بِجَانِبِهِۦ وَإِذَا مَسَّهُ ٱلشَّرُّ فَذُو دُعَآءٍ عَرِيضٍ ﴿٥١﴾﴾

[فُصِّلَت: ٥١]

﴿And when We show favour to man, he withdraws and turns away, but when evil touches him, then he has recourse to long supplications.﴾ *(Qur'an 41: 51)*

The Panic Button

In his book *Deep Healing*, Emmett Miller relates an experiment performed at NASA (the U.S. National Aeronautics and Space Administration). One of the training procedures that each astronaut had to go through before being considered qualified for space travel was a difficult simulation experiment in which he or she was put in a situation resembling an actual burning spaceship. The trainee had to be capable of handling this emergency situation and getting everything under control in the shortest time possible.

During the experiment, various biological parameters of the astronauts (such as blood pressure, heart rate and pulse) were measured to determine their levels of stress. The astronauts were divided into two groups, only one of which was given a 'panic button'. Pushing this button would immediately end the experiment.

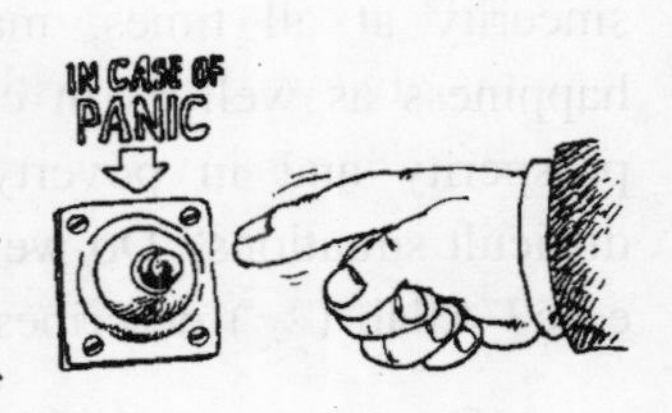

At the end of the experiment, it was found that the group who had the panic button had shown much lower levels of stress, as indicated by the measured biological parameters. Not only that, but their level of performance was much better than the group who had no way out of the experiment — even though none of them actually used the panic button.

Just knowing that there is a way out, that there is a satisfactory end for our seemingly unbearable situation, can help us control our reactions, keep our state of calmness, and even normalize our biological functions.

In real life, do you have a panic button — a way out of your distress and misery?

You sure do! We all possess a built-in panic button. It is our **sincere faith**, our deep belief in Allah (ﷻ), our certainty that our Creator is All-Powerful and All-Wise.

Allah (ﷻ) describes the pious and righteous believers as:

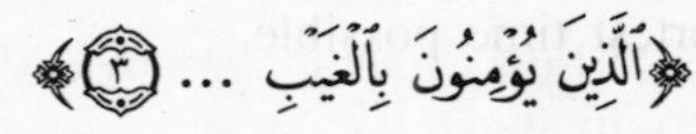

﴿الَّذِينَ يُؤْمِنُونَ بِالْغَيْبِ ... ﴿٣﴾﴾ [البَقَرَة: ٣]

﴿those who believe in the unseen...﴾ *(Qur'an 2: 3)*

They are those who believe deep inside their hearts that Allah (ﷻ) is always there for them. They believe that whatever calamity befalls them has some benefit and is a blessing in disguise:

﴿مَآ أَصَابَ مِن مُّصِيبَةٍ فِى ٱلْأَرْضِ وَلَا فِىٓ أَنفُسِكُمْ إِلَّا فِى كِتَـٰبٍ مِّن قَبْلِ أَن نَّبْرَأَهَآ ۚ إِنَّ ذَٰلِكَ عَلَى ٱللَّهِ يَسِيرٌ ﴿٢٢﴾ لِّكَيْلَا تَأْسَوْا۟ عَلَىٰ مَا فَاتَكُمْ وَلَا تَفْرَحُوا۟ بِمَآ ءَاتَىٰكُمْ ۗ وَٱللَّهُ لَا يُحِبُّ كُلَّ مُخْتَالٍ فَخُورٍ ﴿٢٣﴾﴾

[الحديد: ٢٢-٢٣]

﴿No calamity befalls on the earth or in yourselves but is inscribed in the Book of Decrees before We bring it into existence. Verily, that is easy for Allah, in order that you may not be sad over matters that you fail to get, nor rejoice because of that which has been given to you; and Allah likes not prideful boasters.﴾ *(Qur'an 57: 22-23)*

Allah the Almighty also says:

﴿إِنَّ ٱلَّذِينَ قَالُوا۟ رَبُّنَا ٱللَّهُ ثُمَّ ٱسْتَقَـٰمُوا۟ تَتَنَزَّلُ عَلَيْهِمُ ٱلْمَلَـٰٓئِكَةُ أَلَّا تَخَافُوا۟ وَلَا تَحْزَنُوا۟ وَأَبْشِرُوا۟ بِٱلْجَنَّةِ ٱلَّتِى كُنتُمْ تُوعَدُونَ ﴿٣٠﴾ نَحْنُ أَوْلِيَآؤُكُمْ فِى ٱلْحَيَوٰةِ ٱلدُّنْيَا وَفِى ٱلْـَٔاخِرَةِ ۖ وَلَكُمْ فِيهَا مَا تَشْتَهِىٓ أَنفُسُكُمْ وَلَكُمْ فِيهَا مَا تَدَّعُونَ ﴿٣١﴾﴾

[فصّلت: ٣٠-٣١]

﴿Verily, those who say: Our Lord is Allah [alone], and then they stand firm and remain steadfast, on them the angels will descend [at the time of their deaths, saying]: Fear not, nor grieve! But receive the glad tidings of paradise which you have been promised! We have been your friends in the life of this world and are so in the hereafter. Therein you shall have [all] that your inner-selves desire, and therein you shall have [all] that you ask.﴾ *(Qur'an 41: 30-31)*

The Struggle

Today, many practicing Muslims live uncomfortably with a struggle between their religious and spiritual practices on one side, and their professional and social lives on the other. They end up choosing one over the other or leading a parallel existence that ruptures their inner peace and creates a continuously stressful internal conflict, a kind of separation that we especially feel when living in a mixed society with different nationalities, religions and traditions. For example, when we try to learn foreign languages, we find that they come with foreign customs. Some are compatible with our beliefs as Muslims, while some are in conflict with those beliefs; others are just confusing.

The best way to determine the right from the wrong, the true from the false, is to always remember the purpose of our creation:

﴿وَمَا خَلَقْتُ ٱلْجِنَّ وَٱلْإِنسَ إِلَّا لِيَعْبُدُونِ ﴿٥٦﴾﴾ [الذاريات: ٥٦]

﴾And I [Allah] created the jinns and humans only so they could worship Me [alone].﴿ *(Qur'an 51: 56)*

This means that the aim of developing the earth's resources and the intention of hard work and positive actions is the worship of Allah. We should seek approval only from Allah (ﷻ). We should always supplicate for His guidance and praise Him (ﷻ) for His blessings. This is the ultimate reference by which we should measure all of our acts and knowledge and determine which to adopt and which to abandon. First, though, we must know the true meaning of worship.

The role of the human being goes far beyond just religious rituals. The true meaning of worship includes two primary elements:[8]

1. The feeling that we are servants of Allah (ﷻ) should be deeply rooted in our hearts. The knowledge that He is our One and Only Creator, and we are His creations, is the absolute truth.

2. We should devote all of our movements and actions, our conscious and subconscious awareness, and our whole lives only to Him. We should avoid associating any worldly idols with Him.

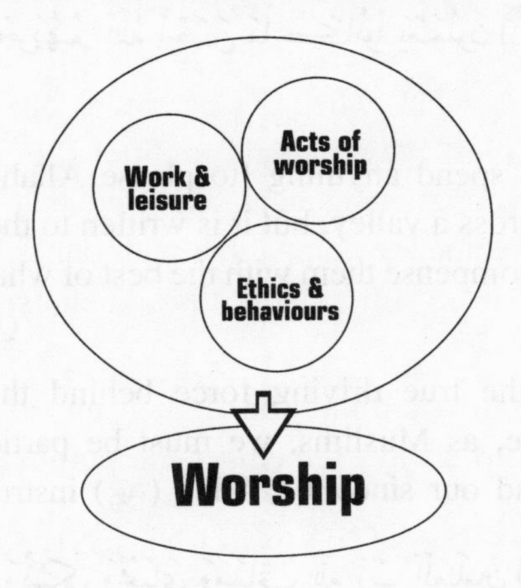

With this meaning engraved in our minds, we can turn any worldly action into an act of worship. With faithful intentions and sincere devotion to Allah (ﷻ), even exercising, working, cooking, playing or any other daily routine can be turned into an act of worship. The intention is the factor that gives true meaning to life and to work; it is what transforms a mere mechanical ritual into true spiritual enlightenment.[9] 'Umar ibn al-Khaṭṭâb (رضي الله عنه) narrated:

---

8 Quṭb

9 Ulwan

«I heard Allah's Messenger (ﷺ) say: The reward of deeds depends upon the intentions, and every person will get the reward according to what he (or she) has intended.» (Bukhari)

The Prophet (ﷺ) also said: «If a man spends on his family sincerely for Allah's sake, then it is a kind of alms-giving in reward for him.» (Bukhari)

Allah (ﷻ) says:

﴿وَلَا يُنفِقُونَ نَفَقَةً صَغِيرَةً وَلَا كَبِيرَةً وَلَا يَقْطَعُونَ وَادِيًا إِلَّا كُتِبَ لَهُمْ لِيَجْزِيَهُمُ ٱللَّهُ أَحْسَنَ مَا كَانُوا۟ يَعْمَلُونَ ﴿١٢١﴾﴾

[التوبة: ١٢١]

﴾Nor do they spend anything [to please Allah] — small or great — nor cross a valley, but it is written to their credit, that Allah may recompense them with the best of what they used to do.﴿ *(Qur'an 9: 121)*

Intention is the true driving force behind the action of any person. Therefore, as Muslims, we must be particularly aware of our intentions and our sincerity. Allah (ﷻ) instructs us, saying:

﴿قُلْ إِنَّ صَلَاتِى وَنُسُكِى وَمَحْيَاىَ وَمَمَاتِى لِلَّهِ رَبِّ ٱلْعَٰلَمِينَ ﴿١٦٢﴾ لَا شَرِيكَ لَهُۥ وَبِذَٰلِكَ أُمِرْتُ وَأَنَا۠ أَوَّلُ ٱلْمُسْلِمِينَ ﴿١٦٣﴾﴾ [الأنعام: ١٦٢-١٦٣]

﴾Say [O Muhammad]: Verily, my prayers, my sacrifice, my living, and my dying are for Allah, the Lord of the worlds [humankind, jinns and all that exists]. He has no partner. This I have been commanded, and I am the first of the Muslims [to submit my life unto Him].﴿ *(Qur'an 6: 162-163)*

With our True Secret, the signpost that illuminates our steps along the way, we can constantly adjust our intentions so that we will not go astray. Following our hearts' desires and finding our path in life does not mean following our whims and aimless passions. Everything has its limits — legitimate, gentle and useful limits; we could call them guidelines that prevent us from straying off the right track. Our True Secret is the light at the end of the tunnel, which shows the direction and leads the way.

Don't be afraid to dream, and don't be intimidated from pursuing your dreams, but always keep your True Secret in its safe place, deep in your heart, to adjust your path.

Body and Soul

Our body is mere clay:

﴿... وَبَدَأَ خَلْقَ الْإِنسَانِ مِن طِينٍ ۝٧ ثُمَّ جَعَلَ نَسْلَهُ مِن سُلَالَةٍ مِّن مَّاءٍ مَّهِينٍ ۝٨﴾ [السَّجدَة: ٧-٨]

﴿And He [Allah] began the creation of man from clay. Then He made his offspring from semen of worthless water.﴾ *(Qur'an 32: 7-8)*

It was worthless until Allah (ﷻ) gave it its true value, its soul:[10]

﴿ثُمَّ سَوَّاهُ وَنَفَخَ فِيهِ مِن رُّوحِهِ ۝٩﴾ [السَّجدَة: ٩]

﴿Then He fashioned him in due proportion, and breathed into him the soul.﴾ *(Qur'an 32: 9)*

Human power and value are supplied by this divine connection, not by earthly bonds. Yet we all tend to focus on the earthly outer 'casing', ignoring our true essence.

Islam does not accept a two-faced person whose deeds are dedicated sometimes to Allah (ﷻ) and at other times to worldly

---

10 Al-Ghazâli, *The Emotional Side of Islam*

goods or idols. Islam totally rejects this sinful dualism, a dualism that regrettably has become very common in contemporary life.[11]

Sincerity is the remedy for this conflicted and ruptured life; it purifies a Muslim's vision, clarifies his or her goals and directs all of his or her deeds for the sake of the One and Only Creator, seeking His pleasure. It unifies the Muslim's body and soul.

Sincerity leads us to a perfect system of life, a system based on balance and moderation, which is perfectly compatible with human nature. The Qur'an stresses the idea of moderation and balance between worldly desires and concern with the hereafter; this is Allah's straight path.[12]

﴿وَكَذَٰلِكَ جَعَلْنَٰكُمْ أُمَّةً ... ﴿١٤٣﴾﴾ [البقرة: ١٤٣]

﴿Thus, have We made of you an Ummah justly balanced...﴾ *(Qur'an 2: 143)*

﴿وَٱبْتَغِ فِيمَآ ءَاتَىٰكَ ٱللَّهُ ٱلدَّارَ ٱلْءَاخِرَةَ ۖ وَلَا تَنسَ نَصِيبَكَ مِنَ ٱلدُّنْيَا ۖ ... ﴿٧٧﴾﴾ [القصص: ٧٧]

﴿But seek, with that [wealth and provision] which Allah has bestowed on you, the home of the hereafter, and forget not your portion of legal enjoyment in this world.﴾ *(Qur'an 28: 77)*

﴿قُلْ مَنْ حَرَّمَ زِينَةَ ٱللَّهِ ٱلَّتِىٓ أَخْرَجَ لِعِبَادِهِۦ وَٱلطَّيِّبَٰتِ مِنَ ٱلرِّزْقِ ۚ قُلْ هِىَ لِلَّذِينَ ءَامَنُوا۟ فِى ٱلْحَيَوٰةِ ٱلدُّنْيَا خَالِصَةً يَوْمَ ٱلْقِيَٰمَةِ ۗ ... ﴿٣٢﴾﴾ [الأعراف: ٣٢]

﴿Say [O Muhammad]: Who has forbidden the adornment with

---

11 Al-Qaraḍâwi, *Intention and Sincerity*

12 Straight path/right way (*aṣ-Ṣirâṭ al-Mustaqeem*): a Qur'anic expression that means Islamic monotheism and all that Islam endorses as a means of living a life that is pleasing to Allah

clothes given by Allah, which He has produced for his slaves, and the good and lawful things [which He provided] for sustenance? Say: They are, in the life of this world, for those who believe, and exclusively for them [believers] on the Day of Resurrection...» *(Qur'an 7: 32)*

The *Sunnah* is a code of life comprising the practice and collected sayings of Prophet Muhammad (ﷺ); together with the Qur'an, it forms the basis of Islamic law. It clarifies this idea and never demands that human beings go beyond their natural limits. Prophet Muhammad (ﷺ) said: «Indeed, I swear by Allah that I am the most fearful among you of Allah, and the most pious. However, I fast and break my fast, I pray and sleep, and I marry women. Whoever refrains from my way is not among my followers.» (Bukhari and Muslim)

In Islamic law, neither exaggeration nor negligence is accepted in a person's duties towards Allah (ﷻ) or in duties towards one's self, family or community. Allah (ﷻ) says:

﴿لَا يُكَلِّفُ ٱللَّهُ نَفْسًا إِلَّا وُسْعَهَا ... ﴿٢٨٦﴾﴾ [البقرة: ٢٨٦]

«Allah does not burden a person beyond his scope...»
(Qur'an 2: 286)

He, the Exalted, also said:

﴿... يُرِيدُ ٱللَّهُ بِكُمُ ٱلْيُسْرَ وَلَا يُرِيدُ بِكُمُ ٱلْعُسْرَ ... ﴿١٨٥﴾﴾
[البقرة: ١٨٥]

«...Allah intends for you ease, and He does not want to make things difficult for you...» *(Qur'an 2: 185)*

In some ways, there may be no big difference in the outer aspects of the lives of Muslims and non-Muslims; they all work, play, marry and raise children. The main and crucial difference lies inside the hearts and souls of the Muslims and in the outcome that can be expected in the hereafter.

Our true and sincere faith and our intention to please Allah (ﷻ) have to be coupled with good deeds in the way we work and perform other activities. Allah (ﷻ) says:

﴿وَمَنْ أَرَادَ ٱلْأَخِرَةَ وَسَعَىٰ لَهَا سَعْيَهَا وَهُوَ مُؤْمِنٌ فَأُولَٰٓئِكَ كَانَ سَعْيُهُم مَّشْكُورًا ﴿١٩﴾﴾ [الإسراء: ١٩]

﴿And whoever desires the [good reward of the] hereafter and strives for it with the necessary effort due for it, while he [or she] is a believer, then such are the ones whose striving shall be appreciated, thanked and rewarded.﴾ *(Qur'an 17: 19)*

The converse is also true: good deeds must be based on true faith and sincere intentions. Allah the Almighty says:

﴿بَلَىٰ مَنْ أَسْلَمَ وَجْهَهُۥ لِلَّهِ وَهُوَ مُحْسِنٌ فَلَهُۥٓ أَجْرُهُۥ عِندَ رَبِّهِۦ وَلَا خَوْفٌ عَلَيْهِمْ وَلَا هُمْ يَحْزَنُونَ ﴿١١٢﴾﴾ [البقرة: ١١٢]

﴿Yes, but whoever submits his face [himself] to Allah and is a *muhsin* [a good-doer with sincere intentions], then his reward is with his Lord [Allah]. On such shall be no fear, nor shall they grieve.﴾ *(Qur'an 2: 112)*

Reminder:

- Make sure that you know your intention for every action you perform.
- Balance your worldly needs with the needs of your soul.
- Be sincere in your intention. Really mean it.

Chapter I
The True Secret in Practice

The True Secret in Practice

In recent years, a number of materials have been published by Western writers telling us that by letting go of life, we can receive more and more, and that by being dedicated in what we do, by thinking positively and strengthening our self-image, we can attain our desires. The more we detach ourselves from life's possessions, they teach, the more prosperity will flow into our lives. This is somewhat true; I cannot argue with that. This is a worldly rule, a law of life that applies to all human beings, Muslims and non-Muslims, believers and non-believers, the faithful and the hypocrites.

By common definition, when you are truly devoted and dedicated to something, your action can be described as sincere. Being sincere in your job in order to gain a promotion to a higher post, or in order to be known by your colleagues as such, will probably lead you to what you intend. However, this is only a worldly pursuit that applies in this transient life; for us as Muslims, being sincere takes on further meaning. Muslims are also required to be sincere in all that we do, but when we use the term 'sincere', we mean that sincerity to Allah is our first and foremost priority.[13]

We apply all worldly rules and life's laws; we take the necessary steps to attract what we want and need. We strive and achieve, but in our hearts we are sincere first to our One and Only Creator, to Allah (ﷻ). This life is not our ultimate goal. Through

---

[13] Al-Ghazâli, *The Revival of Religious Knowledge*

positive thinking, self-confidence, ethics, moral values, other learned skills and detachment from worldly possessions, we can achieve worldly happiness and success. Without sincerity though, without true faith and devotion to Allah (ﷻ), this achievement is but a mirage, a transient acquisition that will not last for long. Allah (ﷻ) says in the noble Qur'an:

﴿فَذَرْهُمْ يَخُوضُوا۟ وَيَلْعَبُوا۟ حَتَّىٰ يُلَـٰقُوا۟ يَوْمَهُمُ ٱلَّذِى يُوعَدُونَ ﴿٤٢﴾﴾ [المعارج: ٤٢]

﴾So leave them to plunge in vain talk and play about, until they meet their Day [the Day of Resurrection and Judgement] which they are promised.﴿ *(Qur'an 70: 42)*

﴿قُلْ هَلْ نُنَبِّئُكُم بِٱلْأَخْسَرِينَ أَعْمَـٰلًا ﴿١٠٣﴾ ٱلَّذِينَ ضَلَّ سَعْيُهُمْ فِى ٱلْحَيَوٰةِ ٱلدُّنْيَا وَهُمْ يَحْسَبُونَ أَنَّهُمْ يُحْسِنُونَ صُنْعًا ﴿١٠٤﴾﴾ [الكهف: ١٠٣-١٠٤]

﴾Say [O Muhammad]: Shall We tell you the greatest losers in respect of [their] deeds? They are those whose efforts have been wasted in this life while they thought that they were acquiring good by their deeds!﴿ *(Qur'an 18: 103-104)*

Their deeds may have been good, but they were not sincere to Allah (ﷻ). Perhaps they forgot Allah (ﷻ) and the reason for their existence, or they had other motivations for their deeds, or they even dedicated their noble actions to someone or something other than Allah (ﷻ) and made that person or thing their 'god'. They were unaware that their work would not get any reward from Allah (ﷻ). Their successes were only limited and temporal; they were just wasting their lives.[14] Allah (ﷻ) says:

﴿أُو۟لَـٰٓئِكَ ٱلَّذِينَ كَفَرُوا۟ بِـَٔايَـٰتِ رَبِّهِمْ وَلِقَآئِهِۦ فَحَبِطَتْ أَعْمَـٰلُهُمْ فَلَا نُقِيمُ لَهُمْ يَوْمَ ٱلْقِيَـٰمَةِ وَزْنًا ﴿١٠٥﴾﴾ [الكهف: ١٠٥]

14 Quṭb

﴿They are those who deny the *âyât* [proofs, evidences, verses] of their Lord and the meeting with Him [in the hereafter]. So their works are in vain, and on the Day of Resurrection, We shall not give them any weight.﴾ *(Qur'an 18: 105)*

Allah (سبحانه وتعالى) also teaches us in the Qur'an:

﴿ٱعۡلَمُوٓاْ أَنَّمَا ٱلۡحَيَوٰةُ ٱلدُّنۡيَا لَعِبٞ وَلَهۡوٞ وَزِينَةٞ وَتَفَاخُرُۢ بَيۡنَكُمۡ وَتَكَاثُرٞ فِي
ٱلۡأَمۡوَٰلِ وَٱلۡأَوۡلَٰدِۖ كَمَثَلِ غَيۡثٍ أَعۡجَبَ ٱلۡكُفَّارَ نَبَاتُهُۥ ثُمَّ يَهِيجُ فَتَرَىٰهُ مُصۡفَرّٗا
ثُمَّ يَكُونُ حُطَٰمٗاۖ وَفِي ٱلۡأٓخِرَةِ عَذَابٞ شَدِيدٞ وَمَغۡفِرَةٞ مِّنَ ٱللَّهِ وَرِضۡوَٰنٞۚ وَمَا
ٱلۡحَيَوٰةُ ٱلدُّنۡيَآ إِلَّا مَتَٰعُ ٱلۡغُرُورِ ٢٠ سَابِقُوٓاْ إِلَىٰ مَغۡفِرَةٖ مِّن رَّبِّكُمۡ وَجَنَّةٍ
عَرۡضُهَا كَعَرۡضِ ٱلسَّمَآءِ وَٱلۡأَرۡضِ أُعِدَّتۡ لِلَّذِينَ ءَامَنُواْ بِٱللَّهِ وَرُسُلِهِۦۚ ذَٰلِكَ
فَضۡلُ ٱللَّهِ يُؤۡتِيهِ مَن يَشَآءُۚ وَٱللَّهُ ذُو ٱلۡفَضۡلِ ٱلۡعَظِيمِ ٢١﴾

[الحديد: ٢٠-٢١]

﴿Know that the life of this world is only play and amusement, pomp and mutual boasting among you, and rivalry in respect of wealth and children, as the likeness of vegetation after rain: the growth of it is pleasing to the tiller, but afterwards it dries up and you see it turning yellow, and then it becomes straw. But in the hereafter [there is] a severe torment [for the disbelievers and evil-doers], and [there is] forgiveness from Allah and [His] good pleasure [for the believers who are good-doers], whereas the life of this world is only a deceiving enjoyment. Race with one another in hastening towards forgiveness from your Lord [Allah] and towards paradise, the width of it is as the width of heaven and earth, prepared for those who believe in Allah and His Messengers. That is the grace of Allah which He bestows on whom He pleases; and Allah is the Owner of Great Bounty.﴾ *(Qur'an 57: 20-21)*

﴿يَوْمَ لَا يَنفَعُ مَالٌ وَلَا بَنُونَ ﴿٨٨﴾ إِلَّا مَنْ أَتَى ٱللَّهَ بِقَلْبٍ سَلِيمٍ ﴿٨٩﴾﴾
[الشُّعَرَاء: ٨٨-٨٩]

﴾The Day on which neither wealth nor children will avail [a person], except for one who brings to Allah a clean heart [clean from polytheism and hypocrisy].﴿ *(Qur'an 26: 88-89)*

By living a life of sincerity, we can face life's pains and struggles, knowing that these are tests and lessons to make us stronger and to wash away some of our sins. We look at calamities as challenges that help us adjust our path and set our priorities straight. When you are struck with a calamity, stop and consider: Is it a blow to my material life or a blow to my religion and faith? Don't get them mixed up.

Money, wealth, power, fame, health, the death of a beloved one, divorce and family breakups are all worldly matters — and yes, they are sometimes painful. Our Prophet (ﷺ) used to supplicate: «O Allah! I seek refuge with You from disbelief and poverty. I seek refuge with You from the torment of the grave. None has the right to be worshipped except You.»[15] (recorded by Abu Dâwood)

He (ﷺ) also advised us: «Ask Allah for forgiveness and health. After faith, nothing is better than health.» (a sound hadith recorded by an-Nasâ'i)

Matters of the material world are not the priorities for Muslims, even the important matter of physical health. It was reported in the above hadith: «After faith, nothing is better than health.» Note that faith ranks first.

Our soul, our divine connection, which is everlasting, is our priority. Any worldly loss is replaceable:

---

15 Abu Dâwood said that the scholars of Makkah kept quiet about this hadith (meaning that they neither fully endorsed it as sound nor renounced it as weak)

﴿مَآ أَصَابَ مِن مُّصِيبَةٍ فِى ٱلْأَرْضِ وَلَا فِىٓ أَنفُسِكُمْ إِلَّا فِى كِتَٰبٍ مِّن قَبْلِ أَن نَّبْرَأَهَآ ۚ إِنَّ ذَٰلِكَ عَلَى ٱللَّهِ يَسِيرٌ ﴿٢٢﴾ لِّكَيْلَا تَأْسَوْا۟ عَلَىٰ مَا فَاتَكُمْ وَلَا تَفْرَحُوا۟ بِمَآ ءَاتَىٰكُمْ ۗ وَٱللَّهُ لَا يُحِبُّ كُلَّ مُخْتَالٍ فَخُورٍ ﴿٢٣﴾﴾

[الحديد: ٢٢-٢٣]

﴿No calamity befalls on the earth or in yourselves but is inscribed in the Book of Decrees before We bring it into existence. Verily, that is easy for Allah, in order that you may not be sad over matters that you fail to get, nor rejoice because of that which has been given to you; and Allah does not like prideful boasters.﴾ *(Qur'an 57: 22-23)*

Always remember the promise of Allah. He rewards good deeds by keeping evil and distress away, and this leads to a pleasant life. Allah (ﷻ) tells us:

﴿فَمَنِ ٱتَّبَعَ هُدَاىَ فَلَا يَضِلُّ وَلَا يَشْقَىٰ ﴿١٢٣﴾﴾ [طه: ١٢٣]

﴿Then whoever follows My guidance shall neither go astray nor fall into distress and misery.﴾ *(Qur'an 20: 123)*

Conversely, He (ﷻ) also warns:

﴿وَمَنْ أَعْرَضَ عَن ذِكْرِى فَإِنَّ لَهُۥ مَعِيشَةً ضَنكًا ... ﴿١٢٤﴾﴾ [طه: ١٢٤]

﴿But whoever turns away from My reminder [and neither believes in this Qur'an nor acts on its orders], verily, for him is a life of hardship...﴾ *(Qur'an 20: 124)*

Allah (ﷻ) says:

﴿مَن كَانَ يُرِيدُ ٱلْحَيَوٰةَ ٱلدُّنْيَا وَزِينَتَهَا نُوَفِّ إِلَيْهِمْ أَعْمَٰلَهُمْ فِيهَا وَهُمْ فِيهَا لَا يُبْخَسُونَ ﴿١٥﴾ أُو۟لَٰٓئِكَ ٱلَّذِينَ لَيْسَ لَهُمْ فِى ٱلْءَاخِرَةِ إِلَّا ٱلنَّارُ ۖ وَحَبِطَ مَا

صَنَعُوا۟ فِيهَا وَبَـٰطِلٌ مَّا كَانُوا۟ يَعْمَلُونَ ﴿١٦﴾﴾ [هُود: ١٥-١٦]

﴿Whoever desires the life of the world and its glitter, to them We shall pay in full [the wages of] their deeds therein, without diminution. They are those for whom there is nothing in the hereafter but fire; and vain are the deeds they did there [in the life of the world], and of no effect is that which they used to do.﴾ *(Qur'an 11: 15-16)*

﴿مَن كَانَ يُرِيدُ حَرْثَ ٱلْـَٔاخِرَةِ نَزِدْ لَهُۥ فِى حَرْثِهِۦ ۖ وَمَن كَانَ يُرِيدُ حَرْثَ ٱلدُّنْيَا نُؤْتِهِۦ مِنْهَا وَمَا لَهُۥ فِى ٱلْـَٔاخِرَةِ مِن نَّصِيبٍ ﴿٢٠﴾﴾ [الشّورىٰ: ٢٠]

﴿Whoever desires [with his deeds] the reward of the hereafter, We give him increase in his reward, and whoever desires the reward of this world [with his deeds], We give him thereof [what is written for him], and he has no portion in the hereafter.﴾ *(Qur'an 42: 20)*

﴿مَّن كَانَ يُرِيدُ ٱلْعَاجِلَةَ عَجَّلْنَا لَهُۥ فِيهَا مَا نَشَآءُ لِمَن نُّرِيدُ ثُمَّ جَعَلْنَا لَهُۥ جَهَنَّمَ يَصْلَىٰهَا مَذْمُومًا مَّدْحُورًا ﴿١٨﴾ وَمَنْ أَرَادَ ٱلْـَٔاخِرَةَ وَسَعَىٰ لَهَا سَعْيَهَا وَهُوَ مُؤْمِنٌ فَأُو۟لَـٰٓئِكَ كَانَ سَعْيُهُم مَّشْكُورًا ﴿١٩﴾ كُلًّا نُّمِدُّ هَـٰٓؤُلَآءِ وَهَـٰٓؤُلَآءِ مِنْ عَطَآءِ رَبِّكَ ۚ وَمَا كَانَ عَطَآءُ رَبِّكَ مَحْظُورًا ﴿٢٠﴾ ٱنظُرْ كَيْفَ فَضَّلْنَا بَعْضَهُمْ عَلَىٰ بَعْضٍ ۚ وَلَلْـَٔاخِرَةُ أَكْبَرُ دَرَجَـٰتٍ وَأَكْبَرُ تَفْضِيلًا ﴿٢١﴾﴾

[الإسراء: ١٨-٢١]

﴿Whoever wishes for the quick-passing [transitory enjoyment of this world], We readily grant what We will for whom We like. Then, afterwards, We have appointed for him Hell. He will burn in it disgraced and rejected [far away from Allah's mercy]. And whoever desires the hereafter and strives for it, with the necessary effort due for it [by doing righteous deeds in obedience to Allah] while he is a believer [in the Oneness of Allah — Islamic monotheism], then such are the ones whose striving shall be appreciated, thanked and rewarded [by Allah]. To each [category] We extend — to these as well as those — from the bounties of your Lord, and never has the bounty of your Lord been restricted. See how We prefer one above another [in this world in terms of provision], and verily, the hereafter will be greater in degrees and greater in preference.﴾ *(Qur'an 17: 18-21)*

Those verses are followed by this precious advice:

﴿لَّا تَجْعَلْ مَعَ ٱللَّهِ إِلَٰهًا ءَاخَرَ فَتَقْعُدَ مَذْمُومًا مَّخْذُولًا ﴿٢٢﴾﴾ [الإسراء: ٢٢]

﴿Set not up with Allah any other god, or you will become censured and forsaken.﴾ *(Qur'an 17: 22)*

Muslims are not seeking just this earthly life. We are striving for eternal paradise, and in this lies the value of our True Secret, sincerity. Our Prophet (ﷺ) taught us: «Allah (ﷻ) has distributed your dispositions among you like He has distributed your material provision, and Allah (ﷻ) grants wealth to whom He loves and to whom He does not love, but He does not grant faith except to one He loves most; and whoever has been granted faith, (Allah) loves him (or her).» (al-Mundhiri; its narrators are trustworthy)

Are you happy?

When I was a young girl, my grandmother used to tell me a bedtime story about a very wealthy and powerful sultan who was always unhappy. All the physicians and alchemists of the kingdom came to heal him, but nothing was wrong with his health. Some of them suggested healthful food, special herbs, holidays... He tried it all but had no success; he was still unhappy.

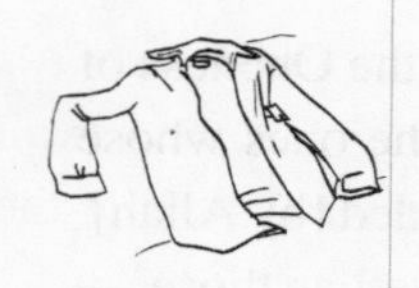

One day a wise man came to the sultan and suggested that he would only find happiness if he took the shirt of a continuously happy person and wore it. All of the sultan's men went out on an extensive search for a person who was continuously happy. It seemed like an easy task in the beginning, but it turned out to be very challenging. None of the people that they questioned could claim continuous happiness. They were happy sometimes, maybe even most of the time, but none of them was happy all the time.

The sultan's men had almost given up. Then, while one of them was walking home through the woods one day, he heard singing. It was the singing of a poor woodchopper who was cutting trees. For days, the sultan's men watched the lowly woodchopper while he happily performed his tremendously exhausting job. He was the one they were looking for. He was always happy.

Finally, they stepped forward and asked the man: "*Are you always happy?*" The woodchopper replied surprisingly: "*Yes, alḥamdulillâh (all praise is for Allah).*" The men were thrilled; they had finally found the cure for their sultan. They offered the woodchopper a bag of gold coins in exchange for one of his shirts. The poor woodchopper replied innocently: "*I'm sorry. I can't give you any shirts.*" The men were taken aback and offered him a large fortune; they even offered him a palace. The poor man replied: "*It's not about money, you see. I'm simply so poor that I don't have any shirts!*"

My grandmother always ended her story with her famous conclusion. The only man in the kingdom who was happy all the time was the poorest one of all. He did not even have a shirt to wear, but that did not stop him from finding continuous happiness.

I have to admit, I did not enjoy this story very much when I was young. It was not funny and not exciting, so what was it all about, I wondered. It was a difficult concept for me to grasp at the time.

My grandmother's story shares an age-old wisdom: you can choose to be happy, if you want to, no matter what your circumstances. Happiness has nothing to do with your wealth, your occupation, or your social position. It is all in your mind. Your happiness is your own decision. It is your decision to accept, acknowledge and embrace the blessings of Allah (ﷻ); it is your decision to be content, grateful and satisfied. Remember the verse in the Qur'an:

﴿فَمَنِ ٱتَّبَعَ هُدَاىَ فَلَا يَضِلُّ وَلَا يَشْقَىٰ ﴿١٢٣﴾﴾ [طه: ١٢٣]

﴿Then whoever follows My guidance shall neither go astray nor fall into distress and misery.﴾ *(Qur'an 20: 123)*

Happiness is an inner feeling; it is the contentment and satisfaction of your soul. You are the only one responsible for your own happiness. I know many people who keep saying, "*If I were richer, I would be happier,*" or "*If I pass this exam, I will be happier*." There is always an 'if' involved. Their happiness is dependent on some worldly objective in their lives, but let me assure you that even 'if' this objective is reached, there will always be another one waiting, further postponing their happiness. Prophet Muhammad (ﷺ) said: «Seek the help of Allah, and do not be frustrated. If something befalls you, do not say: If I had done this, such and such would have happened. Say: Allah decreed, and what Allah wills, He does. Indeed, the word 'if' opens the door for evil.» (Muslim)

The great scholar Ibn al-Qayyim al-Jawziyah classified happiness into three types:

1. External happiness, resulting from wealth, power, prestige or the possession of worldly material goods. This type, he noted, is the lowest stage of happiness because it is a momentary pleasure that can vanish in an instant. Allah (ﷻ) says:

﴿ٱعْلَمُوٓا۟ أَنَّمَا ٱلْحَيَوٰةُ ٱلدُّنْيَا لَعِبٌ وَلَهْوٌ وَزِينَةٌ وَتَفَاخُرٌۢ بَيْنَكُمْ وَتَكَاثُرٌ فِى ٱلْأَمْوَٰلِ وَٱلْأَوْلَٰدِ ۖ كَمَثَلِ غَيْثٍ أَعْجَبَ ٱلْكُفَّارَ نَبَاتُهُۥ ثُمَّ يَهِيجُ فَتَرَىٰهُ مُصْفَرًّا ثُمَّ يَكُونُ حُطَٰمًا ۖ وَفِى ٱلْءَاخِرَةِ عَذَابٌ شَدِيدٌ وَمَغْفِرَةٌ مِّنَ ٱللَّهِ وَرِضْوَٰنٌ ۚ وَمَا ٱلْحَيَوٰةُ ٱلدُّنْيَآ إِلَّا مَتَٰعُ ٱلْغُرُورِ ﴿٢٠﴾﴾ [الحديد: ٢٠]

﴿Know that the life of this world is only play and amusement, pomp and mutual boasting among you, and rivalry in respect of wealth and children, as the likeness of vegetation after rain: the growth of it is pleasing to the tiller, but afterwards it dries up and you see it turning yellow, and then it becomes straw. But in the hereafter [there is] a severe torment [for the disbelievers and evil-doers], and [there is] forgiveness from Allah and [His] good pleasure [for the believers who do good works], whereas the life of this world is only a deceiving enjoyment.﴾

(Qur'an 57: 20)

2. Happiness originating from the physical body, from its health, mood and strength. This type of happiness is more related to who we are than the first type, but it is still an external type of happiness, which can come to an end at any time. Allah (ﷻ) states in His noble Book:

﴿لَقَدْ خَلَقْنَا ٱلْإِنسَٰنَ فِىٓ أَحْسَنِ تَقْوِيمٍ ﴿٤﴾ ثُمَّ رَدَدْنَٰهُ أَسْفَلَ سَٰفِلِينَ ﴿٥﴾﴾

[التين: ٤-٥]

﴿Verily, We created the human in the best stature [and mould]. Then We reduced him to the lowest of the low.﴾

(Qur'an 95: 4-5)

3. Moral happiness, which originates in the heart and the soul. This is true happiness, and it results from useful knowledge, good manners, strength of character and faith. Allah (سبحانه وتعالى) teaches us:

﴿قُلْ بِفَضْلِ ٱللَّهِ وَبِرَحْمَتِهِۦ فَبِذَٰلِكَ فَلْيَفْرَحُوا۟ هُوَ خَيْرٌ مِّمَّا يَجْمَعُونَ ﴿٥٨﴾﴾

[يونس: ٥٨]

﴾Say: In the bounty of Allah, and in His mercy, let them rejoice. That is better than what [wealth] they amass.﴿ *(Qur'an 10: 58)*

The scholar Muhammad al-Ghazâli further explains that the real reasons for happiness reside in the soul. Once it is present there, this happiness can be served by the physical body and its health and strength, and then it can be served by the fulfilment of other external worldly desires, like wealth and children. Whoever follows this order in seeking happiness attains real bliss.[16] Achieving contentment and cheerfulness is a matter of adjusting one's priorities; always remember:

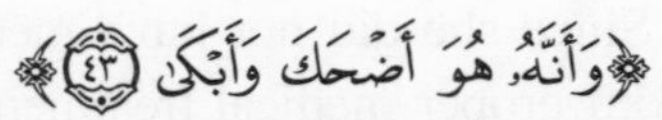

[النجم: ٤٣]

﴾It is He [Allah] Who makes [whom He wills] laugh and makes [whom He wills] weep.﴿ *(Qur'an 53: 43)*

Reminder:

- Happiness is your decision. You have the choice to be happy and content or to remain an unfortunate victim of your current situation, because you are responsible for your own happiness.
- BE HAPPY and spread good feelings and cheer around you!

---

16 Al-Ghazâli, *Renew Your Life*

Many Muslims are practicing the True Secret and are enjoying its tremendous benefits in their lives. I want to share with you some of their stories. I will not tell you stories about millionaires or famous stars; instead, I will share with you some real life experiences of people like you and me. These are people who seek happiness, health, peace of mind and success, but at the same time, they have recognized the truth and identified their priorities; they are sincere to Allah (ﷻ) in their approach to any situation that they encounter in life.[17]

The True Secret & Health

Sameerah is a working class woman. She was a single mother of three school-aged children when she was first diagnosed with breast cancer. Sameerah was working very hard to support her family. Her children had no one else to depend on, and they had no other income except the tiny wage she was getting for cleaning houses all week long.

Since she did not have medical insurance, Sameerah could not afford proper medical treatment. "*Either I pay for my chemotherapy, or I feed and educate my kids. This is not a hard choice to make, is it?*" she asked me.

Sameerah was a sincere believer; she believed that since death has an appointed time and place for each of us, she should focus first on what she could do in her role on earth. She put her priorities in order. She felt that her primary role was to take care of those children and to provide them with a good education so that they would not face the same difficulties in life that she had faced, and she vowed to do that until her last breath. "*If I am meant to die, Allah will take care of my children, but I have to do my part*

---

[17] Names in these stories have been changed to respect privacy.

first," she said. Sameerah completely ignored her cancer and carried on with her mission in life. Allah (سبحانه وتعالى) says:

﴿وَلْيَخْشَ ٱلَّذِينَ لَوْ تَرَكُوا۟ مِنْ خَلْفِهِمْ ذُرِّيَّةً ضِعَـٰفًا خَافُوا۟ عَلَيْهِمْ فَلْيَتَّقُوا۟ ٱللَّهَ وَلْيَقُولُوا۟ قَوْلًا سَدِيدًا ﴿٩﴾﴾ [النّساء : ٩]

﴿And let those [executors and guardians] have the same fear in their minds as they would have for their own, if they had left weak offspring behind. So let them fear Allah and speak right words.﴾ *(Qur'an 4: 9)*

Today, Sameerah is a grandmother. Her daughter is happily married, and her elder son is a successful engineer working to support his mother and his younger brother, who is a university student. There is no sign left of her cancer. Since the rate of spontaneous remission in cancer (meaning cancer that goes away on its own, without any medical intervention) is as low as one in twenty thousand cases,[18] Sameerah's case puzzles the contemporary medical system.

Sameerah healed her soul by being sincere to Allah (سبحانه وتعالى) and being devoted to her true mission in life with faith, dedication, honesty, and absolute surrender to the divine will. Allah (سبحانه وتعالى) took care of her physical body.

This does not mean that every sincere purification of the soul necessarily ends with a physical cure; of course it does not. Our healing and health conditions occur according to the decree of Allah (سبحانه وتعالى). Sometimes physical ailments serve as lessons or challenges along the way to strengthen our faith and resolve. Sometimes ailments and trials are meant to wash away our sins and qualify us for a higher rank in paradise. Prophet Muhammad (ﷺ) said: «If a station (in paradise) has been prescribed by Allah

---

[18] Chopra

for a worshipper that he has not attained by his deeds, Allah tries him through his body or his wealth or his children and causes him to persevere patiently with [these trials] until he finally attains the position that Allah has prescribed for him.» (Abu Dâwood; al-Albâni said it is sound)

Our part is healing our souls and taking care of our bodies, but curing the body is in the hands of Allah (ﷻ). We do our part by maintaining our health, and we seek the required medical treatment available to us, as our Prophet (ﷺ) said: «O servants of Allah, seek treatment, for Allah did not create an illness unless He also created its cure — except for one ailment: aging.» (a sound hadith recorded by Aḥmad, Abu Dâwood and Ibn Mâjah)

Reminder:

- Patience during sickness washes away your sins.
- Heal your soul while seeking the cure for your body.

The True Secret & Wealth

I was once watching an Egyptian television program that discussed contemporary life problems and issues. The presenter related the case of a young man who urgently needed a bone marrow transplant operation that cost one million Egyptian pounds.[19] Members of the audience started calling the show to offer donations, and in less than an hour, the donations reached eight hundred and fifty thousand pounds.

---

[19] At the time of this writing, one million Egyptian pounds was worth about $175,000 U.S. or 138,000 Euros. [Editor]

Then a young man called in and donated fifteen pounds. The young man, Shareef, apologized for the meagre sum he was donating. "*This is half of all the money I possess in this world,*" he said. After a few minutes, a man called the show to donate a large sum for the transplant case and added one thousand pounds. "*For the young man who has just given the fifteen pounds,*" he explained. Another man soon called, and with his donation, he added another five hundred pounds for Shareef. Subḥân Allâh! Shareef donated fifteen pounds, and it was returned to him in less than an hour, multiplied by one hundred.

In the next week's episode, Shareef was the guest on the show, and he related his story. When he was watching the previous program, Shareef asked his mother how much money they had. "*Thirty pounds, and we still have not paid the electricity bill. Why are you asking?*" she replied. Shareef told her about what he was watching on the show and asked her permission to participate by giving half of their possessions to the sick man. "*Why not, my son? When you are ill, you feel the pain of the others,*" replied the mother, who was suffering from cardiac problems herself. This was when Shareef called and donated their fifteen pounds, and Allah (سبحانه وتعالى) rewarded him one hundred times.

The story did not end there, though. On that second episode, during the interview with Shareef, he mentioned that he had studied to be a cameraman and was still looking for a job after having graduated. This is when the second surprise happened. The Minister of Information called and gave orders to hire Shareef immediately to work at the TV station.

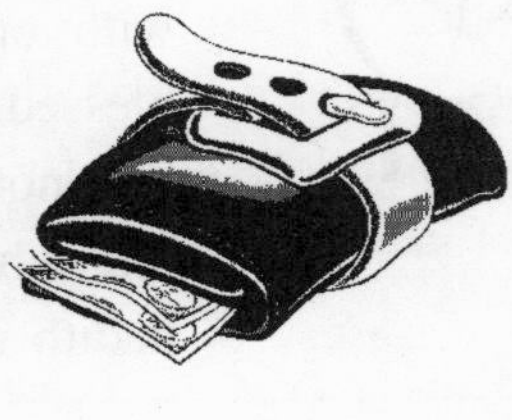

Ameenah and her husband were facing some financial problems. She was sitting at home trying to figure out how they were going to come up with their next house payment when she received a phone call from her mother, who was not aware of their financial difficulties.

Her mother was calling to tell her about a distant relative whose husband had died in a car crash. The woman had no income and was supporting three young girls, and she urgently needed help to pay their school fees. The family had managed to come up with most of the required sum; only two thousand pounds were left. Her mother asked if she could help. "*This is not the time... I am in deep trouble myself,*" Ameenah thought at first, but she could not ignore her conscience, which was advising her to give to this family that was in need. She willingly sent the money.

That day, Ameenah's husband came home late from work, and she completely forgot to tell him about the incident. The next day, her husband called from work to tell her: "*A very strange thing happened today. When I received my pay slip, it had two thousand extra pounds. I thought it was a mistake, but when I reviewed it with the accountant, he informed me that the company decided to raise my salary by two thousand pounds, starting this month.*"

Allah (ﷻ) is the best of providers.

Reminder:

Prophet Muhammad (ﷺ) said: «The bounty of this life is green and beautiful. Whoever takes it with open-handedness, his sustenance will be blessed. Whoever takes it with haughtiness, it will not be blessed for him, and he will be like one who eats and is never satisfied.» (a sound hadith recorded by Abu Dâwood)

The True Secret & Careers

A friend once told me the story of an accountant who worked in a nightclub at an international hotel. He was not very comfortable with his work since he saw drunk customers and belly dancers every night. He tried desperately to find another job, but although he looked everywhere, he was unsuccessful.

One day he met a religious scholar and complained to him about his situation. The shaykh said: "*You are trying the wrong way, my son. Allah says:*

﴿وَمَن يَتَّقِ ٱللَّهَ يَجۡعَل لَّهُۥ مَخۡرَجٗا ٢﴾ [الطّلَاق : ٢]

﴾And whoever fears Allah and keeps his duty to Him, He will make a way for him to get out [from every difficulty].﴿

(Qur'an 65: 2)

You cannot reverse the verse. You should fear Allah and obey Him first, and then He will provide you with a way out — not the opposite."

The shaykh meant that the man should quit his job first, and then Allah (ﷻ) would provide him with another job. This was a very difficult decision for the accountant to make. He had a family to support and had absolutely no other income. The man thought long and hard and finally decided to fear Allah (ﷻ) and quit this job. He would rely on Allah (ﷻ) and entrust his family and his life to Him, the Exalted.

On that same night after his shift ended, he went to his boss's office to tender his resignation. To his surprise, his boss was actually waiting for him; he had news to deliver: "*The branch of our hotel in Saudi Arabia is asking for an accountant, and I nominated you for the job.*" What a relief! A better job with a much better salary, in an alcohol-free environment. Subḥân Allâh!

He did not even have to resign. His sincere intention was enough for Allah (ﷻ) to provide him with a way out.

The father of a friend of mine owned a set of five-star hotels at the site of a well-known tourist attraction. When my friend was a young girl, her father decided that he would no longer sell any alcoholic beverages in his hotels. As a result, they no longer qualified for a five-star ranking, according to international standards. This would mean a much lower income from the hotels and perhaps fewer customers.

His hotel's rankings were reduced from five to four stars, but the man did not care. He refused to listen to others who advised him that he was making a big mistake; he only listened to the commands of Allah (ﷻ). At the end of that year, he swore that he had never made more money in his whole life than he did that year. This story is a clear demonstration of Allah's promise:

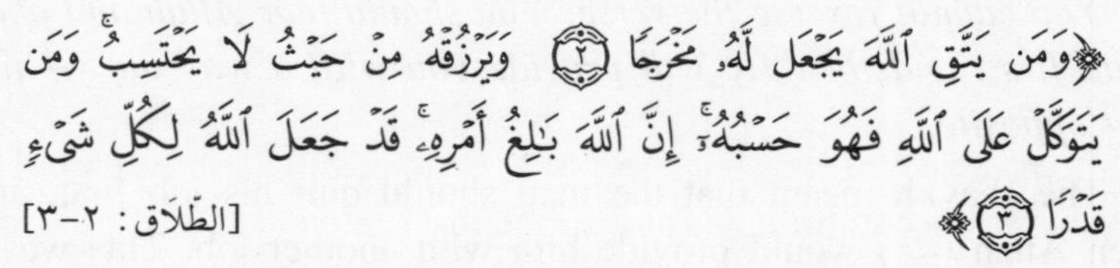
﴿وَمَن يَتَّقِ ٱللَّهَ يَجۡعَل لَّهُۥ مَخۡرَجٗا ٢ وَيَرۡزُقۡهُ مِنۡ حَيۡثُ لَا يَحۡتَسِبُۚ وَمَن يَتَوَكَّلۡ عَلَى ٱللَّهِ فَهُوَ حَسۡبُهُۥٓۚ إِنَّ ٱللَّهَ بَٰلِغُ أَمۡرِهِۦۚ قَدۡ جَعَلَ ٱللَّهُ لِكُلِّ شَيۡءٖ قَدۡرٗا ٣﴾ [الطلاق: ٢-٣]

﴿And whoever fears Allah and keeps his duty to Him, He will make a way for him to get out [from every difficulty]. And He will provide for him from [sources] he never could imagine. And whoever puts his trust in Allah, then He will suffice him. Verily, Allah will accomplish His purpose. Indeed Allah has set a measure for all things.﴾ *(Qur'an 65: 2-3)*

Reminder:

Prophet Muhammad (ﷺ) said: «Allah (ﷻ) likes that when one of you does a job, he perfects it.» (a reliable hadith recorded by al-Bayhaqi)

- Care about what you are doing and always do your best, while seeking only the pleasure of Allah (ﷻ).

The True Secret & Relationships

I have a friend who married while in her early twenties. Her husband already had three sons, the eldest of whom was a teenager; they lived with their mother in another country.

Immediately after my friend's honeymoon, her husband's ex-wife sent the boys to him, stating that she did not want them to live with her anymore. The boys came to live in their father's house, and they were stressed, confused and very much troubled by the presence of their new stepmother. The situation in the house was far from comfortable, and problems started.

I was going to make a pilgrimage to Makkah at that time, and my friend called me and said: "*Please pray for me while you are there*." I thought that she would ask Allah (ﷻ) for the mother to change her mind and take the boys back, or even just ask Allah (ﷻ) for a solution and a way out of this burdensome responsibility, but she did not. She simply said: "*Pray for them to love me. I want them to love me as their own mother. I know that their living with us will make my husband happy. Ask Allah for love to fill our home.*"

After I returned from the pilgrimage, I visited her. I felt the serenity and peace that filled their home. The boys were now calling her 'Mum'. They loved her dearly and had stopped complaining and causing trouble. The sincere love that she had in her heart was enough to share with the whole family.

When I first got married, I used to get very angry whenever a misunderstanding arose between my husband and me. This state of anger made me remember each and every mistake he had made since I first met him, and I would temporarily forget all the good things he had done. Then one day, I read this hadith: «The Prophet said: I saw hellfire, and I have never seen a scene like it. I saw that most of its people are women. They [the Companions] asked: O Messenger of Allah, why? He said: Because of their disbelief. They asked: Do they disbelieve in Allah? He replied: They are ungrateful to their husbands and ungrateful for what they provide for them. If you are kind to one of them for ages, then she sees you make some mistake once, she says: I never saw any good from him.» (Bukhari)

"*Oh my God,*" I thought. "*That is exactly what I have been doing!*"

What was the solution then? The solution is mentioned in the hadith itself: "*...saw any good from him...*" Since that day, whenever I have a disagreement with my husband, I just sit quietly and think of all his good deeds towards me, my children, and my family, or even towards other friends and relatives. At the same time, I also remind myself of this saying: "Seek seventy excuses for your brother."

Amazingly, these simple but sincere exercises, practiced for just a few minutes, utterly change my emotional state from one of anger and resentment to one of peace and forgiveness. Anger cannot resolve problems; it blocks our ability to think rationally. In contrast, tranquillity and serenity enable us to think clearly and to find wise solutions to our problems.

Reminder:

- To love, in the true Islamic meaning, is to relate everything we love to Allah (ﷻ).
- Love for the sake of Allah (ﷻ), and be sincere in your love.

The True Secret & Difficult Situations

When she told me her story, Sanâ' was in her late eighties. She was a great-grandmother living happily, well taken care of by her extended family. Sanâ's husband had passed away when she was only twenty-five years old, leaving her with five young children and no source of income whatsoever. Being from a traditional high class family, Sanâ' had not gone to school. She had received private tutoring at home, so she had no certificates or diplomas to enable her to work and support her children.

Alḥamdulillâh, Sanâ' had been blessed with a good Muslim family. She had four brothers. The two older ones were married and had children of their own, but they decided to take on the financial responsibility for their sister's children. They paid for schooling — the same international school tuition that they paid for their own children — and clothing, and they took the children for entertainment and weekend trips whenever and wherever they took their own children. Sanâ's two younger brothers, on the other hand, took another kind of responsibility. They monitored the children's progress in school and played the roles of caring and loving uncles, so that the children would not feel deprived in any way.

Sanâ' was very grateful to Allah (ﷻ) and to her brothers for this wonderful support. She prayed and thanked Allah (ﷻ) day and night and took great care of her little family, teaching her children true Islamic ethics and values and strengthening their sense of family ties.

Still, the situation was not as perfect as it might seem. There was one person who was not a bit satisfied: Sanâ's sister-in-law, Mahâ. Although Mahâ had a comfortable life — her husband was very wealthy, her children happy and healthy — she was always complaining about everything, even about her husband's financial support of his sister.

Sanâ' tried to be friends with her sister-in-law. She even tried to teach her how to be grateful for all of Allah's blessings. Sometimes she asked her brother to reduce his generous support to avoid problems with his wife, but nothing made Mahâ any happier. Sanâ' still recalls Mahâ's reaction when she was advising her to be grateful to Allah (ﷻ). Her sister-in-law replied angrily: "*What should I be grateful for? What did He give me that is so special, for me to thank Him?*"

Years passed, and I saw Sanâ's children highly established in their careers. They had families of their own, and at the same time, they took very good care of their mother.

I also saw Mahâ, leading a lonely life in her spacious, expensive house. Her children had migrated to other countries and occasionally, maybe seldom, asked about their mother. She had money, and she had many servants and maids, but she had lost love and support. Mahâ recently passed away as lonely as she lived, after years of struggle with a debilitating illness.

It is not easy to be sincere in the most difficult of situations, and it is also not easy to be sincere in the most comfortable of circumstances. Sometimes our luxurious, happy and healthy lives shield us from recognizing the true source of our blessings.

Difficult situations may not always mean deprivation, grief or melancholy. They may, on the contrary, mean happiness, extravagance, abundance and riches.

Allah (ﷻ) says:

﴿وَأَنذِرْهُمْ يَوْمَ ٱلْحَسْرَةِ إِذْ قُضِىَ ٱلْأَمْرُ وَهُمْ فِى غَفْلَةٍ وَهُمْ لَا يُؤْمِنُونَ ﴿٣٩﴾﴾

[مَريَم : ٣٩]

﴿And warn them [O Muhammad] of the day of grief and regrets [the Day of Judgement], when the case has been decided, while [now] they are in a state of carelessness, and they believe not.﴾ *(Qur'an 19: 39)*

Our Prophet Muhammad (ﷺ) taught and reminded us: «There is nothing more honourable to Allah than supplication in times of ease.» (a reliable or sound hadith recorded by al-Mundhiri)

He (ﷺ) used to say this invocation: «O Allah! I seek refuge with You from... the evil of the affliction of wealth, and I seek refuge with You from the affliction of poverty.» (Bukhari)

Reminder:

- Sincerity is a complete way of life.
- Be sincere to Allah (ﷻ) in each and every act and word, even in the most difficult situations.

The True Secret & the World

Allah (ﷻ) says:

﴿وَإِذْ قَالَ رَبُّكَ لِلْمَلَـٰٓئِكَةِ إِنِّى جَاعِلٌ فِى ٱلْأَرْضِ خَلِيفَةً ... ﴿٣٠﴾﴾

[البَقَرَة: ٣٠]

﴾Behold, your Lord said to the angels: I will create a vicegerent on earth...﴿ *(Qur'an 2: 30)*

We human beings are appointed by Allah (ﷻ) to a position of responsibility to apply His laws on earth. Thus Adam (*'alayhi as-salâm* — peace be upon him) and his descendants are responsible for establishing the law of Allah on earth and ruling according to that law, keeping the earth ordered and peaceful, as Allah (ﷻ) wants it to be. We want to make this world a better place to live, and our True Secret is our way of fulfilling this mission.

The stories of Muslim sincerity that helped change our world for the better can fill volumes and volumes of books. There are innumerable examples in history that show how sincerity has helped Muslims to achieve this sacred goal.

I want to recall here one of the most important events in Muslim history, the Battle of Badr, which took place in the month of Ramadan, 2 AH.[20] The Prophet did not want to start a fight with the *Quraysh* (the dominant tribe in Makkah, to which the Prophet belonged; at that time, most of them were polytheists who fervently opposed the Muslims). They outnumbered the Muslims and were well equipped and prepared, but in the end, there was no choice. The Muslim side was able to muster an army of about

---

[20] AH: after *hijrah*, the migration from Makkah to Madinah by Prophet Muhammad (ﷺ) and his Companions that marks the start of the Islamic calendar. [Editor]

three hundred men, with seventy camels and only two or three horses. On the other side, the Quraysh had about one thousand fighters, seven hundred camels and one hundred horses.[21] As we know by now though, victory does not depend on the number of soldiers and their fighting equipment; it depends on sincerity and faith, on spiritual strength and moral values. The fighting was very intense, but Badr ended in a victory for the Muslims. Allah says:

﴿وَلَقَدْ نَصَرَكُمُ ٱللَّهُ بِبَدْرٍ وَأَنتُمْ أَذِلَّةٌ ۖ فَٱتَّقُوا۟ ٱللَّهَ لَعَلَّكُمْ تَشْكُرُونَ ﴿١٢٣﴾ إِذْ تَقُولُ لِلْمُؤْمِنِينَ أَلَن يَكْفِيَكُمْ أَن يُمِدَّكُمْ رَبُّكُم بِثَلَٰثَةِ ءَالَٰفٍ مِّنَ ٱلْمَلَٰٓئِكَةِ مُنزَلِينَ ﴿١٢٤﴾ بَلَىٰٓ ۚ إِن تَصْبِرُوا۟ وَتَتَّقُوا۟ وَيَأْتُوكُم مِّن فَوْرِهِمْ هَٰذَا يُمْدِدْكُمْ رَبُّكُم بِخَمْسَةِ ءَالَٰفٍ مِّنَ ٱلْمَلَٰٓئِكَةِ مُسَوِّمِينَ ﴿١٢٥﴾ وَمَا جَعَلَهُ ٱللَّهُ إِلَّا بُشْرَىٰ لَكُمْ وَلِتَطْمَئِنَّ قُلُوبُكُم بِهِۦ ۗ وَمَا ٱلنَّصْرُ إِلَّا مِنْ عِندِ ٱللَّهِ ٱلْعَزِيزِ ٱلْحَكِيمِ ﴿١٢٦﴾﴾

[آل عِمرَان: ١٢٣-١٢٦]

﴿And Allah has already made you victorious at Badr, when you were a weak little force. So fear Allah much [abstain from all kinds of sins and evil deeds which He has forbidden and love Allah much and perform all kinds of good deeds which He has ordained] that you may be grateful. [Remember] when you [Muhammad] said to the believers: Is it not enough for you that your Lord [Allah] should help you with three thousand angels sent down? Yes, if you hold on to patience and piety, and the enemy comes rushing at you, your Lord will help you with five thousand angels having marks [of distinction]. Allah made it not but as a message of good news for you and as an assurance to your hearts; and there is no victory except from Allah, the All-Mighty, the All-Wise.﴾

(Qur'an 3: 123-126)

---

21 As-Sibâ'ie

It was the true faith, pure intention and sincerity of these few early Muslims that made it possible for Islam to be established in Madinah and from there to spread around the whole world. They made it possible for Islamic teachings to reach us and to stay alive among the people until now and until the end of time, inshallah.

Another notable example of sincerity that changed the world is the story of the noble caliph 'Umar ibn 'Abdul-'Azeez, commonly known as the fifth of the Rightly-guided Caliphs. As a member of the Umayyad dynasty, he was raised in luxury, comfort, ease and wealth, but as soon as he was appointed as caliph, he set his priorities straight. Assuming the responsibility for the whole Ummah was far from easy; it required hard work, dedication, patience, wisdom, and above all sincerity. 'Umar developed all of these traits in himself.

His rule lasted for only two years, five months and forty days,[22] during which time he was able to spread justice, fight corruption, and encourage scholars and scientists. He took care of the poor and the orphans, helped the needy, and closely guarded Islamic values and integrity.

'Umar ibn 'Abdul-'Azeez was known for his patience and flexibility. He was sincere in his motives, and he was also compassionate and wise in his decisions and actions. He did not overburden his people and never rushed for results just to achieve a rapid — but temporary — worldly victory. Instead, he was seeking real reform. He cared for the whole Ummah so much that he wanted Muslims to follow the right path without being forced into it. He wanted them to love the truth, not have the truth imposed on them. He once advised his son: "*Do not rush things, my son. Allah warned about alcoholic drinks in the Qur'an twice*

---

22 Abu al-'Aṭṭâ

before He prohibited it in the third mention. I am afraid to force people towards the truth in such a way that they reject it and cause misguidance."[23]

'Umar ibn 'Abdul-'Azeez used compassion and mercy to teach and guide his people. He advised his friends: "*Never use cauterization if you can find a cure for your brother other than cauterization,*"[24] which also indicates that you should never be harsh with a person if you can guide him or her with love and mercy.

By being sincere in his intentions, trustworthy, caring, loving and compassionate, 'Umar ibn 'Abdul-'Azeez gained the love and trust of his nation, and they soon followed his guidance and teachings. He left an honourable legacy that is still remembered today. His sincerity overflowed and spread to his subjects, giving rise to a strong, faithful Muslim community that reached, during his time, an unprecedented level of abundance and prosperity. It was a community in which justice prevailed, and love and mercy roamed freely.

Reminder:

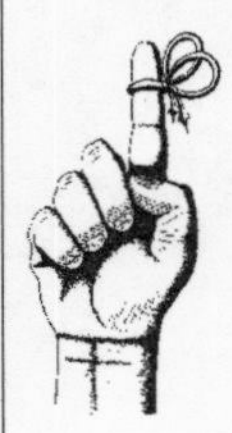

- By being sincere, you are helping to make our world a better place to live.

---

[23] Ibid.

[24] Ibid.

Chapter II

Find Your Path with Your True Secret

Find Your Path with Your True Secret

Do you ever feel that you can accomplish more in life than what you are actually doing?

Do you ever feel that you have some hidden, undiscovered or unfulfilled talents, skills and dreams?

Do you want to get more out of your life?

In this chapter, I will give you tools and guidelines that show how you can attain success, happiness, well-being and fulfilment in your life, while following and acknowledging your True Secret at each step along the way. I will try to help you uncover and unlock your powers and potential and put them into practice.

Every one of us is special in our own way. Each one of us has talents and strengths, whether we are aware of them or not. Every one of us is perfectly tailored to assume our responsibility as a vicegerent on earth. Our Almighty Creator gave each and every one of us the required potential and abilities to fulfil our missions in life. Whether you have already discovered this potential or not, it does exist, believe me. Allah (ﷻ) is always just, and He would not expect something from us without giving us the potential to realize it.

Most of us were raised with a Western-type mentality, ruled by the logical, analytical mind that concentrates on facts and figures while ignoring dreams, imagination and intuition. This left-brain oriented mentality often keeps creativity at bay. We are discouraged from daydreaming and following our instincts or the feelings deep in our hearts. We are forced into a pre-set mould that shapes our thinking and constrains our potential. Finding our path entails shedding these rigid mental settings and having an open mind and open heart to the universe.

The chapter at a glance

Did you ever go on a treasure hunt when you were a child? I did, many times, and I enjoyed it very much. This chapter is like a treasure hunt. You will be hunting for the treasure buried inside your heart, a long lost treasure. It is there. You can find it if you have the perseverance and the right tools to dig it up.

The following chart summarizes the journey on which you are about to embark. It shows the steps towards finding your path and fulfilling your responsibilities:

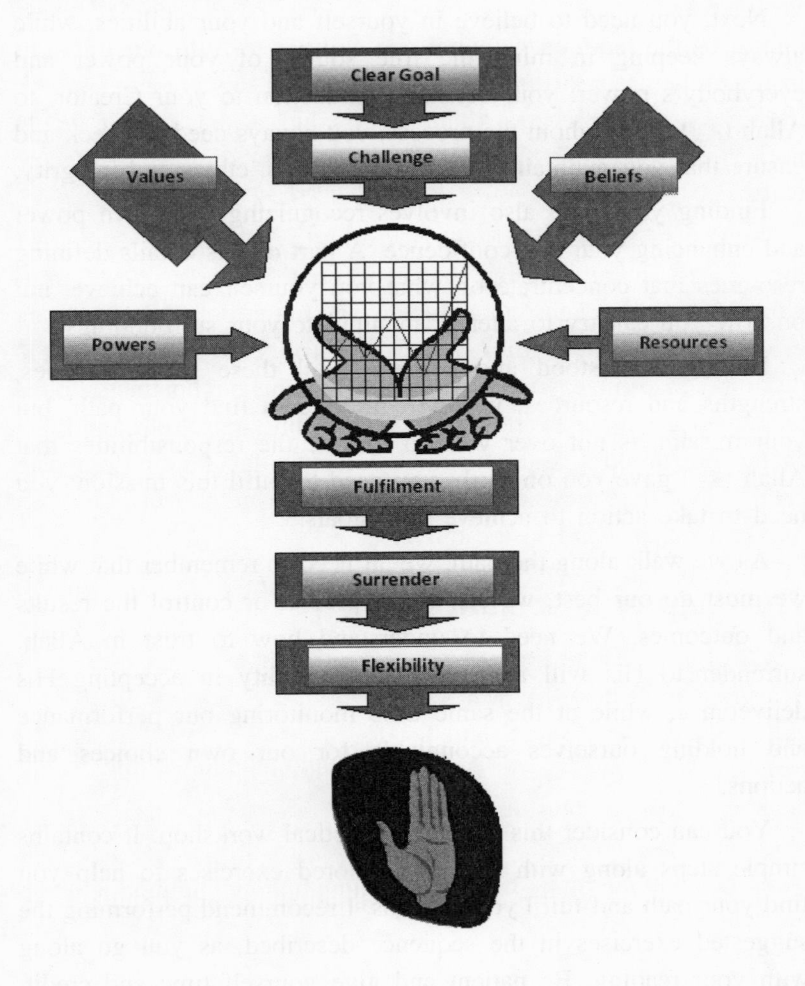

The first step in your journey is defining your goal and mission in life. To assume your responsibility, you need to have a clear goal and purpose in mind. You need to know where you are going and WHY you are heading there. You also need challenges to keep you going, sub-goals that are slowly but steadily conquered.

Next, you need to believe in yourself and your abilities, while always keeping in mind the true source of your power and everybody's power: your constant connection to your Creator, to Allah (ﷻ). Throughout the process, you always need to check and ensure that you maintain your Islamic values, ethics and integrity.

Finding your path also involves recognizing your own power and enhancing your self-confidence. A part of this entails defining resources that concentrate on what you yourself can achieve, not on how you can try to alter or manipulate your surroundings.

Having understood and addressed all these goals, abilities, strengths and resources, you will be able to find your path, but your mission is not over yet. To assume the responsibilities that Allah (ﷻ) gave you on earth, you need to fulfil this mission: you need to take action to achieve your goals.

As we walk along the path, we all need to remember that while we must do our best, we can never predict or control the results and outcomes. We need to understand how to trust in Allah, surrender to His will and maintain flexibility in accepting His deliverance, while at the same time monitoring our performance and holding ourselves accountable for our own choices and actions.

You can consider this chapter a practical workshop. It contains simple steps along with specially tailored exercises to help you find your path and fulfil your dreams. I recommend performing the suggested exercises in the sequence described, as you go along with your reading. Be patient and give yourself time and credit. Changing long-held mental attitudes and assuming a new lifestyle requires hard work, dedication and time. Please do not be discouraged; it is perfectly normal to feel frustration or helplessness at any step along the way. I encourage you to keep trying and to follow your path through to the end.

It may help to perform the exercises with a group or to learn each step and then teach it to friends and family members, or even to your children, while at the same time applying it to your own life. The exercises are simple and easy, yet their effect is very powerful. They can be applied directly or tailored slightly to fit any age group, place or setting.

Why are there so many steps?

You are trying to build a habit, step by step, integrating small but meaningful changes into your life, but let me make one thing clear first: I do not have a magic wand that I can wave to — POOF! — change your entire life and shape your career. In fact, I do not have answers to most of your questions.

"*What? You do not have answers? So why am I reading this?*" you might be asking.

Well, my role is to help you find your own answers. No one can choose your path for you. No one can shape your future or find out what you are able or willing to do. YOU are the only one who has all the answers. Only YOU can choose which path to take. Only YOU can determine your pace and your steps. And let me warn you, it is not going to be easy. This lifelong journey needs patience, perseverance, hard work and — of course — **sincerity**! But don't worry. We will take it one step at a time, and you will have lots of support on the way. Together we can release the potential that is stored inside of each one of us. Are you ready to start?

You will need a journal

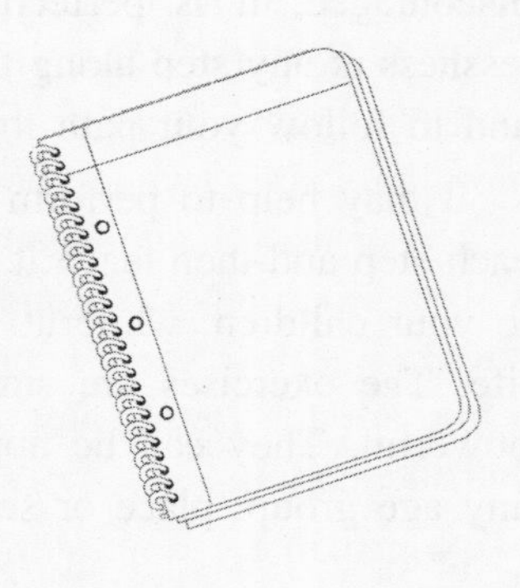

Every one of us has probably kept a journal at some time in our lives. Even children love to use journals to draw, colour, scribble, doodle and write letters to their 'mean' parents or siblings. Simply put, a journal acts as a safety valve to let off excess emotions and frustrations, thus avoiding accidental 'explosions'. It is also a powerful exploratory tool that lets you understand your feelings and release your emotions.

Before embarking on your journey towards finding your path, I highly recommend that you get a new journal.

You will be using your journal for the exercises we will be working on in the course of this book. These include devising plans and goals, describing your heart's desires and long-held dreams, brainstorming and other activities. You can also add your own feelings and variations to any exercise.

In addition to the exercises we will go through, I encourage you to use your journal daily, as Julia Cameron advised in her book *The Artist's Way*. Think of it as signing in every morning. You will need a daily entry that takes no more than five or ten minutes. This is time for yourself alone, time for thinking and awakening your mind, digging into your heart for long hidden desires, hopes, depressions or stresses.

If your mind is blank on some days and you find it difficult to write, try shifting to another activity — any activity that you like and that clears your mind and re-energizes your powers. You could try morning walks, stretching, meditation, drawing or doodling, gardening or baking (but not formal chores). Avoid activities that engage your mind in active thinking. I want your thoughts to run wild, to be totally free. I do not want you to hold them back. Don't judge, critique or censor; just get fully immersed in your morning activity while your mind gradually readjusts and arranges its clutter and chaos. Again, do not rush the process. For some of us, this re-arrangement and clearing of the mind could take a few days, while for others it may require weeks or months, especially if you are not used to any act of self-exploration such as journaling and meditation.

Notice that I am asking you to perform these actions in the morning. Try to set a specific time and place for yourself every day. You may need to adjust your schedule or wake up ten to fifteen minutes earlier, before your children wake up or before the start of your daily routine. These minutes are for you, so be generous with yourself. You really need these few minutes of silence and self-acknowledgment. At first, it may seem difficult to make this part of your regular schedule, but you will soon get used to it and realize its value. I actually long for these minutes of calm and reflection every morning.

Why in the morning? Mornings carry with them a tremendous amount of energy. They are the start of a totally new day, offering new hope and sunshine. Make use of this powerful energy. Don't waste it. Our Prophet (ﷺ) used to supplicate: «O Allah! Bless the early rising of my people.»[25]

Remember, this is your personal journal. No one has to look at it unless you allow it. You have the choice of sharing it with others or keeping it totally to yourself. Rules of grammar, fancy vocabulary and neat handwriting are all optional. In fact, they are

---

[25] At-Tirmidhi, Abu Dâwood and Ibn Mâjah. It has a chain of narrators that includes one narrator who is unknown; however, corroborating evidence for the hadith is found in narrations by 'Ali, Ibn 'Umar, Ibn 'Abbâs, Ibn Mas'ood and others.

discouraged because they bring about interference from the left side of your brain, which hinders the free flow of creative thinking, inspiration and the intuitive feelings of your right-brain hemisphere.

You will need some 'apples'

To live a balanced, holistic life, each area in our lives needs some of our attention. When we are carried away with our daily chores and responsibilities — such as work, study, the house, our spouse and children — we can easily forget about a very important aspect of our lives: our inner selves.

I learned firsthand the consequences of neglecting my inner self. When I graduated at the top of my class, I was immediately hired as a teaching assistant in the same university where I studied. I loved my job, but it took most of my time and energy. After I got married, my husband's job kept him busy most of the day, so I got even more involved in and dedicated to my work. When I had my first son, I had to take maternity leave. Then my daughter came along, and I was now too busy parenting and doing housework to find any time for my academic work.

I loved my children, and I enjoyed playing with them and reading them stories. I also loved cooking, so it was fun preparing food for the family and creating new recipes. My husband was a fine, caring man who was responsible and supportive. Strangely, though, I was feeling depressed. I was crying almost every day. I did not know what was wrong with me until I read a book that turned my life around: *Nurturing Yourself and Others*.

In her book, Lee Schnebly explained how she was suffering from the same symptoms when, like me, she had every reason to be happy in her life. Her counsellor described it for her in a simple, beautiful way. He advised her to think of herself as an apple barrel. The apple barrel is only useful if it actually holds some apples. If we keep distributing our apples to our children, relatives and friends, we will soon run out of apples and feel worthless. To restore our function in life, we have to replenish our supply of apples.[26]

«Salmân (رضي الله عنه), one of the Prophet's Companions, once said to Abu Dardâ' (رضي الله عنه): Allah has a right over you, your own self has a right over you and your partner has a right over you; so give everyone his (or her) due right. When the Prophet (ﷺ) was informed of what he had said, he replied: Salmân has spoken the truth.» (Bukhari)

You have to find the source of your apples. What makes you really relaxed and replenishes your depleted energy? For you, it might be reading a book, memorizing the Qur'an, spending some time with a friend, playing with your children, getting a haircut, or meditating in front of the wide open sea. Think and make a list of activities that rejuvenate you. We will be using this list during our exercises along the way. These apples are the things you love, things that lift your spirit, cheer you up and make you feel happy. Your apples are different from mine and from those of your friends and family. They are unique to you. You love them for a reason; they hold special meaning for you. They may also reveal some hobby, talent, passion or potential. They are the first key in deciphering your treasure map, so take your time in making a list of the sources of your apples.

---

[26] Schnebly, 2000

Take a moment to... discover your 'apples'

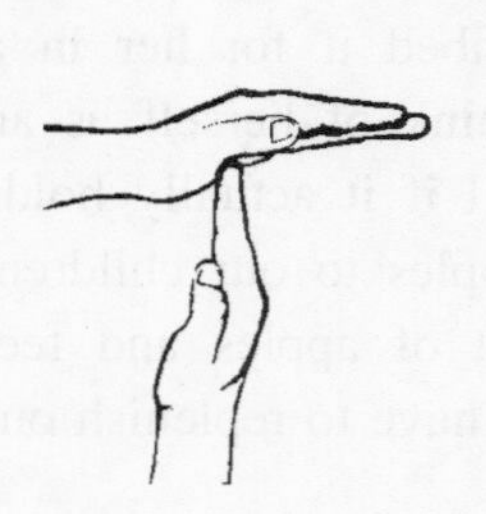

- Close your eyes. Slow down your breathing. Relax for one or two minutes.
- Open your eyes. Write down twenty things that you would like to do, want to do or always dreamed of doing. Write the first things that come into your mind. Don't give them a second thought or judge them, however crazy they might seem. Avoid engaging your left-brain logical critic. Just write them down.
- Now take a deep breath. Open a new double spread page of your journal, and write at the top: My Apples. Start your list.
- During the next week, keep your journal on your desk, open to this page. Look at the list frequently, whenever you have time, and add any more apples that come to mind. Don't remove anything from your list, no matter how ridiculous it seems. The list can be as long as you wish, but not shorter than fifteen or twenty items.

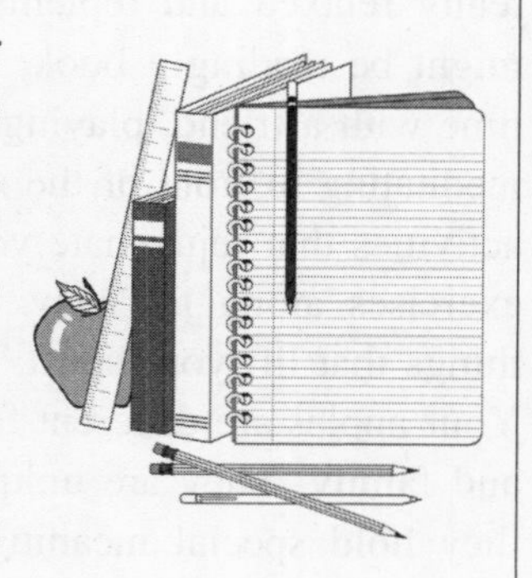

- Pick one apple from your list and reward yourself by doing it at the end of this week. You have now taken the first step on your path. Congratulations!

Starting your journal

Before going further, let's make another entry in our new journal.

Take a moment to... take stock of yourself

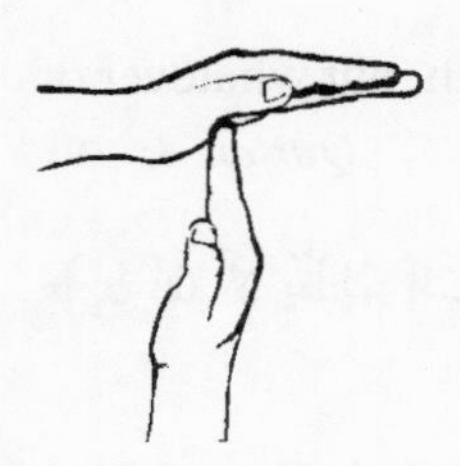

- Reflect on your responsibilities: What is your role around the house, at work, at college, with your family and friends? Record your responsibilities in your journal. Take your time to think about each one of them. Record any tasks that you feel you should be doing.
- Specify your abilities: What are your skills and abilities? Write about your talents and strengths.
- Acknowledge your limitations: Reflect upon your weaknesses and flaws. What, in your opinion, is holding you back? What do you think is missing in your life?

In other words, I am asking you to take stock of where you are today. Keep this journal entry in a safe place. You are going to use it later on.

Finding your path in life entails acknowledging and fulfilling, as much as possible, all your responsibilities. Our Prophet (ﷺ) said: «You are all guardians and are responsible for those under your care.» (Bukhari)

You are responsible for your happiness, for your own actions, for your own life. You are responsible for what you choose to feel or think. You cannot make excuses and blame others for the choices you have made. Assuming responsibility protects and nurtures both your physical health and your emotional well-being. Allah (ﷻ) said in the Qur'an:

﴿مَّآ أَصَابَكَ مِنْ حَسَنَةٍ فَمِنَ ٱللَّهِ وَمَآ أَصَابَكَ مِن سَيِّئَةٍ فَمِن نَّفْسِكَ ... ﴿٧٩﴾﴾

[النِّسَاء : ٧٩]

﴾Whatever of good reaches you is from Allah, but whatever of evil befalls you is from yourself...﴿ *(Qur'an 4: 79)*

﴿إِنَّ ٱللَّهَ لَا يَظْلِمُ ٱلنَّاسَ شَيْـًٔا وَلَٰكِنَّ ٱلنَّاسَ أَنفُسَهُمْ يَظْلِمُونَ ﴿٤٤﴾﴾

[يُونس : ٤٤]

﴾Verily, Allah will not deal unjustly with man at all. It is man that wrongs his own soul.﴿ *(Qur'an 10: 44)*

If you do not accept personal responsibility, you risk developing a hostile and angry attitude towards everyone around you. You will become overly dependent on others for approval and acceptance. You will chronically feel self-pity, weakness and depression.

Stop looking for answers outside yourself. Allah (ﷻ) says:

﴿وَمَآ أَصَٰبَكُم مِّن مُّصِيبَةٍ فَبِمَا كَسَبَتْ أَيْدِيكُمْ وَيَعْفُواْ عَن كَثِيرٍ ﴿٣٠﴾﴾

[الشّورىٰ : ٣٠]

﴾Whatever misfortune happens to you is because of the things your hands have wrought, and He [Allah] pardons much.﴿ *(Qur'an 42: 30)*

It is not what happens that matters, but how you choose to respond to it. You have the free will to choose your path. Allah (ﷻ) says:

﴿إِنَّآ أَنزَلۡنَا عَلَيۡكَ ٱلۡكِتَٰبَ لِلنَّاسِ بِٱلۡحَقِّۖ فَمَنِ ٱهۡتَدَىٰ فَلِنَفۡسِهِۦۖ وَمَن ضَلَّ فَإِنَّمَا يَضِلُّ عَلَيۡهَاۖ وَمَآ أَنتَ عَلَيۡهِم بِوَكِيلٍ ٤١﴾ [الزُّمَر: ٤١]

﴿Verily, We have sent down to you [O Muhammad] the Book [this Qur'an] for humankind in truth. So whoever accepts the guidance, it is only for his own self, and whoever goes astray, he goes astray only for his [own] loss. And you [O Muhammad] are not a *wakeel* [trustee or disposer of affairs or keeper] over them.﴿ *(Qur'an 39: 41)*

﴿مَّنۡ عَمِلَ صَٰلِحٗا فَلِنَفۡسِهِۦۖ وَمَنۡ أَسَآءَ فَعَلَيۡهَاۗ وَمَا رَبُّكَ بِظَلَّٰمٖ لِّلۡعَبِيدِ ٤٦﴾ [فُصِّلَت: ٤٦]

﴿Whoever does righteous good deeds, it is for [the benefit of] his own self, and whoever does evil, it is against his own self, and your Lord is not at all unjust to [His] slaves.﴿

(Qur'an 41: 46)

﴿إِنۡ أَحۡسَنتُمۡ أَحۡسَنتُمۡ لِأَنفُسِكُمۡۖ وَإِنۡ أَسَأۡتُمۡ فَلَهَاۚ ... ٧﴾ [الإسراء: ٧]

﴿If you do good, you do good for your own selves, and if you do evil [you do it] against yourselves...﴿ *(Qur'an 17: 7)*

It is up to you to choose the course you will follow, but from Allah (ﷻ) comes the guidance. If you choose to live sincerely and faithfully, Allah (ﷻ) will guide you to His right path.

Specify your abilities and acknowledge your limitations. Even if you cannot change your outer environment and circumstances, you certainly are able to have absolute control over your own behaviour, attitude and actions. Every one of us has a built-in instinct to know right from wrong:

﴿إِنَّا هَدَيۡنَٰهُ ٱلسَّبِيلَ إِمَّا شَاكِرٗا وَإِمَّا كَفُورًا ٣﴾ [الإنسان: ٣]

﴿Verily, We showed him [humankind] the way, whether he be grateful or ungrateful.﴾ *(Qur'an 76: 3)*

﴿وَنَفْسٍ وَمَا سَوَّىٰهَا ﴿٧﴾ فَأَلْهَمَهَا فُجُورَهَا وَتَقْوَىٰهَا ﴿٨﴾ قَدْ أَفْلَحَ مَن زَكَّىٰهَا ﴿٩﴾ وَقَدْ خَابَ مَن دَسَّىٰهَا ﴿١٠﴾﴾ [الشمس: ٧-١٠]

﴿[I swear] by the soul, and Him Who perfected it in proportion, then He inspired it to understand what is wrong for it and what is right for it. Indeed, he who purifies it [his own soul/self] succeeds, and indeed he who corrupts it fails.﴾

(Qur'an 91: 7-10)

This instinct of knowing right from wrong, which is part of your inborn or natural state instilled by Allah (ﷻ), will guide you through. It will show the way for improvement and give a red-light warning when you cross the line.

Still, there is an important point to stress here. Being responsible is not about punishing yourself and feeling guilty whenever a calamity befalls you. It is not about feeling sinful or assuming that you must have done something wrong whenever you are confronted with a problem or a health concern. Being responsible includes seeking forgiveness from Allah (ﷻ), accepting challenges, surrendering to the divine will, and feeling content and satisfied, both with the blessings you receive and with the challenges you have to work through along the way. It also involves taking real and practical steps towards improving yourself and your own life's circumstances. Being responsible is about applying all of the skills we will be learning in this chapter. Allah (ﷻ) says:

﴿لِّلَّذِينَ أَحْسَنُوا الْحُسْنَىٰ وَزِيَادَةٌ ... ﴿٢٦﴾﴾ [يونس: ٢٦]

﴿To those who do good is the best [reward] and even more!﴾ *(Qur'an 10: 26)*

Now that we have considered these important foundational concepts, made a list of the things that re-energize us, and assessed our responsibilities, strengths and weaknesses, let's get down to the details of correcting our path.

1. Define your objectives

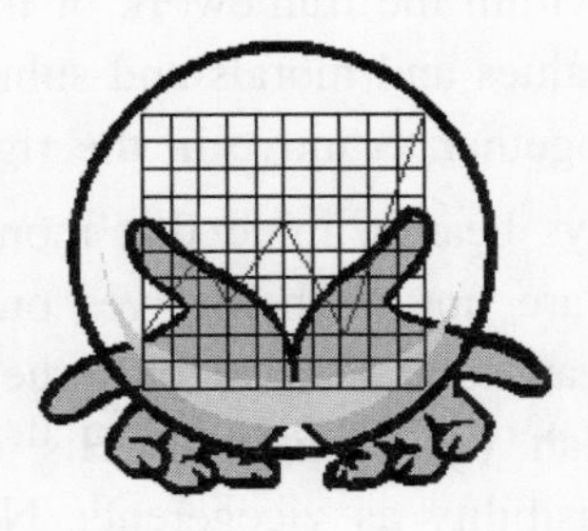

As we start to become more conscious of applying sincerity to our everyday lives, we can take the steps necessary to find our paths. We should first and foremost define our objectives. Each and every person needs to have a purpose for his or her life, an objective that prevents our actions from being barren and meaningless. If there is no reason for what you are doing, nothing will be worthwhile. Allah (ﷻ) says:

﴿أَفَمَن يَمْشِي مُكِبًّا عَلَىٰ وَجْهِهِۦٓ أَهْدَىٰٓ أَمَّن يَمْشِي سَوِيًّا عَلَىٰ صِرَٰطٍ مُّسْتَقِيمٍ ﴿٢٢﴾﴾ [المُلك : ٢٢]

﴾Is he who walks prone on his face [without seeing] more rightly guided, or he who [sees and] walks upright on the straight path?﴿ *(Qur'an 67: 22)*

Who is better: the one who goes through life struggling randomly or the one who knows his path and leads his way with steady, clearly defined steps?[27] The answer is obvious.

Pause for a moment and ask yourself: *What is my objective? What am I seeking out of this life?*

If your answer is anything other than '*to attain the approval of Allah'*, you have to reconsider your values. The ultimate goal for all Muslims is the pleasure of Allah (ﷻ). Being sure of this one essential goal leads you onto the straight path. All the other goals of your life will fit within the framework of this fundamental goal as you adjust your values and morals and submit your heart, mind and body to work together to move in the right direction.

We have to always bear in mind that money, wealth, success, career and the like are not in themselves our goals or purpose. They are merely means that lead to our true purpose: achieving the pleasure of Allah (ﷻ), applying His rules on earth and assuming our responsibility as vicegerents. Nevertheless, worldly endeavours are very important means that we cannot and should not neglect.

It is perfectly fine to have temporary goals that help you along the journey leading to the final objective. These temporary goals are in areas like your studies, your job, or your responsibilities to your spouse, parents and children. Always bear in mind, however, that these intermediate goals are only helpers along the way. The final goal is clear, obvious and irreplaceable. Remember that we are created for a purpose, and each and every event in our lives

---

27 As-Sâbooni

should be well planned and organized to serve this purpose. Allah (ﷻ) says:

﴿وَمَا خَلَقْتُ الْجِنَّ وَالْإِنسَ إِلَّا لِيَعْبُدُونِ ۝٥٦﴾ [الذاريات: ٥٦]

﴾And I [Allah] created the jinns and humans only so they could worship Me [alone].﴿ *(Qur'an 51: 56)*

As we discussed earlier, worshipping does not mean only praying and fasting. Every action in the life of a true Muslim is considered an act of worship, and it is the right intention and sincerity that turn a mere physical or social ritual into an act of worship and obedience to the Almighty.[28] Having this clear picture in mind ensures that our short-term goals are always compatible with the ultimate purpose of our creation.

The more we focus on our final goal, the easier it will be for us to overcome life's inconveniences and the troubles that we face along the way. As al-Ghazâli noted, peace of mind and satisfaction come from acknowledging the fact that we are travellers on this earth, who will reach our final destination someday. Thus, focusing on the journey, rather than keeping our eyes on the final target, may distract us and cause us to risk losing our way. As a traveller, he advised, enjoy your journey, but never lose sight of your final destination.

Always focus
on your
Final Goal!

[28] Ulwan

This focus will allow us to always see the 'Big Picture', as Zarabozo puts it in his book *Purification of the Soul.* It will become the true driving force behind all of our behaviours and actions.

I once read in the newspaper a sad story about a young boy. On his eighth birthday, his present was an airplane — a real one. The next day, the boy committed suicide and left a note asking why he should live any longer when he already had everything he could ever dream of in this life. From his social and cultural surroundings, he had picked up a totally distorted idea about the goals of life.

For many people, material achievements are the definition of success. The main issue in their lives is seeking money and power; that's it. But when they get it, what's next? Some people fall into a vicious cycle of greed and keep struggling for more, while others experience what is commonly known as a 'midlife crisis'. After achieving a good career position, a respectable social status and a secure income, or after having their children grow up and leave the house to start life on their own, many adults stop to ask themselves for the first time: *Why am I here? What am I seeking out of this life? What am I longing for?* This midlife crisis is a major cause of resentment and depression.

What you are doing in life is not as important as **why** you are doing it. Whether you are a physician, a bus driver, a waiter, a writer, or a teacher... what's important is who you really are. Are you self-confident, focused on your goals, optimistic, objective? Do you know exactly what you want in life and what you are meant to achieve?

Have you taken the time to reflect on crucial issues such your attitude towards facing challenges and surmounting obstacles? Are you a good father/mother/son/daughter? Are you — or will you be

— a positive example for your own children to follow? What mindsets do you need to change to achieve all that?

Put your priorities in order. Before embarking on a new mission, you should first organize your priorities. Know why you are choosing this mission. Check your True Secret and adjust your intention.

Let's zoom in

Now that we have set the Big Picture straight, let's zoom in and start thinking about our individual lives.

Worldly efforts are very important means that we cannot and should not neglect. Allah (ﷻ) said:

﴿... ٱعْبُدُوا۟ ٱللَّهَ مَا لَكُم مِّنْ إِلَٰهٍ غَيْرُهُۥ ۖ هُوَ أَنشَأَكُم مِّنَ ٱلْأَرْضِ وَٱسْتَعْمَرَكُمْ فِيهَا فَٱسْتَغْفِرُوهُ ثُمَّ تُوبُوٓا۟ إِلَيْهِ ... ﴿٦١﴾﴾ [هود: ٦١]

﴿...Worship Allah. You have no other god but Him. He brought you forth from the earth and made you settle in it. So ask forgiveness of Him and turn to Him in repentance...﴾

(Qur'an 11: 61)

Notice that this is a divine order, not just a request.

Planning

Now it is time to start devising some plans. Plans can look a bit like a pyramid with our Big Picture at the base, forming the most important foundation upon which the pyramid will stand:

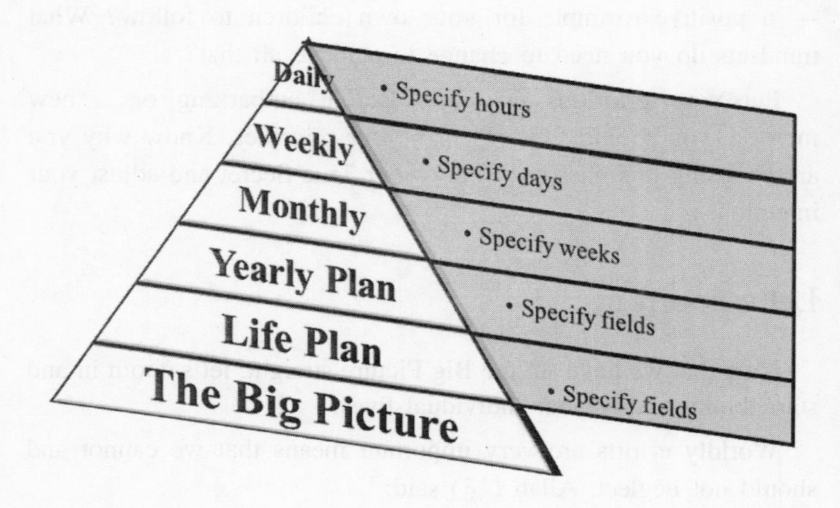

We can divide our planning into long-term and short-term plans:

1. Long-term plans:

When you are considering your long-term plans (from one year to a lifetime), remember that we placed the Big Picture at our base, so every action and thought has to stem from it. When you start writing out your long-term plans, there are some important factors to keep in mind. I want you to consider all the following topics:

1. My Islamic Ummah (What are you contributing to the welfare of Islam and the Muslims? Your contribution can be in any field, be it science, education, physical health, charity work, entertaining, finance, media...)

2. My religious and spiritual development (How am I improving or evolving spiritually and religiously? This includes your worship, ethics, values, purification of the soul, extent of following the prophetic teachings...)

3. My health (exercise, nutrition, adequate sleep, dealing with any addictions or bad habits...)

4. My family (spouse, children, parents, other relatives...)

5. My social life (neighbours, friends, society, environment...)

6. My personal development (What new skills, knowledge or information will I acquire? How will I evolve mentally, intellectually and emotionally? What new books could I read to learn and grow? What new fields or topics might I consider investigating?)

7. My work/career (ambitions, clear goals, setting an example as a successful and respectable Muslim...)

8. My life (money earned and spent; wasted time; entertainment; *zakât*, the obligatory 'alms tax' on wealth; voluntary charity; investments for the future...)

2. Short-term plans:

Short-term plans are our monthly, weekly and daily plans. As you go up the pyramid, the fields will gradually narrow as you integrate more specific details into your life plans. You break the fields down into specific tasks to be performed on specific dates, one at a time or step-by-step. For example:

- My monthly plan includes a rough estimate of the progress required in my work/career and family life (specific issues to work on this month) and any major plans like holidays or travelling.
- My weekly plan includes any appointments that I have, my shopping times and lists, my cooking plans for each day of the week, errands to run, any communications needed and steps required for making progress on my goals. An exact date should be specified for each action.
- My daily plan includes specified times for everything to be performed on this day.

Revising and updating your plans:

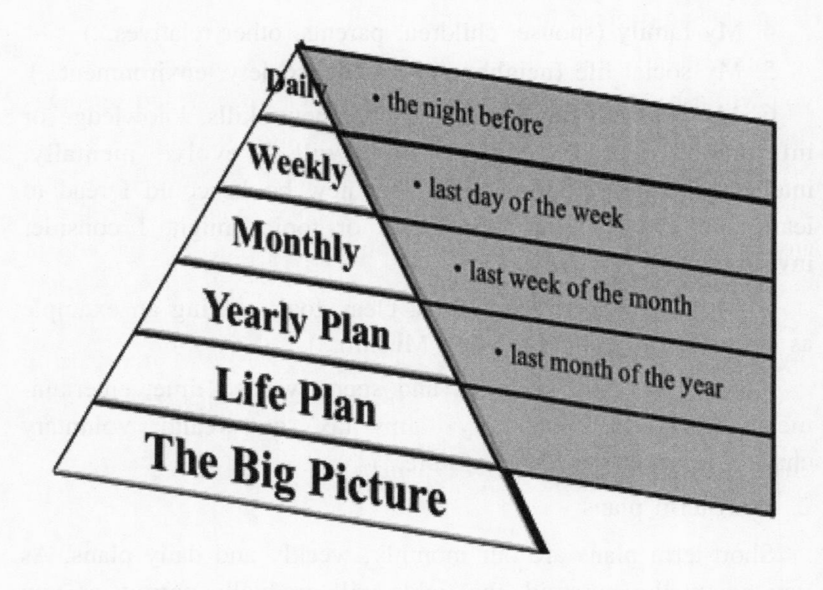

Each night before going to bed, make a quick evaluation of your plan for that day. What did you achieve? What needed to be shifted to the next day? Why? Did you procrastinate? Did you waste your time somehow? Or did you do your best, but this task was not meant to be finished on that specified date? Don't get discouraged. Assess the reasons and just try your best. We cannot control the results; we can only control the actions we perform. Achievements are up to our Creator, the Exalted. Sketch out a plan for the next day, being sure to include a specific timetable for getting things done.

On the last day of the week, just before the start of the new week, sit down for ten or twenty minutes to review the previous week's accomplishments. Start to schedule your next week and organize your thoughts.

In the last week of each month, review your month's achievements. (I also review my monthly budget and spending.) Then schedule plans for the next month.

Subsequently, once a year, at a time that is appropriate for you, you will assess your progress over the previous year and set goals for the following year. For me, it works best to start the new year in January.[29] I usually revise my yearly plan at the start of the school year in September, so that I still have time to catch up on any forgotten or behind-schedule plans before reaching the end of the year. In December, the last month of my year, I revisit my yearly plan to check, analyze and evaluate. How well did I follow my plan? Did my plan take me a step forward towards my life goals? Did I hold tight to my True Secret? Did I miss accomplishing my targets in any of my specified fields? Which one(s)? Why? Finally, I devise a plan for the next year.

My Planning Rules:

P for Patience and Planting seeds of love and compassion in people's hearts

L for Learning constantly and Living in the moment

A for Awareness and Adding meaning and dimensions to life

N for Never losing hope and Never giving up

S for Setting Smart goals and Surrendering to the divine will

---

[29] You might choose to start your new year in the Islamic months of Muḥarram or Ramadan or at another time that better fits your lifestyle.

Take a moment to... devise your plans

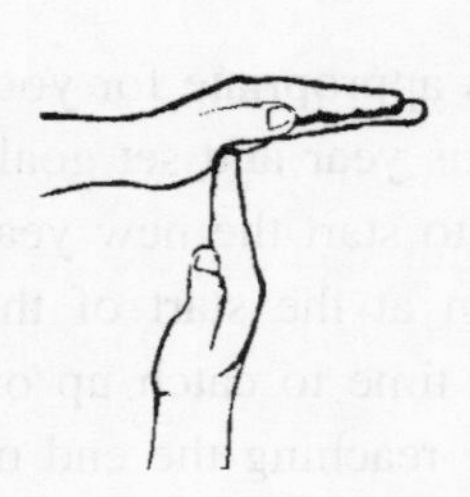

- In your journal, write down your **plan for tomorrow.** (For example: go to the bank and supermarket, cook chicken and rice for dinner, pick up the children...)
- On another page, write **next week's missions**. Write the days of the week in order, leaving several lines after each. Then write your plan for each day. Start with regular fixed activities, such as your work schedule, 'cleaning day' and class times. Then add your other missions, like going to the gym or studying before exams.

- Open a third spread page for **this month's plans** (visit friends or family, finish some studies...)

- A fourth page is for what you would like to achieve throughout the **coming year**. Consider all aspects of your life (the eight fields that we discussed under long-term plans; feel free to add any other topics you want). Take your time.

- Let's go even further. Close your eyes for two minutes. Calm your mind, feel each breath. Imagine yourself travelling in time. **Where do you see yourself twenty years from now?** What are your bigger plans, your dreams? Do not criticize, censor or judge just yet. Write it all down, however far off or crazy it may seem. (You may dream of being the president of your country or the founder of the first hotel apartments on the moon).

Visualize your ideal:

1. Activities/work/career
2. Environment/surrounding/social life
3. Intentions behind what you are achieving (ending world poverty, teaching youth, leading Muslims to the right path...)

Be as specific as you can. Visualize all the details; feel them, touch them, smell them and see them. Now open your eyes and write down your dream.

- Hold on to your dream and read further.

Remember to always consider your intention before implementing any of your plans, and be sincere in your intention. Always make sure that your plans are consistent with your ultimate goal in life: pleasing Allah (ﷻ), and implementing your True Secret.

2. Keep yourself challenged

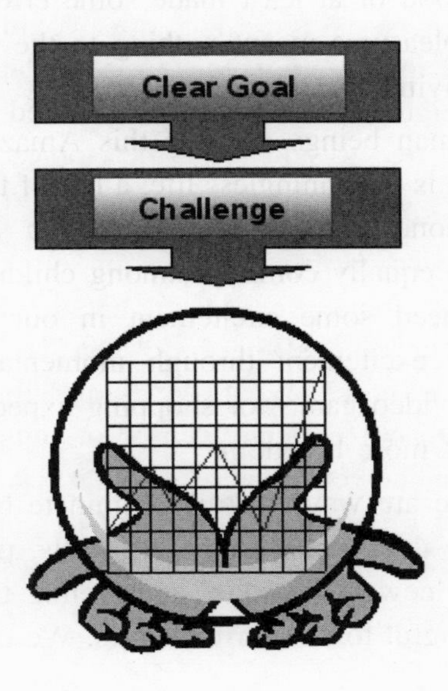

We need the challenge

Martin Seligman related an interesting story in his book *Authentic Happiness*. It is the story of one of his teachers, Julian, who kept an Amazonian lizard as a pet in his laboratory. For weeks after he got the lizard, it totally refused to eat. He offered it everything: lizard foods, fresh fruits and vegetables, insects, meat, food from the supermarket... Nothing worked. The lizard was starving itself to death.

One day Julian was eating a sandwich, and he put it on the table while he read the day's newspaper. When he finished reading, he threw the paper down, and it fell over the sandwich. In the blink of an eye, the lizard jumped, tore the paper to pieces and devoured the sandwich in one bite.

The lizard had refused to eat unless it was challenged, unless it hunted its own food or at least made some effort in acquiring it. Easily acquired pleasures meant nothing to the lizard. They were not even worth living for.

In a way, human beings are like this Amazonian lizard. Life without challenge is a meaningless life, a life of total boredom. We often hear someone saying: "*I'm bored to death.*" It is an expression that is equally common among children, teenagers and adults. We all need some excitement in our lives. Often, we wrongly get this excitement through momentary pleasures like television series, video games or shopping expeditions... but what follows is usually more boredom.

However, there are ways to truly eliminate boredom from our lives. We can do this by learning new skills, pushing our limits further, acquiring new knowledge, and feeling that we contribute something meaningful to our surroundings. We need to feel useful to ourselves, our families and our society. We need to fulfil our mission on earth. That's why our internal instincts will not be satisfied with less than continuous achievements. These achievements do not need to be big, but they have to be ongoing and cumulative. They need to be meaningful, at least to us. They need to be part of our lifelong quest to develop our potential and seek the pleasure of Allah (ﷻ).

This is why a very important part of defining your goals is to keep yourself constantly challenged. If your objectives are too easy to reach, you will get bored after a while and become dissatisfied. As soon as you reach your goals, you might lose interest in them, feel unmotivated and lose momentum. On the other hand, if your challenges are well suited to your abilities, and if you are gradually meeting your goals, you will be self-fulfilled and satisfied. Constantly meeting your short-term goals gives you the required stamina and driving force to continue your pursuit of bigger and higher goals. It gives you the excitement and delight that is necessary to stimulate your willpower and keep you going.

If you have too many dreams and big ambitions, don't get discouraged or disappointed. Take a moment to assess your capabilities and resources, adjust your priorities and carefully plan your next step.

Consider the story of a young man who was walking by the seashore. He stopped to look at some fishermen who were casting their nets and collecting their catch. One fisherman was selecting the small fish from his net and putting them in his basket, while throwing the big fish back into the sea. The young man was puzzled.

He approached the fisherman. "*Excuse me,*" he said. "*May I ask what you are doing?*"

"*Catching fish for dinner,*" the fisherman replied.

"*So why are you throwing away all those big fish?*"

"*I'm not that rich, you know. I only have a tiny frying pan,*" answered the fisherman.[30]

How many times have you thrown away big dreams and opportunities because you were convinced that they were just not 'right' for you or that this was not the 'right' time for change and growth?

Take a moment to... consider making some changes

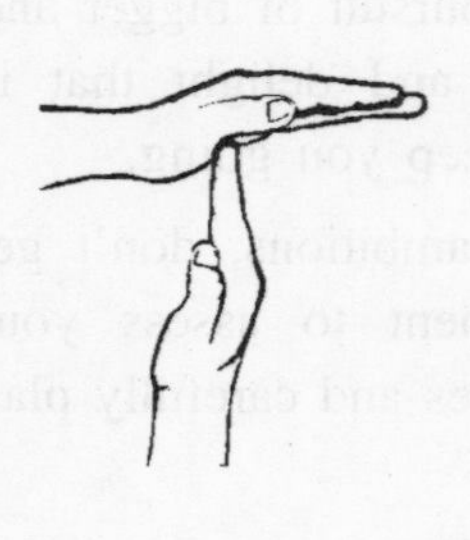

- In your journal, list twenty changes (or new activities) you would like to adopt, whether big or small.[31] Quickly write whatever crosses your mind. Don't stop or assess; just record the first twenty thoughts that come to your mind. They may be anything: get a haircut, buy a new set of china, find a better friend, join an art class, learn to sew, repaint the house, take computer programming courses, write a novel, go back to college, fly an airplane, start a scout movement...
- Select two of them and commit yourself to doing them, or at least taking the first step towards accomplishing them, this week.

---

[30] Doane and Sloat

[31] Cameron

Some people avoid big dreams so that they will not get frustrated if they fail to achieve them. A fifty-year-old woman once advised her friend to pursue a college degree in teaching, since her friend loved working with young children.

"*Do you know what age I will be when I get my degree?*" her friend exclaimed.

"*Exactly the same age you would be if you didn't get it,*" the lady replied.

Taking on a new challenge, switching careers, or following a new path can be done at any time in life. As the saying goes, better late than never. Our Prophet (ﷺ) taught us: «If the Day of Resurrection comes while a seedling is in the hand of one of you, let him plant it.» (Aḥmad; al-Albâni graded it as sound)

Allah (ﷻ) also says in the Qur'an:

﴿فَإِذَا فَرَغْتَ فَٱنصَبْ ۝٧﴾ [الشَّرح : ٧]

﴿Therefore, when you are free [from your immediate task], still labour hard.﴾ *(Qur'an 94: 7)*

We must always remember the next verse, too, because it completes the meaning of the previous one:

﴿وَإِلَىٰ رَبِّكَ فَٱرْغَب ۝٨﴾ [الشَّرح : ٨]

﴿And to Allah [alone] turn [all your intentions and hopes and] your invocations.﴾ *(Qur'an 94: 8)*

You should live in the moment and enjoy your achievements, but at the same time set intentions for your future goals, and always remember to be sincere in your intentions.

When I talk about challenges, I always hear two main complaints:

1. "*I don't have time.*" We will be discussing some time management tips in the resources section, but for now, the basic idea is to not procrastinate. Organize and simplify your life, and most importantly, put your priorities straight.

2. "*I have no special talent.*" In my first book, *Healing Body and Soul*, I related the story of a friend who complained to me about being a true loser. She was convinced that she was good at nothing, that she possessed no talents whatsoever. I sat with her and tried to make her think about all the things that she really enjoys doing, her hobbies and what she was good at. After a long discussion, she only came up with two skills: she loved shopping at expensive department stores and enjoyed eating in fancy, five-star restaurants.

I could not conceive of any possible way to help her out, so I left, urging her to think of other and more 'useful' things to do. A few days later, I was looking at a job recruitment site when my eyes fell on a very strange career category. A renowned company was seeking a 'mystery shopper'. The job description went as follows: "The person required has to love shopping and dining in the highest standard stores and restaurants. He/she will then be charged with writing reports evaluating these places in terms of service quality and employee efficiency." That was it! There was actually something there waiting especially for my friend, demanding her particular passion and total dedication. With her unique talents, she could excel at helping different companies in the hospitality industry to improve their quality standards.

This example may be extreme, but it illustrates perfectly how we all have hidden potential just waiting to be explored. Never underestimate the value of your hobbies and interests. Never think that you have nothing to contribute. If you are having trouble determining what you are good at, dig deeper, look around you, ask friends to help you and consider investigating different fields and topics that have sparked your interest.

Take a moment to...
broaden your horizons through reading

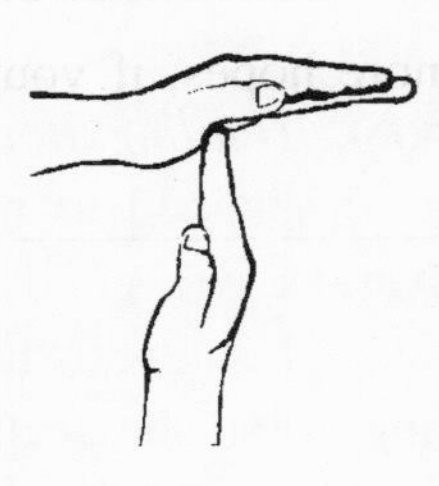

Go to a bookstore or a library this week and give yourself enough time to browse through a number of books. Look at some new topics. Then choose a book that looks interesting and, at the same time, is in a totally new field that you are curious to learn about. It can be anything from science, computers, math, literature, journalism, cooking, nutrition, medicine, fashion, interior design... Enjoy your reading and see what thoughts or inspirations the book will bring out of you.

Take a moment to... review and revise

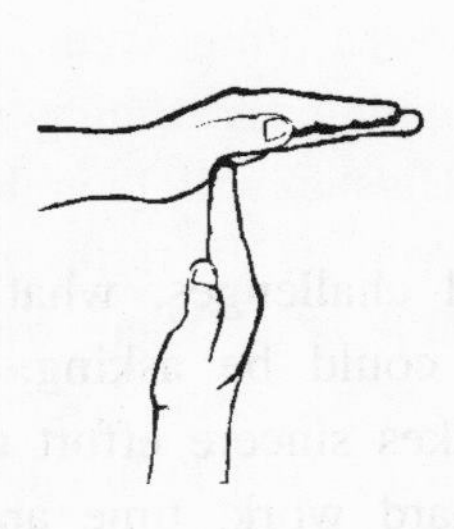

- Reconsider the next yearly plan that you developed in the previous exercises. Are your plans the right size for you? Too big (because you do not want to get frustrated or overwhelmed and risk giving it all up)? Too small (because you do not want your potential to go untapped and rust away)? Did you challenge yourself enough?
- Reread your time-travelling trip to twenty years in the future. Would you like to add something?
- Now refer back to your list of apples. Is there anything in common between those lists? Are your plans and life dreams conforming to your passions?

- Do any of your plans and dreams stir up in you extra fervour and enthusiasm? Do any of your apples constitute a hidden dream that you are longing to execute? Write it down.
- Add more apples, more dreams, or more hopes, if you feel like it. Don't be afraid to dream.

3. Be a believer

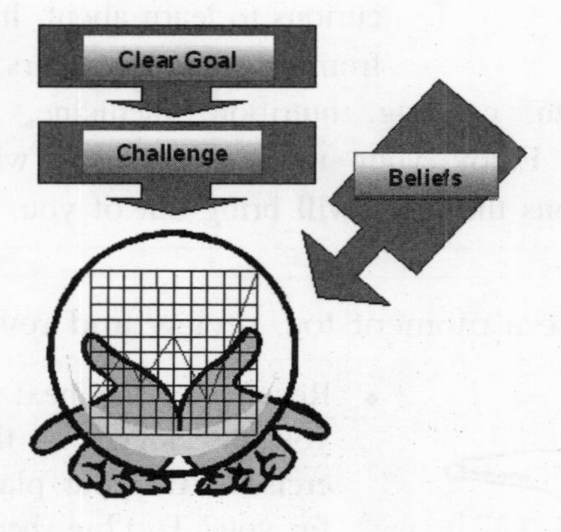

Now that you have set some goals and challenges, what's next? "*How can I actualize them?,*" you could be asking. I know, it is easy to talk and dream, but it takes sincere effort to turn those dreams into reality. It requires hard work, time and patience, but most of all it requires **belief**. By belief here, I mean two things. First is the belief in your Creator, in Allah (ﷻ), belief that all power, success and wisdom comes according to His will. This is the essence of our True Secret and the Big Picture that we instilled in our minds and hearts. The second required belief here is belief in yourself. To be able to achieve your goals and fulfil your dreams, you have to believe in yourself and your abilities. Later, we will deal with self-confidence and personal power in more detail, but in this section, I want you to feel and see that this power and self-esteem stem only from your sincere faith. I want you to know deep inside that believing in your Creator is the first step in believing in yourself and your abilities.

Inner thoughts and beliefs

Your thoughts and beliefs dictate your actions, and your actions, in turn, shape your reality.

We acquire and store beliefs over the years from our environment, our parents, our friends, our culture, our educational system, our experiences of success or failure, the events we encounter, the books we read and the information we are exposed to on the internet or from the media. Those beliefs generate a tremendous amount of power, which may be positive or negative, according to their nature.

The more you choose to have gracious, wholesome, constructive and inspirational thoughts towards yourself and others and towards every event that you encounter in daily living, the more you will generate blissful reactions in your life. Your wisdom resides within yourself; stop seeking answers elsewhere. Purify your heart and soul, believe in yourself and your abilities, and have total, unconditional faith in your Creator. Only then will you change your life for the better.

Our Prophet Muhammad (ﷺ) related that Allah (ﷻ) says: «I am as My servant thinks I am, and I am with him if he calls for Me...» (Bukhari and Muslim)

Dr. Albert Ellis outlined an 'ABC' system to help people adjust their state of mind:[32]

A = Action

B = Belief

C = Consequential feeling

We usually think that actions or events that we encounter are the only causative agents behind our feelings. For example, if I lose my job, this will lead to and be the reason for a feeling of low self-esteem: *I am not good enough, and I will never be successful in my life*. This shows the importance of 'B' in the formula. If I believe in myself, I will have confidence, and I can change my consequential feelings 'C' in a positive direction: *This is a new challenge, a given opportunity to learn and to further improve myself and reveal my hidden talents and gifts.*

Do not accept failure. It is up to you to turn your failures into successes by always trying one more time.[33] It is not what happens that matters, but how you choose to respond to it. Learn from your experiences and have total belief in your abilities and potential. Be open to new possibilities and directions as they come into your life. Evaluate them. Don't be distracted by every tangent, but consider alternatives as they present themselves. Are they consistent with your major goals in life? Are they better ways of reaching your unique potential than the way you are currently following?[34]

---

32 Schnebly

33 Dyer

34 There will be more about flexibility later in this chapter.

I read an interesting story that illustrates how your perception of problems or incidents can really make all the difference. According to the source, this is a true story of something that happened between the customer of a famous car company and its customer-care executive.[35]

This car company received a very strange complaint from a customer who stated that his family was used to having ice cream every day after dinner. After finishing their meal, they would decide which ice cream flavour they fancied and then drive to a nearby store to fetch it. The problem was that whenever the flavour was vanilla, their new car would not start when they wanted to go back home. This problem did not occur when they bought any other flavour of ice cream.

The client's problem seemed ridiculous; nevertheless, after receiving two complaint letters, the department president decided to send an engineer to the man's house to check it out.

At the client's house, the engineer was surprised to find that the owner of the car was a decent, well-educated man who seriously repeated the same strange complaint. After checking the car, they drove together to the store, and to the surprise of the engineer, the owner's complaint was entirely accurate. Each time they bought vanilla ice cream, the car refused to start, but it had no problem with any of the other flavours. The engineer repeatedly visited the client's house and arranged frequent trips to purchase ice cream.

[35] Subordinate Courts of Singapore

He had no clue whatsoever that could lead to discovering the reason behind this strange phenomenon.

Sometimes thinking logically and focusing so much on the problem (in this case, the car) can make us blind to other sides of the story. Open-minded attitudes and a broader view — what is now called creative thinking — can help, so this is exactly what the engineer used. He set aside his 'common sense' beliefs for a moment and assumed a broader perspective. Let's check the store, not the car, he thought (thus introducing 'B' in the formula).

The store had the vanilla flavoured ice cream arranged in aisles close to the checkout counters, while all the other flavours were found in the back aisles. How could this affect the car trip? This meant that it took much less time for the man to purchase the vanilla than any other flavour. Aha!

Now the problem became strictly a mechanical one, and the answer could be easily found. The extra time needed to purchase the other flavours allowed the engine more time to cool down, and the car restarted easily, while this was not the case when buying vanilla ice cream.

Strange as it might seem at first glance, the problem was real, and an answer could be found with the right mental attitude. If the engineer had persisted with an inflexible attitude that only considered what was obviously logical, he could not have located the problem. Your mental attitude — in other words, your beliefs — can alter your world view and help you find real solutions.

Allah (ﷻ) teaches us this in the Qur'an:

﴿... إِنَّ ٱللَّهَ لَا يُغَيِّرُ مَا بِقَوْمٍ حَتَّىٰ يُغَيِّرُوا۟ مَا بِأَنفُسِهِمْ ... ﴿١١﴾﴾

[الرّعد: ١١]

﴾...Verily, Allah will never change the condition of a people until they change what is in themselves...﴿ *(Qur'an 13: 11)*

To create change in your life, you have to start working on your thoughts and beliefs. It is all up to you. Learn a lesson from each failure, and search for the message behind every problem. Believe that Allah (ﷻ) wills only what is best for you and that the door to His guidance and mercy is always open. Visualize a joyful life and serene surroundings. Remember that a perfect life is not defined by material possessions and riches. Visualize yourself being happy, productive and successful; you will find yourself subconsciously working on that perfection once you believe in it.

Start working on your thoughts and beliefs.

Take a moment to... consider your inner beliefs

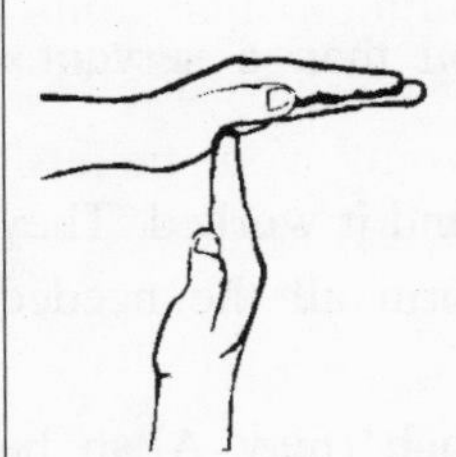

- Do you believe in yourself and your abilities?
- What deeply held beliefs do you need to change in order for you to improve your feeling of self-worth and your outlook on life?
- Always make sure that your beliefs are consistent with your True Secret. Be sincere even in your most deeply held thoughts.

Think positively

It is crucial to give your mind consistently positive and harmonious thoughts. If you keep concentrating on how poor, unhappy, weak or incapable you are, then mental images of vulnerability and weakness — along with apprehension and incompetence — will be conveyed to all the body tissues. They, in turn, will be affected by these destructive vibrations, and your body will hinder you with illnesses, imbalances in the various physical systems and lack of motivation or energy.

The idea of subconscious suggestion can be seen in the behaviour of many early Muslims. The Prophet (ﷺ) even taught his own daughter Fâṭimah (رضي الله عنها) this technique when she came with her husband, 'Ali (رضي الله عنه), to ask the Prophet (ﷺ) to help them acquire a servant, as the housework was becoming too much for them to bear. Prophet Muhammad (ﷺ) sat gently beside them and taught them a form of *dhikr Allâh* (remembering Allah through praising and supplicating to Him) to say every night just before going to bed:

Subḥân Allâh (Glory be to Allah) – 33 times

Alḥamdulillâh (All praise be to Allah) – 33 times

Allâhu akbar (Allah is the Greatest) – 34 times

He (ﷺ) told them: «That is better for you than a servant.» (Aḥmad; al-Albâni graded it as sound)

They tried it with absolute faith and belief, and it worked. They found within themselves the strength to perform all the needed work.

These are not mere words: 'Ali and Fâṭimah (may Allah be pleased with them) believed completely in them and in the power and will of Allah (سبحانه وتعالى). There is an actual blessing in these words, and **sincere faith** was the key to receiving that blessing. Of course, we must still remember that any benefit arising from certain supplications and dhikr comes only by the will of Allah (ﷻ). We do not have the knowledge of how Allah (ﷻ) brings this about, but we know and believe that it is true and effective.

Prophet Muhammad (ﷺ) taught us to make dhikr, and he (ﷺ) gave us many examples of phrases to use. Some of these are to be recited specifically in the morning and evening. These are not just meditation exercises; they are a continuous active remembrance of the power of Allah (ﷻ) and a regeneration of our faith and belief. If you practice them regularly and faithfully, they constitute a type of autosuggestion, protecting you from poverty, disease and evil thoughts. This opens in front of you the doors to a prosperous, happy and healthy life in this world and to a promised eternal reward beyond all human limitations and boundaries.

Take a moment to... learn some phrases of dhikr

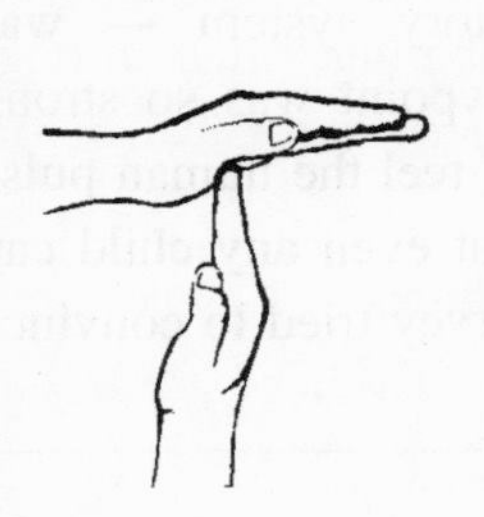

- Go through the different phrases of praise and remembrance of Allah (ﷻ) that our Prophet (ﷺ) taught us. You will find hundreds of them. There are dhikr or supplications to be said for waking up, for going to bed, for putting on new clothes, for undressing, for entering and leaving the bathroom, for entering or leaving the mosque and for entering the market (or 'mega mall', as the case may be). There are supplications and dhikr for eating, visiting the sick, sneezing and travelling; others for cases of fear, physical pain, panic, anger or distress; and others to say in case of delight or amazement, or upon receiving pleasant news.[36]

[36] For more details, see al-Qaḥṭâni, *Fortification of the Muslim: Supplications from the Qur'an and Sunnah.*

- Copy some phrases of dhikr into your journal. Try to memorize them and use them in your everyday life. You can also write them on small pieces of cardboard and post them where you can easily see them. Feel their empowering action and enjoy the positive mindset that they convey.

Reflect on your beliefs

Until the early seventeenth century, the world regarded as 'commonsense' the writings of the Roman/Greek philosopher and physician Galen (129-199 CE). His anatomical explanation of the body was the only one that was accepted. According to him, the role of the heart was to introduce heat into our bodily systems, and the function of the brain was to balance this by cooling the system down. Because of these strongly held beliefs, the idea proposed by William Harvey in 1628 CE — that the heart was a pump that pushed the blood within a closed circulatory system — was strongly rejected. The belief in Galen's viewpoint was so strong that the medical doctors at the time could not feel the human pulse or hear the beating of the heart — things that even any child can now feel and hear — no matter how hard Harvey tried to convince them.[37]

Take a moment to...
examine your 'commonsense' beliefs

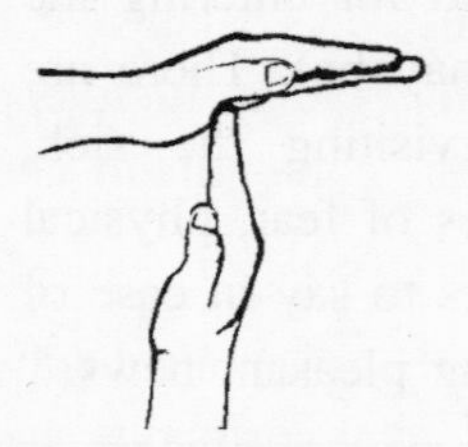

- List some 'commonsense' beliefs that you have held for a long time, whether they were inherited or picked up from your environment or through daily experiences. (Some of mine were

[37] Radin

things like: talent cannot be acquired, you are either born with it or not; one person cannot change the world; and I am not so special.)

- Write them down. Now go through them, one by one, and reflect on their meanings. Are they completely true, unable to be changed and challenged, or are they subject to opinion, moods and circumstances? Is any of them holding you back?

- Think about which ones you need to keep and which ones need to be changed.

- Compare your beliefs with your long-term plans. Do you see any contradiction? If so, check your intention and True Secret again. Re-visualize your Big Picture and adjust your path.

Take a moment to... visualize your happiness

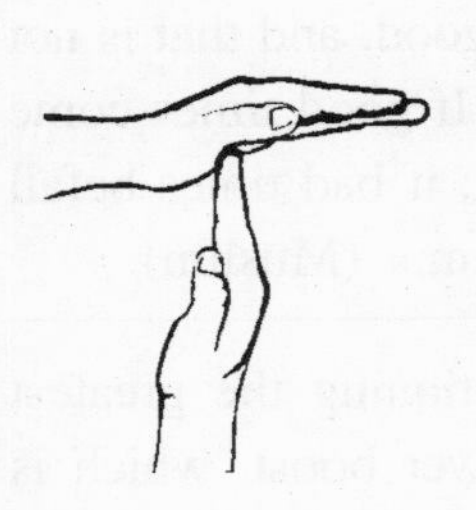

- Before going to bed, think of something pleasant. Always visualize a prosperous, happy life in which you are relieved of your daily hassles and worldly distress. Then leave your subconscious mind to manage your affairs for you, and depend on and trust in Allah (ﷻ). Don't be impatient for results. Just keep practicing it every night with total faith, contentment and patience.

- Then, when your problems are solved and your happy endings are reached, always remember to give thanks and praise to Almighty Allah (ﷻ) who can, by His will, make anything happen:

﴿إِنَّمَآ أَمۡرُهُۥٓ إِذَآ أَرَادَ شَيۡـًٔا أَن يَقُولَ لَهُۥ كُن فَيَكُونُ ﴿٨٢﴾﴾

[يٓس: ٨٢]

﴿Verily, His Command, when He intends a thing, is only that He says to it: Be! And it is!﴾ *(Qur'an 36: 82)*

• Remember that any calamity that befalls you is of your own doing (although at first you may not recognize it), and that anything good is from Allah (ﷻ):

﴿مَّآ أَصَابَكَ مِنۡ حَسَنَةٖ فَمِنَ ٱللَّهِۖ وَمَآ أَصَابَكَ مِن سَيِّئَةٖ فَمِن نَّفۡسِكَۚ ... ﴿٧٩﴾﴾

[النِّساء: ٧٩]

﴿Whatever of good reaches you, it is from Allah, but whatever of evil befalls you, is from yourself...﴾

(Qur'an 4: 79)

• Also remember that there is always good in everything that happens to a Muslim. Our Prophet (ﷺ) said: «The believer's affair is amazing; it is all for the good, and that is not the case with anyone other than a believer. If good times come to him, he is thankful, so it is good for him; if bad times befall him, he is patient, so it is also good for him.» (Muslim)

I should not end this section before mentioning the greatest positive thought of all Muslims, our real power boost, which is Allah's promise of paradise for the believers. No matter what happens in this life, there is no more positive thought for the Muslim than this. Our most tremendous blessing is to be guided to Islam, and this fact alone gives joy and hope to the life of the Muslim.

﴿فَمَآ أُوتِيتُم مِّن شَيۡءٖ فَمَتَٰعُ ٱلۡحَيَوٰةِ ٱلدُّنۡيَاۖ وَمَا عِندَ ٱللَّهِ خَيۡرٞ وَأَبۡقَىٰ لِلَّذِينَ ءَامَنُواْ وَعَلَىٰ رَبِّهِمۡ يَتَوَكَّلُونَ ﴿٣٦﴾﴾

[الشّورى: ٣٦]

﴿Now whatever you have been given is but a passing comfort for the life of the world, and that which Allah has is better and more lasting for those who believe and put their trust in their Lord.﴾ *(Qur'an 42: 36)*

﴿سَابِقُوٓاْ إِلَىٰ مَغۡفِرَةٖ مِّن رَّبِّكُمۡ وَجَنَّةٍ عَرۡضُهَا كَعَرۡضِ ٱلسَّمَآءِ وَٱلۡأَرۡضِ أُعِدَّتۡ لِلَّذِينَ ءَامَنُواْ بِٱللَّهِ وَرُسُلِهِۦۚ ذَٰلِكَ فَضۡلُ ٱللَّهِ يُؤۡتِيهِ مَن يَشَآءُۚ وَٱللَّهُ ذُو ٱلۡفَضۡلِ ٱلۡعَظِيمِ ٢١﴾ [الحديد: ٢١]

﴿Race one with another for forgiveness from your Lord and a garden [in paradise], the breadth of which is as the breadth of the heavens and the earth, which is in store for those who believe in Allah and His Messengers. Such is the bounty of Allah, which He bestows upon whom He wills, and Allah is the Owner of Infinite Bounty.﴾ *(Qur'an 57: 21)*

4. Watch your values and ethics

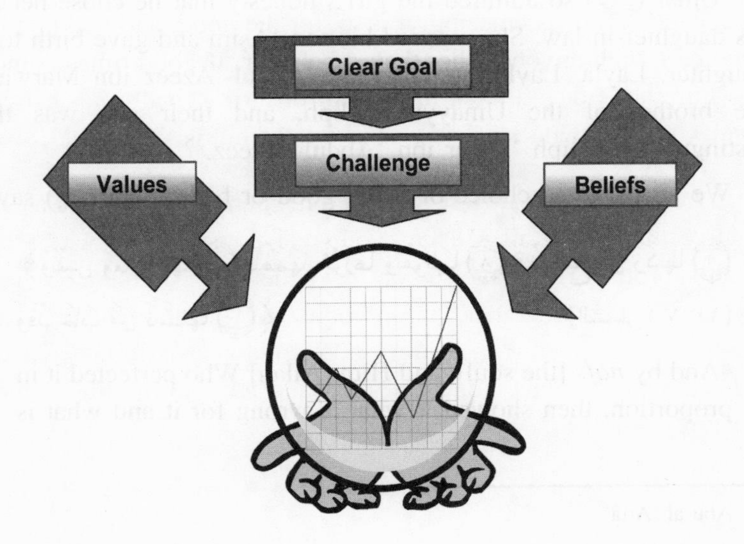

Being ethical does not mean just following the rules, as in: "*I do not steal because if I got caught, I would be put in jail,*" or "*I do not lie because if someone found out, it could be publicly humiliating.*" Statements like these cannot in any way be described as ethical. Being ethical is choosing to do the right things because they are the right things to do, and doing them only for the sake of Allah (ﷻ).

True ethics are illustrated in many incidents that occurred among the Prophet's Companions (may Allah be pleased with them). For example, one night, 'Umar ibn al-Khaṭṭâb (رضي الله عنه) was walking in Madinah when he heard a woman, a milk seller, ordering her daughter to mix water with the milk before heading to the market. The daughter refused, stating that Caliph 'Umar (رضي الله عنه) had prohibited this kind of treachery. The mother replied: "*O my daughter, 'Umar cannot see you doing it.*" The daughter responded, "*If 'Umar cannot see me, 'Umar's God surely can. I cannot obey Him in public and disobey Him in private.*"

'Umar (رضي الله عنه) so admired the girl's honesty that he chose her as his daughter-in-law. She married his son 'Âṣim and gave birth to a daughter, Laylâ. Laylâ later married 'Abdul-'Azeez ibn Marwân, the brother of the Umayyad caliph, and their son was the distinguished caliph 'Umar ibn 'Abdul-'Azeez.[38]

We all have the choice of being good or bad. Allah (ﷻ) says:

﴿وَنَفْسٍ وَمَا سَوَّىٰهَا ۝٧ فَأَلْهَمَهَا فُجُورَهَا وَتَقْوَىٰهَا ۝٨ قَدْ أَفْلَحَ مَن زَكَّىٰهَا ۝٩ وَقَدْ خَابَ مَن دَسَّىٰهَا ۝١٠﴾ [الشّمس: ٧-١٠]

﴿And by *nafs* [the soul], and Him [Allah] Who perfected it in proportion, then showed it what is wrong for it and what is

[38] Abu al-'Aṭṭâ

right for it. Indeed he who purifies his own self [soul] succeeds; and indeed he who corrupts his own self fails.﴿

(Qur'an 91: 7-10)

Unethical actions do not show their consequences only in the hereafter; the punishment is received in this world as well. Allah the Almighty says:

﴿إِنَّ ٱلَّذِينَ يُبَايِعُونَكَ إِنَّمَا يُبَايِعُونَ ٱللَّهَ يَدُ ٱللَّهِ فَوْقَ أَيْدِيهِمْ ۚ فَمَن نَّكَثَ فَإِنَّمَا يَنكُثُ عَلَىٰ نَفْسِهِۦ ۖ وَمَنْ أَوْفَىٰ بِمَا عَـٰهَدَ عَلَيْهُ ٱللَّهَ فَسَيُؤْتِيهِ أَجْرًا عَظِيمًا ﴿١٠﴾﴾ [الفتح : ١٠]

﴾Then whoever breaks his pledge, breaks it only to his own harm; and whoever fulfils what he has covenanted with Allah, He [Allah] will bestow on him a great reward.﴿

(Qur'an 48: 10)

﴿أَفَأَمِنَ ٱلَّذِينَ مَكَرُوا۟ ٱلسَّيِّـَٔاتِ أَن يَخْسِفَ ٱللَّهُ بِهِمُ ٱلْأَرْضَ أَوْ يَأْتِيَهُمُ ٱلْعَذَابُ مِنْ حَيْثُ لَا يَشْعُرُونَ ﴿٤٥﴾ أَوْ يَأْخُذَهُمْ فِى تَقَلُّبِهِمْ فَمَا هُم بِمُعْجِزِينَ ﴿٤٦﴾﴾ [النحل : ٤٥-٤٦]

﴾Do then those who devise evil plots feel secure that Allah will not sink them into the earth or that the torment will not seize them from directions they perceive not? Or that He may catch them in the midst of their going to and fro, so that there is no escape for them [from Allah's Punishment]?﴿

(Qur'an 16: 45-46)

I know of a man who started his career as a middle class government employee. His meagre salary was not enough to satisfy his family's needs and desires, so the man found an easy way out: bribes. Since he was a civil engineer, his post with the government allowed him to deal with many wealthy contractors and businessmen. He started by accepting any offered 'gifts', and then the whole matter progressed rapidly until he refused to sign any document without taking his 'share'.

It did not take long for his financial status to improve dramatically. He thought this improvement would bring happiness to his family, but he was wrong. His wife, a pious Muslim woman, warned him repeatedly against wrongful deeds and tried in vain to stop him, but the newfound luxury and riches blinded him and only made him long for more. He forgot the order of Allah (ﷻ):

﴿وَلَا تَأْكُلُوٓا۟ أَمْوَٰلَكُم بَيْنَكُم بِٱلْبَٰطِلِ وَتُدْلُوا۟ بِهَآ إِلَى ٱلْحُكَّامِ لِتَأْكُلُوا۟ فَرِيقًا مِّنْ أَمْوَٰلِ ٱلنَّاسِ بِٱلْإِثْمِ وَأَنتُمْ تَعْلَمُونَ ﴿١٨٨﴾﴾ [البقرة: ١٨٨]

﴿And eat up not one another's property unjustly [in any illegal way, such as stealing, robbing or deceiving], nor give bribes to the rulers that you may knowingly eat up a part of the property of others sinfully.﴾ *(Qur'an 2: 188)*

Years have passed, and the man is now relating his story. He is sitting near his vast swimming pool in his luxurious villa, but he is sitting alone. His wife has left, his only son is in a sanatorium receiving treatment for drug addiction, and his daughter lives with her husband and wants nothing to do with her father.

Unethical behaviours may bring temporary riches, but they never bring true happiness or satisfaction. They may feed one's greed, but they surely deplete one's soul.

In Islam, practicing good ethics and morality is highly stressed. Allah (ﷻ) describes His Messenger by saying:

﴿وَإِنَّكَ لَعَلَىٰ خُلُقٍ عَظِيمٍ ﴿٤﴾﴾ [القلم: ٤]

﴿And verily, you [O Muhammad] are on an exalted standard of character.﴾ *(Qur'an 68: 4)*

Prophet Muhammad (ﷺ) also taught us: «A bad person in the sight of Allah (ﷻ) is he who does not behave courteously, and people shun his company because of his bad manners.» (Bukhari)

Many good moral qualities are taught to us in the Qur'an and Sunnah. Here are but a few examples from among the sayings of Allah's Messenger (ﷺ): «Let him who believes in Allah (ﷻ) and the Last Day speak good or keep silent; and let him who believes in Allah (ﷻ) and the Last Day be generous to his neighbour; and let him who believes in Allah (ﷻ) and the Last Day be generous to his guest.» (Bukhari and Muslim)

«Truthfulness leads to righteousness, and righteousness leads to paradise. A person remains truthful until he is written as truthful with Allah (ﷻ). Lying leads to iniquity, and iniquity leads to the fire. A person keeps lying until he is written as a liar with Allah (ﷻ).» (Bukhari and Muslim)

«The signs of the hypocrite are three: when he speaks, he lies; when he makes an oath, he breaks it; and when he is entrusted with something, he betrays that trust.» (Bukhari and Muslim)

«Whoever guarantees for me that which is between his legs (meaning he guards the chastity of his private parts) and that which is between his two jaw bones (meaning he guards his tongue from acts of indiscretion), I guarantee for him paradise.» (Bukhari)

«On the Day of Judgement, there are three types of people to whom Allah (ﷻ) will not speak nor make flourish, nor will He look at them, and for them is a painful torment: an old man who commits fornication, a king who is a liar, and a poor person who is arrogant.» (Muslim)

«Many a community ruined itself in the past because they only punished the poor and ignored the offences of the privileged. By Allah, if (even) Muhammad's (my) daughter Fâṭimah had committed theft, her hand would have been severed (according to the punishment for theft decreed by Allah).» (Bukhari)

In the noble Qur'an, we also find many statements from Allah (ﷻ) that instruct us to live moral and ethical lives:

﴿ ۞ إِنَّ ٱللَّهَ يَأۡمُرُ بِٱلۡعَدۡلِ وَٱلۡإِحۡسَٰنِ وَإِيتَآيِٕ ذِي ٱلۡقُرۡبَىٰ وَيَنۡهَىٰ عَنِ
ٱلۡفَحۡشَآءِ وَٱلۡمُنكَرِ وَٱلۡبَغۡيِۚ يَعِظُكُمۡ لَعَلَّكُمۡ تَذَكَّرُونَ ٩٠ ﴾
[النّحل : ٩٠]

﴿Verily, Allah enjoins justice [and worshipping none but Him alone], and the doing of good [to others as well as being patient in performing your duties to Allah, totally for Allah's sake and in a perfect manner], and giving to kith and kin [all that Allah has ordered you to give them, such as wealth, visiting them, looking after them, or any other kind of help] and forbids *faḥshâ'* [all shameful deeds, like illegal sexual acts, disobedience of parents, polytheism, telling lies, giving false witness, and killing a life without right], and *munkar* [all that is prohibited by Islam: every kind of evil deed], and *baghy* [all kinds of oppression]. He admonishes you that you may take heed.﴾ *(Qur'an 16: 90)*

﴿ إِنَّمَا ٱلۡمُؤۡمِنُونَ إِخۡوَةٞ فَأَصۡلِحُواْ بَيۡنَ أَخَوَيۡكُمۡۚ وَٱتَّقُواْ ٱللَّهَ لَعَلَّكُمۡ
تُرۡحَمُونَ ١٠ يَٰٓأَيُّهَا ٱلَّذِينَ ءَامَنُواْ لَا يَسۡخَرۡ قَوۡمٞ مِّن قَوۡمٍ عَسَىٰٓ أَن يَكُونُواْ خَيۡرٗا
مِّنۡهُمۡ وَلَا نِسَآءٞ مِّن نِّسَآءٍ عَسَىٰٓ أَن يَكُنَّ خَيۡرٗا مِّنۡهُنَّۖ وَلَا تَلۡمِزُوٓاْ أَنفُسَكُمۡ وَلَا
تَنَابَزُواْ بِٱلۡأَلۡقَٰبِۖ بِئۡسَ ٱلِٱسۡمُ ٱلۡفُسُوقُ بَعۡدَ ٱلۡإِيمَٰنِۚ وَمَن لَّمۡ يَتُبۡ فَأُوْلَٰٓئِكَ هُمُ
ٱلظَّٰلِمُونَ ١١ يَٰٓأَيُّهَا ٱلَّذِينَ ءَامَنُواْ ٱجۡتَنِبُواْ كَثِيرٗا مِّنَ ٱلظَّنِّ إِنَّ بَعۡضَ ٱلظَّنِّ إِثۡمٞۖ
وَلَا تَجَسَّسُواْ وَلَا يَغۡتَب بَّعۡضُكُم بَعۡضًاۚ أَيُحِبُّ أَحَدُكُمۡ أَن يَأۡكُلَ لَحۡمَ

أَخِيهِ مَيْتًا فَكَرِهْتُمُوهُۚ وَٱتَّقُوا۟ ٱللَّهَۚ إِنَّ ٱللَّهَ تَوَّابٌ رَّحِيمٌ ﴿١٢﴾﴾

[الحُجرات: ١٠-١٢]

﴿The believers are nothing other than brothers [in the religion]. So make reconciliation between your brothers, and fear Allah, that you may receive mercy. O you who believe! Let not one group scoff at another group; it may be that the latter are better than the former. Nor let [some] women scoff at other women; it may be that the latter are better than the former. Nor defame one another, nor insult one another by nicknames. How bad it is to insult one's brother after having faith. And whoever does not repent, then such are indeed wrong-doers. O you who believe! Avoid much suspicion; indeed some suspicions are sins. And do not spy, nor backbite one another. Would one of you like to eat the flesh of his dead brother? You would hate it [so hate backbiting]. And fear Allah. Verily, Allah is the One Who accepts repentance, Most Merciful.﴾ *(Qur'an 49: 10-12)*

﴿وَلَا تَسْتَوِى ٱلْحَسَنَةُ وَلَا ٱلسَّيِّئَةُۚ ٱدْفَعْ بِٱلَّتِى هِىَ أَحْسَنُ فَإِذَا ٱلَّذِى بَيْنَكَ وَبَيْنَهُۥ عَدَٰوَةٌ كَأَنَّهُۥ وَلِىٌّ حَمِيمٌ ﴿٣٤﴾﴾ [فُصّلت: ٣٤]

﴿Repel [evil] with that which is better [Allah orders the faithful believers to be patient at the time of anger, and to excuse those who treat them badly]. Then verily, the one whom between you and him there was enmity will become as though he were a close friend.﴾ *(Qur'an 41: 34)*

Take a moment to... evaluate your conscience

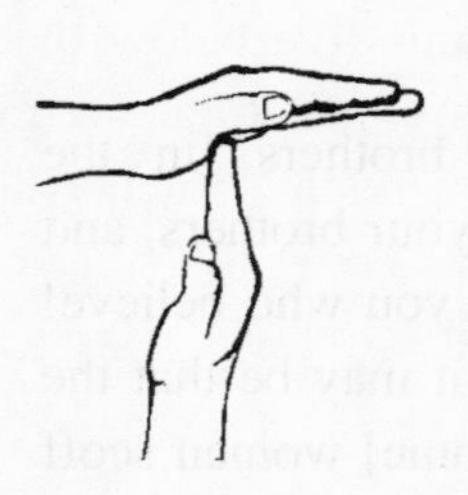

- Every night before you sleep, perform a Conscience Exam. Reconsider your actions of the day. How will the people you dealt with today describe you or think of you? (Include your spouse, children, co-workers, friends, neighbours, strangers you met on the street). Probably most of us — thanks be to Allah (ﷻ) — have pretty good manners, but we need to go even beyond that. We need to purify our hearts before purifying our actions. We need our True Secret to guide every step of our lives.
- Watch your tongue; it often reflects what is in your heart.
- Pause and think before you act or respond, especially to perceived offences.

Try this...
Talking Furniture Journaling

- Sit in a comfortable place with your journal. Close your eyes and relax for two minutes. Imagine that your furniture and household items could speak as soon as you stepped out of your home. What would they say about you? Will the living room sofa complain of the long hours wasted in front of the television? Will your computer tell about your negligence of your spouse and children? Will the telephone mention your backbiting? Will your wardrobe complain about too many unused clothes while millions of Muslims live below the poverty line? Will your cookware say that they were satisfied with the way you treated your servant? What will your bathroom mirror tell about you? Your TV? Your balcony? Your plants? Your pet, if you have one?

- Open your eyes. Write it all down in your journal.
- Think about what you need to change.

Take a moment to...
perform your IPC (In Process Control)

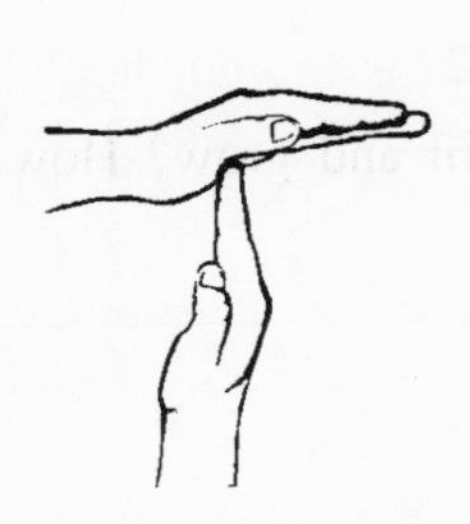

- When a pharmaceutical company produces a batch of medicine, it cannot wait until the end of production to analyze the quality of the finished product. If anything was found to be wrong then, the whole batch would have to be rejected, which of course would be very costly. The manufacturers perform what is called IPC (In Process Control) to regularly assess the medicine at each step in its production, so that any deviation from standard requirements can be noticed and fixed before it is too late.

- Being a pharmacist by trade, I highly recommend IPC. During the course of our workshop — as we go through this book — we will be regularly assessing our progress and monitoring the changes that we are undergoing.

The following are some IPC checkups:

- In your journal, explore:

  Your feelings

  Your outlook on life and on those around you (more/less optimistic, compassionate, forgiving...)

  Your enthusiasm

  Your self-esteem

  Your goals

  Your planning

  Your faith

  Your values

  Your priorities

  Your intention and True Secret

  Are you saying your dhikr regularly?

  Are you reading more books to learn and grow? How many have you read so far?

5. Be powerful

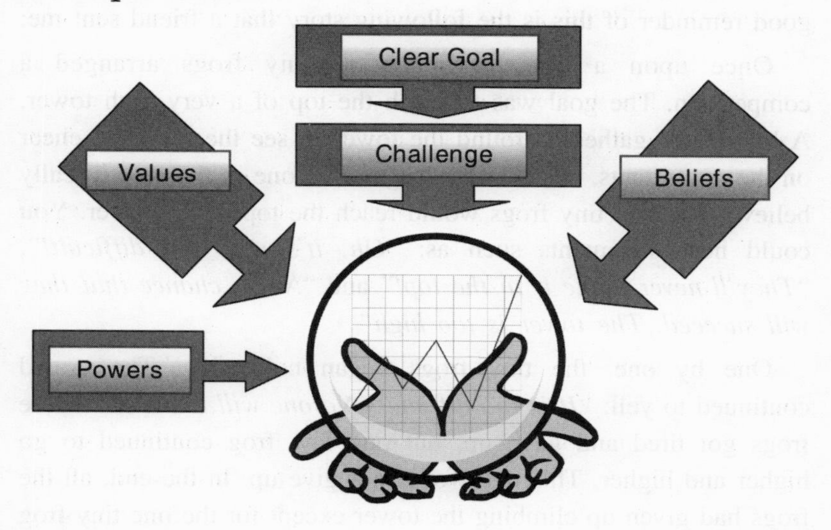

The Prophet Muhammad (ﷺ) is reported to have said: «The strong believer is more loved by Allah (ﷻ) than the weak one, though there is good in both.» (Muslim)

The meaning of strength in this saying of the Prophet (ﷺ) encompasses both physical and moral strength. Being powerful means overcoming our fears and self-doubts, exploring new challenges and fulfilling our duties and responsibilities.

Each of us is special. Each one of us is blessed with innumerable talents, faculties and potential strengths. The true challenge is to dig deep into your soul to explore these faculties and make the most out of them. You cannot fulfil your role on this earth unless you improve your sense of self-worth; by doing that, you unlock your potential and free your creative powers.

Have confidence in yourself and recognize that Allah (ﷻ) created you with many capabilities. Don't ever let people discourage you or lead you away from your important goals. A good reminder of this is the following story that a friend sent me:

Once upon a time, a bunch of tiny frogs arranged a competition. The goal was to reach the top of a very high tower. A big crowd gathered around the tower to see the race and cheer on the contestants, and the race began. No one in the crowd really believed that the tiny frogs would reach the top of the tower. You could hear statements such as: "*Oh, it's way too difficult!*", "*They'll never make it to the top!*" and "*Not a chance that they will succeed. The tower is too high!*"

One by one, the tiny frogs began collapsing. The crowd continued to yell: "*It is too difficult! No one will make it!*" More frogs got tired and gave up, but one tiny frog continued to go higher and higher. This one would not give up. In the end, all the frogs had given up climbing the tower except for the one tiny frog who, after great effort, finally reached the top!

All of the other frogs naturally wanted to know how this one frog managed to do it. One of the contestants asked the tiny frog how he had found the strength to succeed and reach the goal. It turned out that the winner was DEAF.[39]

The moral of this story is to never listen to discouraging and pessimistic opinions. Remember the little, deaf frog. Be confident of your abilities and always try your best.

Give your self-esteem a boost

Let's look at some practical ways to increase your self-confidence.

---

[39] This anecdote, along with several others related in this book, is one of many such stories circulating via e-mail. The author is unknown to me, and I hope I am excused for using it as an illustrative example.

1. Believe in your self-worth and your potential

Hold tightly to your faith in your Creator. Always remind yourself that Allah (ﷻ) is with you and that if you are on the right path, nothing can defeat you.

'Abdullah ibn 'Abbâs (رضي الله عنه), a young Companion of the Prophet (ﷺ), narrated that one day he was riding behind the Prophet on a mount, and the Prophet said to him: «Young man, I shall teach you some words (of advice). Be mindful of Allah (ﷻ), and Allah will protect you. Be mindful of Allah, and you will find Him in front of you. If you ask, ask of Allah. If you seek help, seek help from Allah. Know that if the people came together to do you a favour, they would be unable to do so unless Allah had prescribed it for you; if they united to harm you, they would not do you any harm unless Allah had prescribed it for you. The pens (that write destiny) have been lifted, and the pages have dried.»[40] (at-Tirmidhi; al-Albâni said it is sound)

Believe deep in your soul that your connection with Allah (ﷻ) is the true source of your power and strength. Allah (ﷻ) says:

﴿وَيَرْزُقْهُ مِنْ حَيْثُ لَا يَحْتَسِبُ وَمَن يَتَوَكَّلْ عَلَى ٱللَّهِ فَهُوَ حَسْبُهُۥٓ إِنَّ ٱللَّهَ بَٰلِغُ أَمْرِهِۦ قَدْ جَعَلَ ٱللَّهُ لِكُلِّ شَىْءٍ قَدْرًا ﴿٣﴾﴾ [الطّلاق: ٣]

﴿And whoever puts his trust in Allah, then He will suffice him. Verily, Allah will accomplish His purpose. Indeed Allah has set a measure for all things.﴾ *(Qur'an 65: 3)*

﴿أَلَيْسَ ٱللَّهُ بِكَافٍ عَبْدَهُۥ وَيُخَوِّفُونَكَ بِٱلَّذِينَ مِن دُونِهِۦ ... ﴿٣٦﴾﴾

[الزُّمر: ٣٦]

---

[40] Meaning that what has been written and decreed cannot be altered

﴾Is not Allah sufficient for His slave? Yet they try to frighten you with those [whom they worship] besides Him!﴿

(Qur'an 39: 36)

Take a moment to... assess your powers

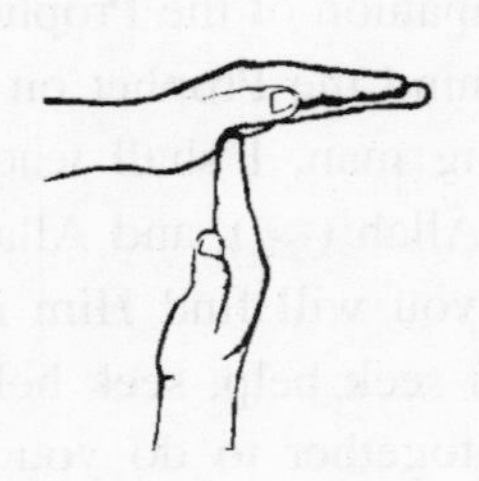

- Sit comfortably with your journal. Close your eyes and take a deep breath. Relax.
- Think about your strengths, abilities, talents, traits, and potential. What are you good at? What can you do?
- Open your eyes. Write down a list of all your potential abilities and good characteristics and traits. Write whatever crosses your mind, whether you think it is useful or not. (Remember the mystery shopper story?) Just write it all down. You can mention your nice smile, good heart and listening skills. You can also write your skills such as shopping, savouring food, writing (even if your high school teacher disagreed), or drawing. Record the skills and knowledge you acquired at school, in college, from friends and family, through experience, from the television, from the internet...Write down everything.

  If you like, you can have a friend help with this exercise. One simple rule applies: we are listing only positive traits here — no negative judgements.

- When you are done, take some time to reflect on your list. We all know more than we think we do. We all have more skills and knowledge than we usually give ourselves credit for.

2. Assess your limitations and work with them

Think about how you perceive yourself. Recognize your own personal limits and acknowledge your human limitations.[41] We are all human, and we all have our flaws — don't be ashamed of yours. Instead, recognize them so that you can figure out how to deal with them or work around them.

Every day, say your dhikr and supplications to Allah (ﷻ) — think of them as 'fortification' — and practice your self-empowering affirmations, like this one to be said three times: «In the Name of Allah, in whose name nothing can cause harm in the earth or the heavens, He is the All-Hearer and the All-Knower.» (a sound or reliable hadith recorded by Abu Dâwood, at-Tirmidhi and al-Mundhiri)

Dhikr, the remembrance and glorification of Allah, rectifies your mental image. In your heart, you visualize yourself as being strong through the strength of Allah and as succeeding with His help and blessings. Dhikr and supplication to Allah can transform your negative thoughts or self-doubts into confidence and strength. They increase your faith in Allah and support your belief in your abilities.

Try this... A Perfect Day

- Imagine a perfect day in your life. Let your imagination run wild on this. Change your home or workplace if you need to or feel like it.
- Write down a detailed timeline for this perfect day. (Don't forget time for your prayers and divine remembrance.) Make time for the whole you, includ-

[41] Seymour and Shervington

ing your physical, intellectual, emotional and spiritual sides.

- Write about the details of this perfect day. Envision an ideal environment, a wonderful time with your spouse/family/friends, ideal behaviour from your children, ideal relationships on all levels, a stress-free, worry-free day with heartfelt acts of worship, a satisfying career, plenty of time for everything... Take your time. Don't be afraid to dream.
- Then analyze your perfect day:[42]

1. What elements of your perfect day are already present in your life? (What activities/work/studies? Which environment or surroundings? Which people whom are you happy to be with now?)

2. What elements of your current life do you really need to work on to attain the desired life/goal/dream of yours? Notice that you need to have your True Secret and your Big Picture fully present before your eyes here. What is the true meaning of happiness? What does 'life' mean to you?

3. Which elements of your imagined day are optional (either you can wait for a while or you can do without them entirely)?

What you are trying to do here is to prioritize your dreams and goals. Try to locate precisely what you feel is missing from your current life. Focus.

- Now, **define your problem.** What is keeping you from having your dream come true? Identify it, because you cannot deal with it until you know what it is. Does it involve money? Education? Time? Self-

42 Sher

confidence? Work? Too much responsibility? Lack of support from family and friends?

Keep this list; we will deal with it later. Writing down your problems takes them off your mind for a while.

3. Visualize your personal success

Imagine performing your tasks well. The better you imagine yourself, the bigger the boost you are giving to your confidence.[43] You are a believer, thus be sure that Allah (ﷻ) will always be there for you. Allah (ﷻ) says in His noble Book:

﴿يُثَبِّتُ ٱللَّهُ ٱلَّذِينَ ءَامَنُوا۟ بِٱلْقَوْلِ ٱلثَّابِتِ فِى ٱلْحَيَوٰةِ ٱلدُّنْيَا وَفِى ٱلْـَٔاخِرَةِ ... ﴿٢٧﴾﴾ [إبراهيم: ٢٧]

﴾Allah will establish in strength those who believe, with the word that stands firm in this world and in the hereafter...﴿

(Qur'an 14: 27)

Try this... remember your dream

- Do you remember the dream of your life twenty years from now, which we envisaged in one of the earlier exercises? Take some time to visualize it.
- Close your eyes, relax, turn your attention to your breathing and again imagine how you would like your life to be twenty years into the future.

Draw a perfect picture of this life in your mind. See

---

43 Seymour and Shervington

and feel every detail. Notice your environment and the people surrounding you. Recognize your contribution to the well-being of your family, your society, your nation and the whole of humankind.

- Feel your True Secret deep in your heart, and feel the power and hope that it supplies to you.

4. Work to achieve your visualized goal

Now comes the most important part in the achievement process: the concrete actions you take to reach your dreams. Allah (ﷻ) says:

﴿... إِنَّ ٱللَّهَ لَا يُغَيِّرُ مَا بِقَوْمٍ حَتَّىٰ يُغَيِّرُوا۟ مَا بِأَنفُسِهِمْ ... ﴿١١﴾﴾

[الرّعد: ١١]

﴿...Verily Allah will never change the condition of a people until they change what is in themselves...﴾ *(Qur'an 13: 11)*

You are the one who is responsible for bringing your dreams to life. You have to take actual steps towards your goals, doing so to the best of your ability. Your performance is directly related to both your level of confidence and to the amount of effort you are willing to put into your work.

No doubt there will be bumps along the way. Some things may go wrong, but don't get discouraged. Perceive 'setbacks' as challenges, and keep trying. Focus on success and always maintain your positive self-image while surrendering to the divine will.

Muhammad al-Ghazâli said: "*Do not ask Allah to reduce your burden, but ask Him to strengthen your back to carry the load.*"[44]

---

[44] Al-Ghazâli, M. 'A Muslim's Manners'

Try this... take action

- Refer back to your plan for the coming year.
- Choose an item and take some serious steps towards achieving it. Do you still think you cannot really accomplish your dreams? Read your list of powers and strengths again.

In addition, achieving your goal will give you a tremendous boost of power for working on your other goals. One triumph can lead to many more successes!

Persistence and perseverance

Another expression of power that we learn from Islamic teachings is persistence and perseverance, as taught and practiced by our dear Prophet (ﷺ) through all his years of calling to the way of Allah (ﷻ). Recall the time when the people of Quraysh refused to give up polytheism and follow the monotheistic faith of Islam, and they tried to forbid the Prophet (ﷺ) from spreading his message. This negative reaction did not deter Prophet Muhammad (ﷺ). He was still determined to continue his mission with total devotion and sincerity, and he never gave up.

He looked for a new territory where the people would accept and welcome the religion of Allah (ﷻ), and thus he went to Ṭâ'if, but there he found the same stubbornness and rejection. The Prophet (ﷺ) left Ṭâ'if with bleeding feet and sought refuge in a nearby garden. According to his biographers, he sat and supplicated to Allah, saying, "If You are not angry with me, I care not (that I have been treated so badly by the people)." His only concern was Allah's pleasure; he was determined to continue his efforts and to fulfil his mission, while at the same time seeking strength only from Allah.[45]

Your True Secret is the source of your strength, confidence, persistence and perseverance. Being sincere to Allah (ﷻ) in each and every act and thought gives us the required stamina to overcome and withstand any obstacles in life.

Erroneous ideas of power

Stubbornness

Being stubborn is completely different from being powerful, especially when the stubbornness is associated with ignorance.

My son has a nice tale in his storybook that illustrates the meaning of this. It is the story of a very tenacious snapping turtle who lived deep in the forest. The snapping turtle had a strange rule: once she seized an enemy, she would not let go until either her adversary admitted defeat or there was thunder.

One day, while crawling among the bushes, a gigantic snake hit the turtle on the back of her shell. This made the turtle angry, so she shouted at the snake, telling him to knock it off or she would bite him and not let go until he apologized or until it thundered. "*And be sure of that*," shouted the turtle. "*I will never let go until one of the two happens!*"

The snake liked a challenge, so he swung on a nearby tree branch and hit the turtle once again. This time, the turtle was furious and opened her jaw wide to firmly seize the snake, but since she had bad eyesight and was competing against a very fast opponent, the turtle caught a tree branch instead.

Being as stubborn as she was, the turtle would not let go until her adversary, this time the seized branch, admitted defeat or until

---

45 As-Sibâ'ie

it thundered. The animals of the forest passed by the turtle, reminding her that it was summertime. "*It won't thunder soon,*" they said. "*And the branch cannot talk and admit defeat,*" they added.

"*I do not care,*" replied the turtle from the back of her throat, not letting go of the branch. "*I will not change my mind; when I say something, I mean it.*"

Days went by, with the turtle's friends trying to convince her to let go. "*Not until it thunders!*" she kept saying.

At the end of the week, the turtle fell helplessly to the ground and died. She did not learn the precious lesson: "There is a great difference between strength of character and plain stupidity."[46]

Arrogance

Arrogance is another faulty expression of power. The most well-known example is the story of Iblees (Satan) when he refused to prostrate to Adam (عليه السلام) upon the command of Allah (سبحانه وتعالى).

﴿إِذۡ قَالَ رَبُّكَ لِلۡمَلَٰٓئِكَةِ إِنِّي خَٰلِقُۢ بَشَرٗا مِّن طِينٖ ٧١ فَإِذَا سَوَّيۡتُهُۥ وَنَفَخۡتُ فِيهِ مِن رُّوحِي فَقَعُواْ لَهُۥ سَٰجِدِينَ ٧٢ فَسَجَدَ ٱلۡمَلَٰٓئِكَةُ كُلُّهُمۡ أَجۡمَعُونَ ٧٣ إِلَّآ إِبۡلِيسَ ٱسۡتَكۡبَرَ وَكَانَ مِنَ ٱلۡكَٰفِرِينَ ٧٤ قَالَ يَٰٓإِبۡلِيسُ مَا مَنَعَكَ أَن تَسۡجُدَ لِمَا خَلَقۡتُ بِيَدَيَّۖ أَسۡتَكۡبَرۡتَ أَمۡ كُنتَ مِنَ ٱلۡعَالِينَ ٧٥ قَالَ أَنَا۠ خَيۡرٞ مِّنۡهُ خَلَقۡتَنِي مِن نَّارٖ وَخَلَقۡتَهُۥ مِن طِينٖ ٧٦ قَالَ فَٱخۡرُجۡ مِنۡهَا فَإِنَّكَ رَجِيمٞ ٧٧ وَإِنَّ عَلَيۡكَ لَعۡنَتِيٓ إِلَىٰ يَوۡمِ ٱلدِّينِ ٧٨﴾ [ص: ٧١-٧٨]

﴿[Remember] when your Lord said to the angels: Truly, I am going to create man from clay. So when I have fashioned him and breathed into him [his] soul created by Me, then you fall down prostrate to him. So the angels prostrated themselves, all

46 Pepper

of them. But not Iblees [Satan]; he was proud and was one of the disbelievers. [Allah] said: O Iblees! What prevents you from prostrating yourself to one whom I have created with My Hands? Are you too proud [to fall prostrate to Adam] or are you one of the high exalted? [Iblees] said: I am better than he; You created me from fire; and You created him from clay. [Allah] said: Then get out from here, for verily, you are outcast, and verily, My curse is on you until the Day of Recompense!》 *(Qur'an 38: 71-78)*

Also remember our Prophet's warning: «The person who has the equivalent of even a grain of arrogance in his [or her] heart will not enter paradise.» (Muslim)

Take a moment to... feel your power

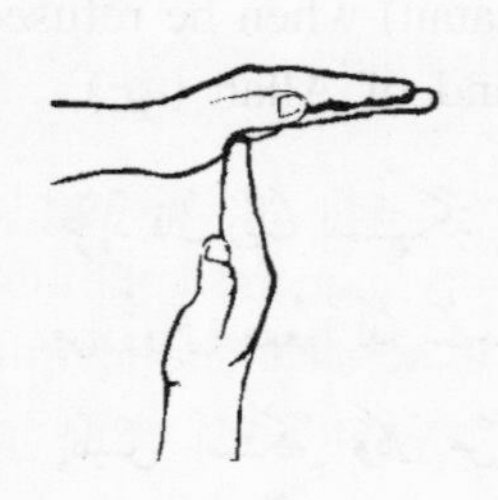

- Think of a situation in which you were powerful. How did it feel?
- Now review your intention at that time. Were you sincere to Allah (ﷻ) and relying on Him for support and strength? Or were you stubborn or arrogant?

Don't be scared to be different

When you are putting your True Secret to work and remembering the Big Picture in all your actions, don't get discouraged by other people's opinions or try to blindly copy them. Don't fear being different. Prophet Muhammad (ﷺ) taught us: «Do not make yourself worthless, so if the people behave well, then you behave too, and if they misbehave, you do the same. Instead, if the people behave well, you behave well also; and if they misbehave, do not [follow them in] acting unjustly.» (at-Tirmidhi, who said it is a reliable hadith, though the transmitter is alone in reporting it)

Consider the life of al-Birooni, one of our great Muslim scientists who lived in Persia more than one thousand years ago. Despite the odds against him — especially the lack of appreciation of science in his day — he had the courage to be unusual and follow his love of nature. He spent hours in the woods studying plants and herbs. He studied under the leading mathematicians and astronomers of his time, and his teachers noticed his love of learning and dedication to it. He excelled in botany, pharmacy, physics, astrology, mathematics, geography, religion and philosophy.

Near the beginning of the eleventh century, civil wars raged within the Islamic empire. Al-Birooni's land was taken over by the Ghaznayids, whose sultan, Maḥmood al-Ghaznâwi, hated science and scientists. He regarded scientific experiments as a kind of disbelief, so he sentenced many scientists to death. Al-Birooni fled and was compelled to live for years in poor financial conditions, fearing for his safety. Still, he was devoted to science and learning; he wrote many books and passed his time by studying geography and trigonometry.

One day, the sultan asked his courtiers to measure the width of his kingdom, a wide realm that extended from India to Persia. They sent workers to literally traverse the vast land and measure it. It was a tremendously exhausting task, not to mention an unavoidably inaccurate method. A wise man mentioned al-Birooni's

knowledge to the sultan and suggested consulting him. Reluctant at first, the sultan eventually decided to seek al-Birooni's advice.

Using his scientific knowledge of astronomy and trigonometry, al-Birooni was able to calculate the required information. The sultan was amazed and was finally convinced of the importance of scientific knowledge and experimentation, as long as they were used in the right cause. Al-Birooni became one of the sultan's main advisers, and today we still recall his name as one of the greatest Muslim scientists.[47]

Robert Solé, in his book *Le Tarbouche*, also relates a very interesting story about Ḥabeeb Sakâkeeni. He was a young member of a modest family from Syria, who migrated to Egypt, without any fortune or diploma, in search of a better living. One day he read in the newspapers a cry for help from Ferdinand de Lesseps, the man responsible for the project of digging the Suez Canal. Enormous rats had attacked the digging site, eating the workers' food, destroying the equipment and spreading diseases. They had tried different methods to get rid of the rats, but nothing worked effectively, so they were offering a valuable prize to anyone who could find a solution.

The young Sakâkeeni offered an answer: Why not bring cats to the site? Everybody belittled his idea, but he was confident that it could work, and after all, he felt there was nothing to lose by trying. Ḥabeeb collected hundreds of cats, put them in cages and shipped them to the Canal Zone, where they were set free to deal with the ferocious rats. Soon the whole site was free of rats.

Ḥabeeb was promoted and given one assignment after another; each time, he used his creativity and self-confidence to excel. Honours were bestowed on him, and the sultan in Constantinople, 'Abdul Ḥameed, offered him a palace in a famous Egyptian district

---

[47] Sabry

which still carries his name 'Sakâkeeni'.[48]

Reflect also on the amazing story of Sir Alexander Fleming. It was Fleming whose discoveries led to the first antibiotic drugs, after he detected the ability of the penicillin mould to kill bacteria.

Before Fleming, researchers were irritated by the 'troublesome green mould' that would grow on their Petri dishes. Literature prior to Fleming's discovery stated this observation more than 140 times.[49] Researchers used to throw out their cultures and repeat their experiments, not realizing that this mould was exactly what the whole world was searching for: a drug that could kill bacteria. Instead of throwing away his cultures, Fleming was inspired to experiment further. When he discovered that the mould prevented bacterial growth, he realized that he had an amazing cure in his hands. He named it 'penicillin'. Because he dared to be different from his colleagues, Fleming's investigations in bacteriology, immunology and chemotherapy were special and distinctive. In 1945, Sir Fleming received the Nobel Prize in medicine. His momentous discovery saved the lives of many people, and it is still saving millions of lives in our present time.

An even greater example of being special and powerful is the story of 'Umar ibn al-Khaṭṭâb (ﷺ) when he first embraced Islam. On his first day as a Muslim, 'Umar was very sincere and directed all his strength to serving this new cause. He asked the Prophet (ﷺ), "*O Messenger of Allah, are we not following the truth whether we live or die?*" Prophet Muhammad replied, "*Yes indeed, by the One in Whose hand is my soul, you are following the truth whether you live or die.*" 'Umar asked: "*So why should we hide? By the One Who sent you with the truth, you should go*

---

48 Solé

49 Chopra

out [and preach openly]."[50]

On that exact day, the call to Islam stopped being a mission that was carried out in private, under secrecy. Islamic monotheism was announced publicly, and Prophet Muhammad (ﷺ) began referring to 'Umar as *al-Farooq*, 'the one who separated the truth from falsehood'. As soon as 'Umar was convinced of the truth of Islam, he went on to announce it loudly and clearly, not caring what the consequences might be. Indeed, Allah (ﷻ) strengthened Islam with 'Umar.

Presenting yourself

Most of the time, we try to give other people a good impression of ourselves, and we may even try to present ourselves in a way that makes us look better than we really are. We spend time and money to rearrange our looks and to improve our communications and social skills.[51]

We cannot say that this is bad behaviour; it is neither good nor bad. In order to fit in and be well integrated into society, we should care about the impression that we make on others and about their opinions of us,[52] at least as a kind of feedback to teach us more about ourselves so that we can adjust our manners and improve our behaviour.

There is also the concept of 'practice makes perfect'. By acting the way that you wish you truly were, you can gradually fix some unwanted characteristics or habits. For instance, you may be a very impatient person, but if you keep practicing patience outwardly, it will eventually affect your inner feeling of patience. Likewise, if you keep practicing kindness, you can turn yourself into a kind

---

50 Sallâbi, *'Umar ibn al-Khattâb: His Life and Times*

51 Santrock

52 Santrock

person; if you practice controlling your temper, you might end up a calmer person. This is, of course, provided that your intention is sincerely to develop honourable qualities within yourself.

Sometimes, however, you may act in a way that portrays you as a certain type of person that is not who you really are or who you are trying to be. When this happens, your concern with the impression you make on others may become an obsession, to the degree that you 'fine-tune' your performance accordingly, changing all your actions and behaviours depending on whom you are dealing with.[53] This process is tiresome and constitutes a burden on your physical health as well as your emotions. Most importantly, it is insincere, and people can sense it easily. It may even lead all the way to hypocrisy.

Be proud of who you are. You only gain the respect and acceptance of others when you are sincere, honest and self-confident.

When I was in university, I went to Germany as part of a student exchange summer camp. There was a young student on our team who always carried with him a small backpack containing a little prayer mat and a compass to determine the direction for prayers. Whenever it was time for prayer, no matter where we were, Muhammad would stop on the side of the road or in a corner of a mall to perform his prayer. This took no more than a few minutes, and he did it so quietly and sincerely that he caused no inconvenience to anyone.

One day we were invited by the mayor of Frankfurt to take a tour of the city. When it was time for the obligatory noon prayer, Muhammad, as usual, stepped aside for a few minutes to perform his prayer. This action did not surprise the mayor much; what

---

[53] Ibid

surprised him more was the reaction of the other students. They kept apologizing to the mayor for keeping him waiting and went on complaining about Muhammad's 'inappropriate behaviour'. The mayor was puzzled. "*Isn't this your religion?*" he asked. All of the students affirmed that it was. "*Then why aren't you praying with him?*" he asked unexpectedly. I guessed that the mayor had more respect for Muhammad than for any of the other students who were just trying to be nice, even though it was at the expense of one of the most important pillars of our religion.

Always remember that Allah (ﷻ) created us — humans — as honourable beings; do not belittle yourself or your religion. Allah (ﷻ) says:

﴿إِذْ قَالَ رَبُّكَ لِلْمَلَٰٓئِكَةِ إِنِّى خَٰلِقٌۢ بَشَرًا مِّن طِينٍ ﴿٧١﴾ فَإِذَا سَوَّيْتُهُۥ وَنَفَخْتُ فِيهِ مِن رُّوحِى فَقَعُوا۟ لَهُۥ سَٰجِدِينَ ﴿٧٢﴾ فَسَجَدَ ٱلْمَلَٰٓئِكَةُ كُلُّهُمْ أَجْمَعُونَ ﴿٧٣﴾﴾

[صٓ: ٧١-٧٣]

﴿[Remember] when your Lord said to the angels: Truly, I am going to create man from clay. So when I have fashioned him and breathed into him [his] soul created by Me, then you fall down prostrate to him. So the angels prostrated themselves, all of them.﴾ *(Qur'an 38: 71-73)*

﴿كُنتُمْ خَيْرَ أُمَّةٍ أُخْرِجَتْ لِلنَّاسِ تَأْمُرُونَ بِٱلْمَعْرُوفِ وَتَنْهَوْنَ عَنِ ٱلْمُنكَرِ وَتُؤْمِنُونَ بِٱللَّهِ﴾

[آل عِمرَان: ١١٠]

﴿You [true believers in Islam and real followers of Prophet Muhammad] are the best of peoples ever raised up for humankind. You enjoin *ma'roof* [Islamic monotheism and all that Islam has ordained] and forbid *munkar* [polytheism, disbelief and all that Islam has forbidden], and you believe in Allah.﴾ *(Qur'an 3: 110)*

Take a moment to... remember

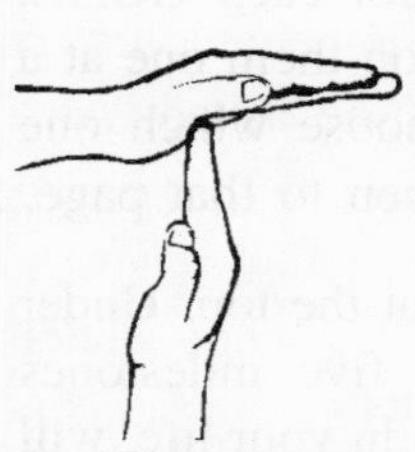

- Remember a time in your life when you tried to fine-tune your behaviour in order to be accepted by others (like during a job interview, for example). Did this behaviour help you to achieve your desired goal?
- Now assess the reasons behind your self-monitoring behaviour. What was your intention? Were you sincere?
- If you could repeat this event, what would you change?

Take a moment to... specify your GOALS

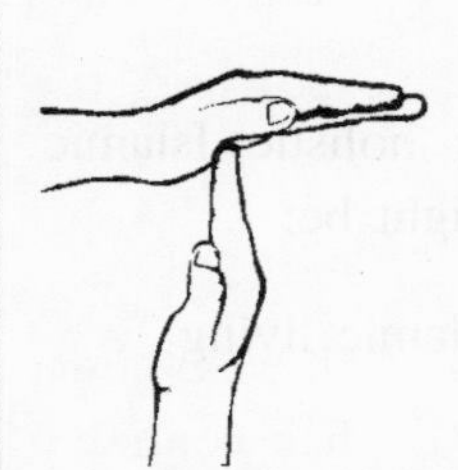

- You now have three lists:
  1. Plans for the year (and lifetime dreams)
  2. Apples
  3. Powers and potentials
- Compare the lists and find common factors. These are your passions, your cravings, your longings, what you really enjoy doing, what you feel you were born to do.
- Make a new list. This one will be the list of your GOALS at this point in your life.
- If the list is long, examine your GOALS and choose only three items to start with (or maybe one or two items, if you feel more comfortable with that).
- Set aside a page or two in your journal for each of your chosen GOALS. Write your GOAL at the top of the first page and leave the rest for now. We will fill in those pages later.

Take a moment to... add milestones

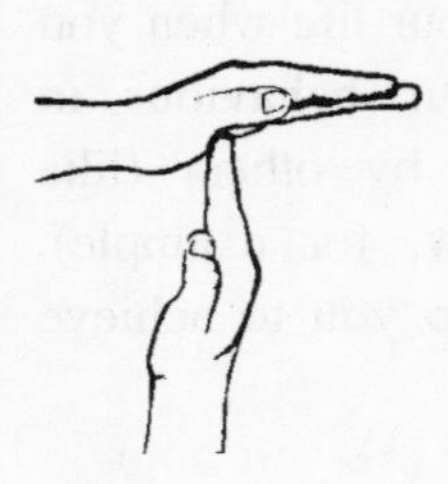

- Now you have a page for each GOAL. You are going to work on them one at a time. Let your heart choose which one to consider first, and open to that page.
- Your GOAL is written at the top. Under the title, write four or five milestones that, when they show up in your life, will indicate to you that you are fulfilling your GOAL. These should be four to five signs that you see or would like to see in your life to show that you are in the process of achieving that GOAL and that you are progressing on the right track. These are not steps that you take to achieve your GOALS; they are smaller goals in the same direction.

For example, if my GOAL is teaching holistic Islamic living worldwide, some of my milestones might be:

- ❖ Write my first book about holistic Islamic living
- ❖ Design a professional website
- ❖ Arrange professional workshops and meet and improve the lives of many Muslims
- ❖ Meet and learn from important Muslim figures
- ❖ Bestselling books and world tours
- ❖ International seminars

Don't think about the rational possibility of these milestones just yet. (I never imagined that I would actually be able to write and publish a book one day.) Just write down what you want and what you would like to see, or imagine seeing, on your way to fulfilling your life's dream.

Try this...

- Sit calmly, close your eyes and relax. Notice your breath.
- I want you to visualize your GOAL and feel your milestones. I want you to live them in the tiniest detail. What are you wearing right now? Where are you? Who is with you? What are you doing? How do you feel? See the faces of the people surrounding you, the colours of the curtains behind you... Visualize everything in the most minute detail.
- Visualization of your milestones at this stage will help you to narrow your choice of passions down to one or two, or at least to prioritize them and decide which path you want to start with. Do not totally reject the other GOALS, though. We will learn about flexibility later. You may find new paths opening with time, or new branches on your path that may lead to other passions. Just keep your eyes and heart open.
- If your nosy self-critic keeps interfering to make judgements, then visualize a big box. Open it, put all your future worries inside it, and then close it tight. You can open it later when we reach the fulfilment stage, when you will need your logical thinking and left-brain analysis. Right now, it is still dream time.

6. Work on your resources

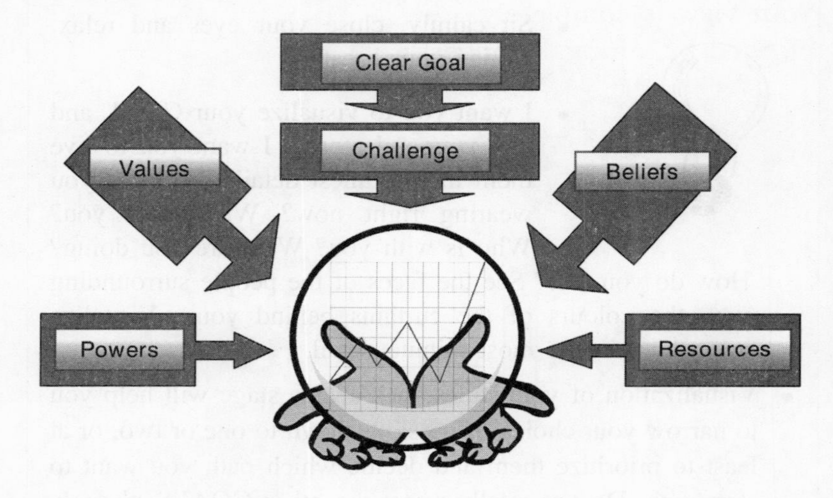

Now that your goals are clear, your plans and challenges are written down, and you have strengthened your self-belief and power, you need to gather your resources. You are going to need twelve resources on your journey: six inner resources and six outer ones.

What are these resources and why do you need them?

If you focus only on your challenges (in our case now, the big GOALS we devised for ourselves), only on the seemingly huge tasks expected from you, your view will be completely blocked by your concerns. Consequently, you might react by feeling self-defensive and/or depressed. This is like standing in front of a concrete wall. If you stand too close to the wall, you will not be able to see anything else. (See Figure A.)

Figure A.
Your view is completely
blocked by your challenges.

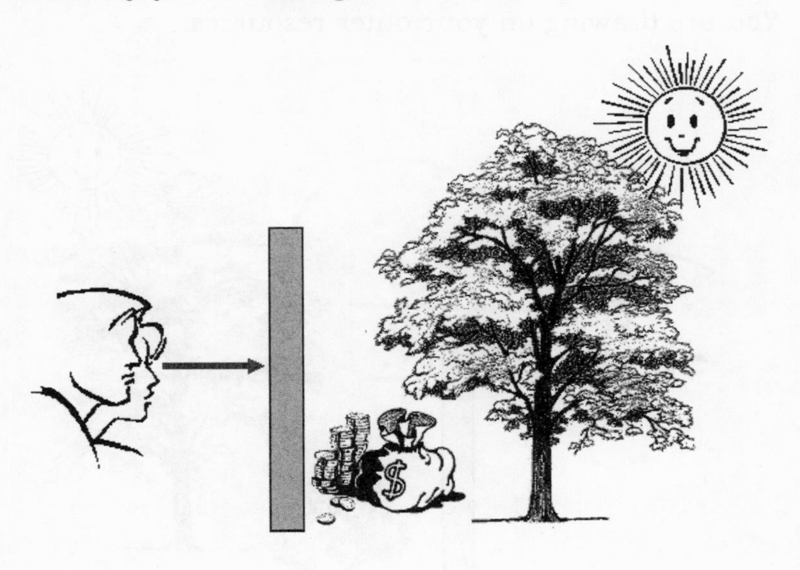

If you change your position to have a wider view, you will be able to see the beauty beyond that wall. The outer resources are the ones that will give you this broader view of your situation. They will show you the sunshine and the beautiful landscape. (See Figure B). They allow you to find real solutions and to take practical actions towards improvement. They will help you to start taking genuine steps towards positive life changes, while being grateful for all the gifts and blessings in your life.

Figure B.
Changing position allows you
a broader view of your situation.
You are drawing on your outer resources.

Now, let's imagine that you can fly above this wall and take a look from up there. (See Figure C). You can see an even wider view now. You can see the hidden treasure behind the wall! This is transcendence, the soul purification process achieved through your inner resources, the ones that let you transcend your challenges and dig up your hidden treasure. Your inner resources allow you to feel and acknowledge your millions of blessings, perceive the hidden lessons behind your challenges, and recognize the countless gifts and bits of help and ease that come to you along the way.

Figure C.
Transcendence allows an even wider view,
drawing on your inner resources.

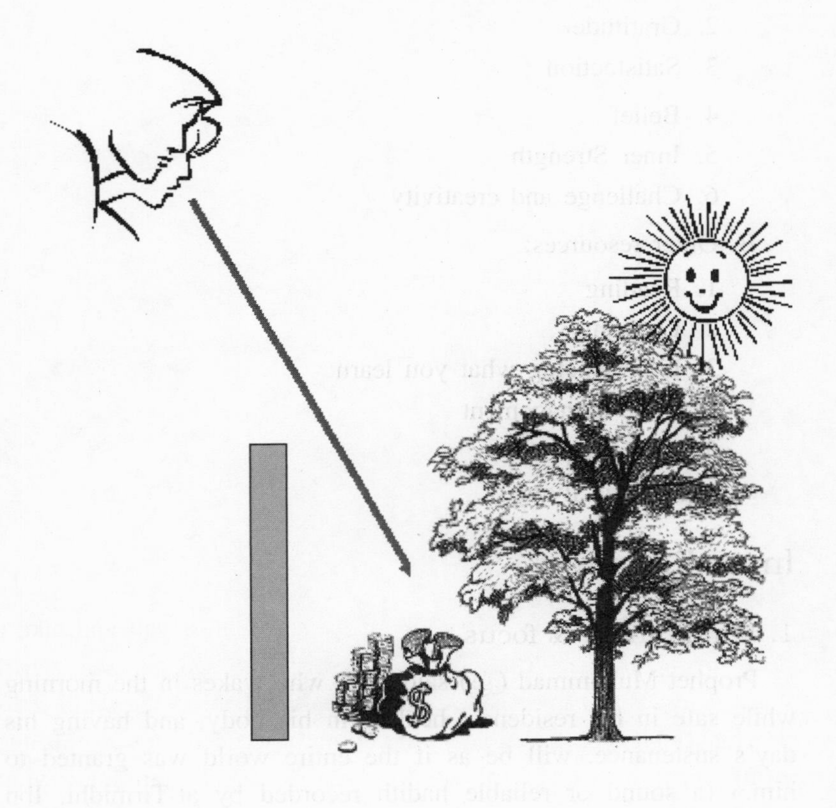

Your Resources

A. Inner Resources:

1. Mindfulness and focus
2. Gratitude
3. Satisfaction
4. Belief
5. Inner Strength
6. Challenge and creativity

B. Outer resources:

1. Reading
2. Learning
3. Experiencing what you learn
4. Time management
5. Social support
6. Holistic living

Inner Resources

1. Mindfulness & focus

Prophet Muhammad (ﷺ) said: «He who wakes in the morning while safe in his residence, healthy in his body, and having his day's sustenance, will be as if the entire world was granted to him.» (a sound or reliable hadith recorded by at-Tirmidhi, Ibn Mâjah and Ibn Ḥibbân)

In this fast-paced world we live in, with our lives spent running and rushing, we rarely stop to truly feel and enjoy our days. Every day seems like the previous one; every task is as tedious as the one that preceded it. Life just passes by, and we act like a traveller on a high speed train who is totally immersed in reading the newspaper, missing all the beautiful scenery. He never even notices or experiences the beauty existing around him. From time to time, when the train slows down at an intersection or stops at a nearby station, he raises his head to take a quick glimpse of the surroundings, but it is a scene that rapidly fades from his memory as the train speeds up again. What a waste!

Life is too precious to let it speed by without noticing; without learning, growing, teaching, and serving; and without assuming our responsibilities. By focusing too much on our concerns and on our past and future troubles and challenges, we lose a very precious gift: the present.

Prophet Muhammad (ﷺ) taught his Companion 'Abdullah ibn 'Umar (رضي الله عنه): «If you reach the evening, do not expect to be alive in the morning, and if you reach the morning, do not expect to be alive in the evening. Take from your life for your death and from your health for your sickness, as you do not know, 'Abdullah, even what your name will be tomorrow.» (Bukhari)

Living mindfully is about enjoying each moment of our lives, with all its positive and negative aspects, with all the gifts and blessings, along with the lessons and challenges it brings. Living mindfully is about acknowledging Allah's blessings all around us and employing all of our senses: feeling, seeing, smelling, touching, tasting and hearing life's endless beauty.

We say our daily dhikr and supplications to remind us that each morning we are facing a new beginning in our lives. Thus, we reconfirm our faith and devotion to Allah (سبحانه وتعالى) and supplicate for health, wealth and happiness in this new day: «We have reached the morning while the dominion of the universe belongs to Allah (سبحانه وتعالى). All praise is due to Allah. None has the right to be worshipped except Allah, Who has no partner. All praise and thanks are due to Allah, Who is able to do all things. O Allah! I ask You to give me the best of this day and the best of what follows it. I seek refuge in You from laziness and senile old age, and I seek refuge in You from the torment of the fire and the punishment of the grave.»[54] (Muslim)

«O Allah! I ask You for knowledge that is useful, for provision that is lawful and for deeds that are acceptable to You.» (a sound hadith recorded by Aḥmad)

There is a similar supplication that can be said each evening: «We have reached the evening, while all dominion belongs to Allah (ﷻ), the God of humankind, the jinn and all that exists. O Allah! I ask You to give me the good of this evening, its triumph and victory, its light, its blessing and guidance. I seek refuge with You from its evil and the evil which follows it.»

Since you can never know what awaits you tomorrow, why waste time and energy with excessive worry? Hold tight to your faith, and renew your commitment to it each night before you go to bed. Ask Allah (ﷻ) for protection, forgiveness and mercy: «O Allah! Verily, You created my soul, and You are able to take its life. To You belong its life and death. If You keep it alive, guard it; and if You cause its death, forgive it. O Allah! I ask You to grant me well-being.» (Muslim)

Living in the moment brings the peace of mind that we all struggle to achieve. It is a relaxing state of mind that helps us to meet and surmount everyday challenges.[55] This mindfulness helps us set our priorities straight, adjust our intention and perfect our sincerity to Allah (ﷻ) on a regular basis.

---

[54] This supplication can also be said in the evening, substituting the word 'evening' for 'morning', as mentioned in *al-Qaḥṭâni, Fortification of the Muslim.* Unless otherwise noted, all the supplications and phrases of dhikr (remembrances) are from this source.

[55] Carter-Scott

Try this... invite yourself over

- Prepare your favourite dish or buy it from a nearby restaurant. Invite a close friend or your spouse, or maybe you would like to have some time just for yourself. Sit at your dinner table and use your best china. Fully savour the moment and do not think of anything else; put all your worries aside for now. Let your taste buds enjoy your food without worrying about the extra calories, just for once.
- How do you feel? How much of your day do you spend fully present and aware? Do you eat when you eat, sleep when you sleep, enjoy the moment of fun when you play with your kids?
- Savour each moment of your life. Read with your heart; let your taste buds enjoy your food; rest when you need it, without worrying about your unfinished chores. Be mindful of every moment of your life. Each moment has its beauty.

The key to understanding yourself is to consciously observe your own actions, thoughts and feelings; to be totally aware of every moment of your life; to be MINDFUL.

Practice your daily dhikr. This remembrance of Allah (ﷻ) is a constant reminder for us to be mindful, to be grateful for the beauty of each moment, to adjust our intentions and see the Big Picture.

Try this... inspire and get inspired

- Did you ever consider that you are a continuous source of inspiration? We all are. Pause and think. Who did you inspire today?

❖ Your kids, by controlling your temper, even when they refused to get up for school?

❖ Your neighbour, by cleaning the front yard, including his path?

❖ The woman in the supermarket parking lot, when you volunteered to put her trolley (shopping cart) back in place?

❖ The cute frowning kid in the car in front of you, when you smiled and waved at him?

And who or what inspired you?

❖ Your husband, when he surprised you with a gift?

❖ The beautiful morning sunshine?

❖ The clear blue sky? Or the grey clouds declaring another polluted day?

❖ A smile from a friend? Or even better, a smile from a stranger?

❖ An early call from your mother?

❖ The man collecting the garbage down the road?

❖ Or maybe the garbage thrown down the road?

❖ The unexpected hug from your teenager?

❖ The flower growing between the broken tiles of the sidewalk?

We inspire and get inspired by everybody and everything around us. Every day and night, there is something new to teach or to learn. We are surrounded by lessons, inspirations, stories and ideas. Open your eyes and your heart to send and receive inspiration, lessons and ideas. You can inspire others to be more careful, grateful, forgiving, helpful, respectful, altruistic, or receptive. Don't underestimate your effect on others, and never overlook the lessons sent to you along your path.

Try this... reflect on your awareness

- Sit comfortably. Close your eyes. Notice your breathing.
- Take some time for mindful reflection on your past week:

❖ What have I been paying most attention to this week?

❖ Was I fully aware of all my responsibilities and roles (as a spouse, son/daughter, parent, at work, with friends, neighbours, family, myself, my Ummah...)?

❖ What area in my life still needs my attention?

❖ What activity needs more awareness?

❖ How often did I remember Allah (ﷻ) and say daily dhikr?

❖ Did I remember to verify — and adjust when necessary — my intention and sincerity before every action I performed this week?

❖ What signs in my life did I notice or fail to notice? (Disguised lessons, hidden messages, new people in my life, unexpected bounties I should be grateful for, tests, challenges, trials...)

Now open your eyes. Get out your journal and write three pages — three full pages — nonstop. Don't pause to think or edit. Get every feeling, thought, reflection or idea on paper. If you feel you need more than three pages, go ahead, but don't use less than three.

After you have finished, close your journal. Don't re-read it now. Save it for the next day, when you will read it carefully and thoughtfully. You will learn a bit more about your feelings and your fears, and perhaps you may discover some milestones or signs that appeared in your life and went unnoticed.

2. Gratitude

Very long ago, in a faraway land somewhere in India, there was a successful and well-off farmer. He lived with his family in a beautiful house, and he cultivated his own land. One day, a monk passed by the farm and stayed for the night. The monk told the farmer lots of stories about his travels. He also talked to him about diamonds, the most precious material on the face of earth, claiming: "*Whoever possesses diamonds becomes happy and prosperous like a king*." The talk went on for a long portion of the night. In the morning, the monk went on his way, leaving behind a very 'poor' farmer. The farmer still had his house and his land. He still had his family and his crops, but now it all seemed like nothing to him. He could only think of diamonds.

That day, the farmer made a momentous decision. He sold his farm and his house, left his wife and children, and embarked on a long journey in search of diamonds. He travelled for many days and nights. He walked, ran, rode on camels and sailed across seas and oceans. Months and years went by, and he exhausted all his savings, all to no avail. The story has it that he drowned in the ocean, hungry, weak and penniless.

However, the story does not end there. An important character is still missing: the man who bought the farmer's land. This man worked on the farm, cultivating it and raising his sheep and camels; he loved the farm and the animals. He took his herd every day to drink from a picturesque lake that ran through his land. One sunny morning, while the camels were drinking from the lake, the man noticed something shining in the sand, a strange but beautiful piece of glass that reflected the rainbow colours of the sky. It was not glass, though; it was a diamond. The farmer's land stood on the largest diamond mine in the whole world, the mine of Golconda.[56]

Subḥân Allâh! All along, the original farmer had had the riches and fortune he was looking for, right under his own feet. He owned it but never noticed it. He sold all his treasures and travelled to and fro in search of something that was like a mirage, while all he truly wanted and needed had been in his own hands.

Look around you. Can you feel your blessings?

Allah's blessings are countless. Enough, on its own, is the blessing of faith, of Islam. Think about all that you have. Think about your senses of sight, hearing, touch, smell, taste; think about your health, wealth, family and friends; think about your children, your parents, and your spouse; think about the sunshine, the moonlight, the greenery and the fresh air. Allah (ﷻ) says in His Book:

---

[56] Conwell

﴿وَءَاتَىٰكُم مِّن كُلِّ مَا سَأَلْتُمُوهُ ۚ وَإِن تَعُدُّوا۟ نِعْمَتَ ٱللَّهِ لَا تُحْصُوهَآ ... ﴿٣٤﴾﴾ [إبراهيم: ٣٤]

﴿And He gave you of all that you asked for, and if you count the blessings of Allah, never will you be able to count them [all]...﴾ *(Qur'an 14: 34)*

Don't ever forget that all blessings come from Allah (سبحانه وتعالى):

﴿وَمَا بِكُم مِّن نِّعْمَةٍ فَمِنَ ٱللَّهِ ۖ ثُمَّ إِذَا مَسَّكُمُ ٱلضُّرُّ فَإِلَيْهِ تَجْـَٔرُونَ ﴿٥٣﴾ ثُمَّ إِذَا كَشَفَ ٱلضُّرَّ عَنكُمْ إِذَا فَرِيقٌ مِّنكُم بِرَبِّهِمْ يُشْرِكُونَ ﴿٥٤﴾ لِيَكْفُرُوا۟ بِمَآ ءَاتَيْنَٰهُمْ ۚ فَتَمَتَّعُوا۟ ۖ فَسَوْفَ تَعْلَمُونَ ﴿٥٥﴾﴾ [النحل: ٥٣-٥٥]

﴿And whatever of blessings and good things you have, it is from Allah. Then, when harm touches you, unto Him you cry aloud for help. Then, when He has removed the harm from you, behold! Some of you associate others in worship with their Lord [Allah]. So [as a result of that] they deny [with ungratefulness] that [Allah's favours] which We have bestowed on them! Then enjoy yourselves [your short stay in the life of this world], but you will come to know [with regrets].﴾ *(Qur'an 16: 53-55)*

We are nothing without Allah (سبحانه وتعالى):

﴿هَلْ أَتَىٰ عَلَى ٱلْإِنسَٰنِ حِينٌ مِّنَ ٱلدَّهْرِ لَمْ يَكُن شَيْـًٔا مَّذْكُورًا ﴿١﴾ إِنَّا خَلَقْنَا ٱلْإِنسَٰنَ مِن نُّطْفَةٍ أَمْشَاجٍ نَّبْتَلِيهِ فَجَعَلْنَٰهُ سَمِيعًۢا بَصِيرًا ﴿٢﴾ إِنَّا هَدَيْنَٰهُ ٱلسَّبِيلَ إِمَّا شَاكِرًا وَإِمَّا كَفُورًا ﴿٣﴾﴾ [الإنسان: ١-٣]

﴿Has there not been over man a period of time when he was nothing to be mentioned? Verily, We created man from drops of mixed semen [discharge of man and woman], in order to try him. So We made him hear and see. Verily, We showed him the way, whether he be grateful or ungrateful.﴿ *(Qur'an 76: 1-3)*

Our Prophet Muhammad (ﷺ) said: «Whoever is not grateful for little will not be grateful for abundance, and whoever does not give thanks to people is not thanking Allah (ﷻ). Speaking about Allah's blessings is considered a sign of gratitude, and abandoning it is a sign of disbelief.» (Aḥmad and al-Mundhiri, who said it is reliable)

Even if you are encountering some problems or inconveniences, think about those who are in a worse condition. The Prophet (ﷺ) advised: «Look at those who are inferior to you, and do not look at the ones above you. This is worthier of you so that you do not see Allah's blessings (upon you) with contempt.» (Muslim)

Allah is the All-Just and All-Wise. Each and every one of us has been given appropriate gifts; you just have to feel and enjoy them. Don't let your life speed by in front of your eyes like a video clip. Enjoy each and every moment, and celebrate each and every blessing.

Allah (ﷻ) promises to reward gratefulness:

﴿وَإِذْ تَأَذَّنَ رَبُّكُمْ لَئِن شَكَرْتُمْ لَأَزِيدَنَّكُمْ وَلَئِن كَفَرْتُمْ إِنَّ عَذَابِي لَشَدِيدٌ ﴿٧﴾﴾ [إبراهيم: ٧]

﴾And [remember] when your Lord proclaimed: If you give thanks, I will give you more [of My blessings]﴿ *(Qur'an 14: 7)*

At the same time, we should also remember the rest of the verse:

﴿وَلَئِن كَفَرْتُمْ إِنَّ عَذَابِي لَشَدِيدٌ ﴿٧﴾﴾ [إبراهيم: ٧]

﴾But if you are thankless, verily, My Punishment is indeed severe!﴿ *(Qur'an 14: 7)*

Allah (ﷻ) tells us in the Qur'an about when Prophet Solomon (ﷺ) spoke with understanding and thankfulness, saying:

﴿هَٰذَا مِن فَضْلِ رَبِّي لِيَبْلُوَنِيٓ ءَأَشْكُرُ أَمْ أَكْفُرُ ۖ وَمَن شَكَرَ فَإِنَّمَا يَشْكُرُ لِنَفْسِهِۦ ۖ وَمَن كَفَرَ فَإِنَّ رَبِّي غَنِيٌّ كَرِيمٌ ﴿٤٠﴾﴾ [النَّمل: ٤٠]

﴾This is by the grace of my Lord to test me whether I am grateful or ungrateful! And whoever is grateful, truly, his gratitude is for [the good of] his own self; and whoever is ungrateful, [he is ungrateful only to the loss of his own self]. Certainly! My Lord is Rich [Free of all wants], Bountiful.﴿

(Qur'an 27: 40)

This is a reminder not to remember Allah (ﷻ) only when you are facing problems, but also to remember Him during good times, indeed at all times. Allah (ﷻ) says:

﴿۞ وَإِذَا مَسَّ ٱلْإِنسَٰنَ ضُرٌّ دَعَا رَبَّهُۥ مُنِيبًا إِلَيْهِ ثُمَّ إِذَا خَوَّلَهُۥ نِعْمَةً مِّنْهُ نَسِيَ مَا كَانَ يَدْعُوٓا۟ إِلَيْهِ مِن قَبْلُ وَجَعَلَ لِلَّهِ أَندَادًا لِّيُضِلَّ عَن سَبِيلِهِۦ ۚ قُلْ تَمَتَّعْ بِكُفْرِكَ قَلِيلًا ۖ إِنَّكَ مِنْ أَصْحَٰبِ ٱلنَّارِ ﴿٨﴾﴾ [الزُّمَر: ٨]

﴾And when some hurt touches man, he cries to his Lord [Allah alone], turning to Him in repentance, but when He bestows a favour upon him from Himself, he forgets that for which he cried before, and he sets up rivals to Allah, in order to mislead others from His path. Say: Take pleasure in your disbelief for a while; surely, you are [one] of the dwellers of the fire!﴿

(Qur'an 39: 8)

How can we thank Allah (ﷻ) for our blessings?

In the Qur'an, Allah (ﷻ) teaches us what we can do to be thankful. He gives us this valuable supplication:

﴿رَبِّ أَوْزِعْنِيٓ أَنْ أَشْكُرَ نِعْمَتَكَ ٱلَّتِيٓ أَنْعَمْتَ عَلَيَّ وَعَلَىٰ وَٰلِدَيَّ وَأَنْ أَعْمَلَ صَٰلِحًا تَرْضَىٰهُ وَأَدْخِلْنِي بِرَحْمَتِكَ فِي عِبَادِكَ ٱلصَّٰلِحِينَ ١٩﴾

[النّمل: ١٩]

﴿My Lord! Inspire and bestow upon me the power and ability that I may be grateful for Your favours which You have bestowed on me and on my parents, and that I may do righteous good deeds that will please You, and admit me [to paradise] by Your mercy among Your righteous slaves.﴾

(Qur'an 27: 19)

• Recognize your innumerable blessings and give thanks to Allah (ﷻ). The Prophet (ﷺ) advised us to say after each prayer: «O Allah! Help me to remember You and thank You, and enable me to worship You properly.» (a sound hadith recorded by an-Nasâ'i, Abu Dâwood and Ibn Ḥibbân)

• Use your blessings for a good cause, seeking the pleasure of Allah (ﷻ). If you are wealthy, you can help the needy. If you have knowledge, teach others and use your knowledge for the benefit of your society and all humanity. If Allah (ﷻ) gave you health and strength, work to cause the land to flourish. If you can smile, use it to brighten someone else's day.

• Be grateful to Allah (ﷻ), and be grateful to all of His creatures. Thank others for the good that they bring into your life, because Prophet Muhammad (ﷺ) said: «One who is not grateful to people is not grateful to Allah.» (a sound hadith recorded by at-Tirmidhi and Abu Dâwood)

Take a moment to... recognize your blessings

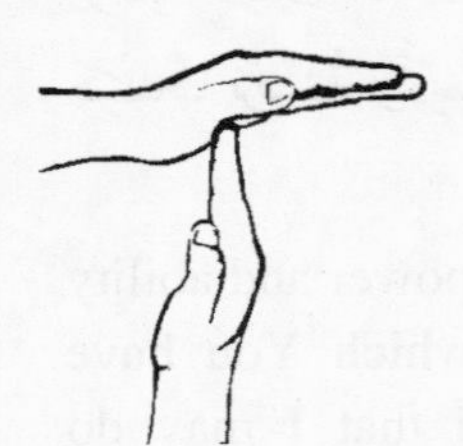

- Reflect on something good that happened to you today. What did you experience today that brought happiness and satisfaction to your heart? It does not have to be a big thing. Did you see a beautiful sunrise? Did you smell a breeze of fresh air or maybe notice a smile on your little child's face? You will find a lot for which you can thank Allah (ﷻ).
- In your journal, open a spread of two pages. On the top of the first page, write this verse:

﴿وَمَا بِكُم مِّن نِّعْمَةٍ فَمِنَ ٱللَّهِ ... ﴿٥٣﴾﴾ [النّحل: ٥٣]

﴿And whatever of blessings and good things you have, it is from Allah...﴾ *(Qur'an 16: 53)*

- Then start a list of your blessings. Record everything that you can think of, but remember to end your list with this verse:

﴿... وَإِن تَعُدُّواْ نِعْمَتَ ٱللَّهِ لَا تُحْصُوهَآ ... ﴿٣٤﴾﴾ [إبراهيم: ٣٤]

﴿...And if you [try to] count the blessings of Allah, never will you be able to count them [all]...﴾ *(Qur'an 14: 34)*

- Reflect upon each item on your list, and feel the meaning of the verses.
- After each of your prayers today, and always, ask Allah (ﷻ) to help you in thanking Him: «O Allah! Help me to remember You and thank You, and enable me to worship You properly.» (a sound hadith recorded by an-Nisâ'i and Abu Dâwood)

Take a moment to...
use your blessings for the good of others

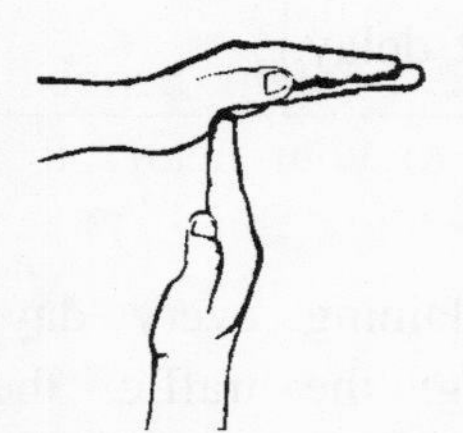

- This week, actively thank Allah (ﷻ) for your blessings by using your blessings in a good cause. Be creative; think of something that you never did before.

Take a moment to... thank someone

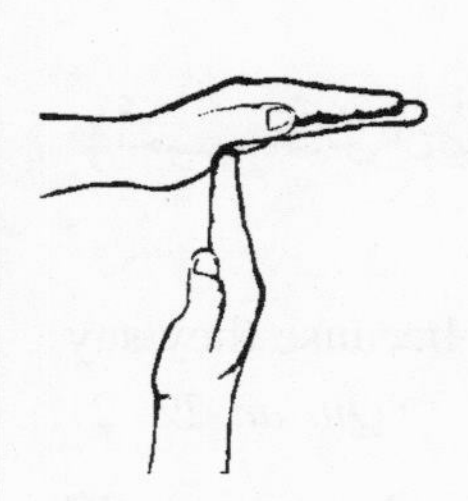

- Call someone today and thank him or her. Choose someone to whom you really feel grateful. The person may not have done anything lately; they may not have done any material thing at all. You may be grateful for a friend's support over the years, for your spouse's tolerance and love, for your child's good behaviour lately, or for your parents' support. You may need to thank your neighbour for being there when you needed some help, or your close friend for his or her good friendship, or the postman for accurate and punctual work, or the child next door for the smile he gives you every morning. Remember that the Prophet (ﷺ) said: «One who is not grateful to people is not grateful to Allah (ﷻ).» (a sound hadith recorded by at-Tirmidhi and Abu Dâwood)

You may feel that they already know you are grateful, or you may feel that the simple words 'thank you' will not make a difference, or perhaps you even feel shy or hesitant. Please believe me: a word of thanks and gratitude makes a HUGE difference! Try it now. Don't procrastinate. Make it a habit to express your gratitude whenever you feel it. If you want to thank someone, even a stranger, do it; don't delay.

3. Satisfaction

How many people do you hear complaining every day, complaining about anything and everything: the traffic, the weather, their children, their spouse, their parents, their boss, their weight, their finances, their health...?

It is true that life's struggles and challenges never end. Allah says:

﴿أَحَسِبَ ٱلنَّاسُ أَن يُتْرَكُوٓا۟ أَن يَقُولُوٓا۟ ءَامَنَّا وَهُمْ لَا يُفْتَنُونَ ۝٢﴾

[العنكبوت : ٢]

﴿Do people think that they will be left alone because they say 'We believe' and will not be tested?﴾ *(Qur'an 29: 2)*

Tests and challenges are a part of the law of existence. They are integral parts of our growth and development. There is a wisdom hidden behind every pain, every struggle and every challenge. Your task is to try to understand the lesson and heed the warning without ever questioning the will of Allah. Prophet Muhammad (ﷺ) cautioned: «Do not try to put Allah on trial about something He preordained.» (a reliable hadith recorded by Aḥmad)

It is very easy to talk and preach about being satisfied, but I know that it is sometimes very hard to practice it. Nevertheless, there is a wonderful addictive sweetness that accompanies satisfaction. When you feel satisfied with Allah's preordainment, when you accept whatever befalls you and act on improving yourself and your life with total gratitude and contentment, the serenity you get in return is incomparable; it is truly priceless.

A friend of mine desperately wanted to have a child, and it took her more than five years to get pregnant. On her expected delivery date, her gynaecologist informed her that the brain of the child she was carrying was malformed. Her daughter suffered from a rare syndrome where the brain of the foetus does not take shape during pregnancy; instead, the skull only fills with liquid. There was nothing that could be done about it. They told her that the child would not survive to leave the hospital.

My friend was totally devastated. She cried for days and nights. This was the child she had tried for so long to have. Family and friends offered words of consolation and advice about acceptance of the will of Allah (ﷻ), satisfaction and gratitude, perseverance and her reward in paradise, inshallah. She understood and intellectually accepted the facts. She prayed and supplicated for guidance and patience, but it was still very hard for her to feel satisfaction deep in her heart.

Against the expectations of the doctors, the child survived and went home with her mother. "*I'm not going to love her,*" my friend constantly announced. "*She will die soon, and if I love her, it will break my heart.*" Still, she could not help but love her baby girl, as Allah (ﷻ) willed, since He is the turner of hearts. My friend's night-long cries and supplications reaped their reward. Allah (ﷻ) granted her satisfaction, love and patience deep in her heart. He granted her sincerity to accept whatever He had predestined for her. A few months later, she was praying and thanking Allah (ﷻ) with her tears wetting the grave of her beloved child. She now felt true contentment and knew deep in her heart that this test held precious wisdom. It brought her closer to Allah (ﷻ) and made her stop to re-examine her life, her priorities and her beliefs. It was a lesson and a blessing.

Many of us do not face such difficult challenges in our everyday lives, but still we complain. Our misery lies in our inability to appreciate all of our blessings. We allow our challenges to build this strong concrete wall that blocks our view and shields our hearts against our God-given gifts.

If you measure your happiness by your material achievements, you may be faced with many disappointments and frustrations, since it is impossible to control the outside world. You only have control over your inner choices, awareness, consciousness and feelings; these are the factors that can change your whole world view. To fail to accept the will of Allah is to deny yourself the opportunity to advance and prosper. Prophet Muhammad (ﷺ) said: «If the son of Adam (that is, a human being) had two valleys full of gold, he would wish for three.» (Bukhari and Muslim)

He (ﷺ) also told us: «He who wakes in the morning while safe in his residence, healthy in his body, and having his day's sustenance, will be as if the entire world was granted to him.» (a sound or reliable hadith recorded by at-Tirmidhi, Ibn Mâjah and Ibn Ḥibbân)

You have to look within your heart to find inner peace and contentment. To help you in your journey towards satisfaction, adopt this dhikr that Prophet Muhammad (ﷺ) taught us, to be said three times in the morning after the obligatory dawn prayer and three times in the late afternoon after the obligatory mid-afternoon prayer: «O Allah! I am satisfied with Allah (ﷻ) as my God, Islam as my religion and Muhammad as my prophet.» (a reliable hadith recorded by Aḥmad and an-Nasâ'i)

Prophet Muhammad (ﷺ) explained that if one says this dhikr at these specified times, Allah (ﷻ) has promised to grant that person satisfaction and contentment.[57]

---

[57] At-Tirmidhi

Another help in your journey towards satisfaction is the adjustment of your free will to the divine will, and this can be achieved through a non-obligatory prayer called *istikhârah*, which means 'seeking what is good'. Prophet Muhammad (ﷺ) taught us that whenever anyone intends to undertake a matter, the person should first offer two units of prayer and then supplicate to Allah (ﷻ) seeking guidance to make the right decision or choose the proper course. This puts one in total agreement with Allah's choice and cultivates satisfaction in one's heart.

Stop the 'Why me?' attitude!

I was really touched by the story of Arthur Ashe, the legendary Wimbledon tennis player. Ashe got infected with HIV (the virus that causes AIDS) through a contaminated blood transfusion given to him during heart surgery. His many fans felt tremendous sorrow for him, and one of them asked him: "*Why has God selected you for such a terrible disease?*"

Ashe's response was: "*When I was holding a cup [after winning a tennis tournament], I never asked God, 'Why me?' And today in pain, I should not be asking God, 'Why me?'*"[58]

Ashe redirected his pain for a useful cause. He started the Arthur Ashe Institute for Urban Health, an institute that deals with issues related to the quality of health care available in vulnerable, underserved communities.

As Muslims, we can take comfort and guidance in the words of Prophet Muhammad (ﷺ): «The bigger the test, the greater the reward. When Allah (ﷻ) loves people, He tests them. If they accept the affliction (cheerfully), then they will achieve contentment (or Allah's pleasure); those who become enraged will only

---

[58] Wikipedia

reap Allah's rage.» (a sound or reliable hadith recorded by at-Tirmidhi, Ibn Mâjah and al-Mundhiri)

No matter how long you complain or grieve, sooner or later, if you wish to thrive, you will have to forgo the matter and get on with your life. A wise man once said: "*On the first day that a calamity strikes, the wise person behaves like the ignorant person behaves only days later.*"[59]

Take a moment to... reflect

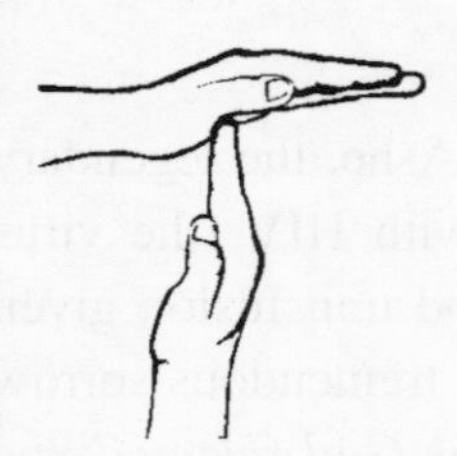

- Remember a calamity that befell you recently. What was your first reaction? Did you complain?
- Do you suffer from the 'Why me?' syndrome?
- When you feel content during an affliction, what are the real reasons behind this attitude? Is it helplessness or true sincerity? Re-evaluate your intention.

Reminder... say this phrase of dhikr:

- «O Allah! I am satisfied with Allah (ﷻ) as my God, Islam as my religion and Muhammad as my prophet. [*Allâhumma inni raḍayt billâhi rabban wa bilislâmi deenan wa bi Muḥammad ṣalla Allâhu 'alayhi wa sallam nabeeyan.*]» (a reliable hadith recorded by Aḥmad and Nasâ'i)

---

[59] Al-Ghazâli, *The Book of Religious Learning*

4. Belief

In his book *Entangled Minds*, Dean Radin relates an experiment performed by psychologists at the University of Illinois. Participants were shown a short video clip of a basketball game between two teams, one wearing white T-shirts and the other wearing black. Each team had its own ball, which was tossed among its players. The participants were required to count the number of times the basketball was tossed among the players on the white team. At some point in the middle of the game, a man dressed in a black gorilla costume stepped calmly onto the court, beat his chest, and then walked away as calmly as he had entered. Guess what? The majority of the participants in the experiment did not even notice the gorilla, since they were so focused on watching the white team. This is what Radin called 'deflected attention'.

Deflected attention acts like our commonly held beliefs, which in many instances 'cause us to become blind to the obvious'.

Adjusted beliefs, the good beliefs that you choose to inculcate into your heart and mind, are very important tools in your resources. The beliefs that all power and success come from Allah (ﷻ) and that all strength is attributed to Him (ﷻ), and then the humble but strong belief in yourself and your abilities, and the positive thoughts and continuous dhikr that reprogram your subconscious mind and help you overcome life's obstacles and challenges — all of these beliefs help you to see the Big Picture and give you strength to assume your responsibilities.

Reminder:

- Don't forget to say about twenty minutes of morning and evening dhikr each day.
- Memorize more phrases of dhikr from the Qur'an and the Sunnah and integrate them into your daily actions.

5. Inner strength

One of my first jobs as a pharmacist was in the scientific office of a well-established pharmaceutical company. My job was to translate the quality control and laboratory analysis documents into French before the products were exported to Morocco and Algeria.

One evening, really exhausted from my morning work at the university, I miscopied some numbers from a quality control sheet. 'Some numbers' in pharmaceutical terms are not mere numbers; a dose error of one microgram could be fatal. I usually reviewed the sheets before submitting them, but this time, my highly meticulous boss asked for the sheets early, and he discovered the mistake before I did. Soon I was called into his office. Knowing that my mistake was quite serious, I was willing to accept any judgement that he deemed suitable. Before meeting him, I was warned by my colleagues about his bad temper and terrible insults. "*Never answer back,*" one of them advised. "*It will only make matters worse. Just nod and apologize. He will eventually calm down,*" another colleague added.

I gathered my strength and went into his office. Before I could say a word, a flow of insults and affronts was thrown into my face. I never expected this treatment. Given my shy and introverted nature, I felt fearfully and apprehensively guilt-ridden at first, but soon I could not withstand the insults. I don't know how I found the strength to stop him. "*Please sir,*" I interrupted politely. "*I know how terrible my mistake is, and I am willing to accept full responsibility for it. You have the right to fire me if you want, but you have no right to personally insult me.*" Silence enveloped the room for a few seconds. I could hear my heartbeat accelerating as I awaited his reply. Suddenly, the man stood up and said firmly, "*I respect your response. I am sorry. Correct these sheets and take better care of your work in the future.*"

This was a great relief. I never made such a mistake again and was afterwards treated with much respect by my boss and all of my colleagues, but more importantly, I felt great respect for myself.

We all possess hidden powers, powers that help us face difficult situations and surmount obstacles. Sometimes we do not even know that we possess this strength until we are faced with a challenge.

Take a moment to... reflect on your own power

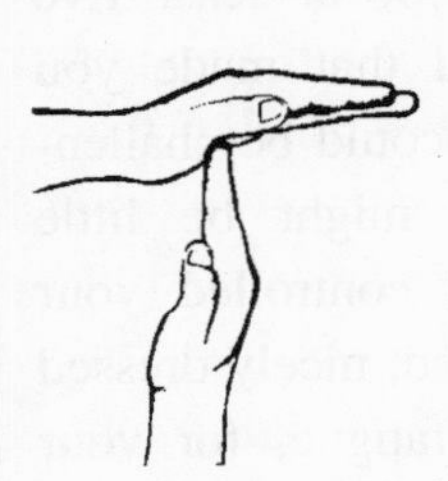

- Think of a situation in which you were powerful, when you surprised even yourself with your reaction. Yes, you surely have at least one memory about that: when you assumed a responsibility and did a great job at handling it, when you travelled alone for the first time, when you moved to a new city, when your loved one got really ill, when you passed a hard exam, or when you got your driving license... Relax and dig it up. Write about it in your journal.

- Remember your feelings at that moment. See yourself, feel your victory.
- See, YOU can do it!
- Now pause for a moment. Review your intention at that time. Were you sincere to Allah (ﷻ) and relying on Him for support and strength? What was the origin of your power? If you were in this situation again, what would be your intention now, and accordingly, would you act any differently?
- Feeling your True Secret in your heart and seeing the Big Picture before your eyes, would you have been stronger?

Try this...

- This is an addition to the Conscience Exam that we already discussed doing each night, but this one will be testing your fairness to yourself.
- Every night, think of at least five things that you did that made you proud. At first, this could be challenging because they might be little things that usually pass unnoticed: you controlled your temper with the children or in traffic; waited, nicely dressed and with a big smile in spite of your fatigue, for your spouse who was late; made a good choice; baked a nice cake; gave something in charity; performed a random act of kindness; noticed hidden bounties and felt grateful...
- Feel special. YOU ARE SPECIAL!

Take a moment to... remember your strengths

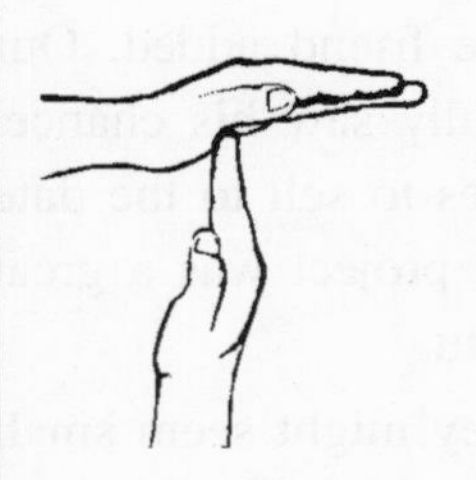

- Sit comfortably with your journal. Close your eyes and take a deep breath.
- Open your journal to the list of your powers, potentials, traits, good characteristics and strengths, which you wrote earlier. Re-read it. Do you want to add anything to the list?
- Think again about what you are good at, what you can do, and all that you have learned over your lifetime, whether at school, at home, from friends or family, from life experiences, from your reading...
- Keep the list in mind for a whole week and add to it anything that you remember. Don't think twice about a potential item on your list; just write it down and let your subconscious work on actualizing it in your life.

6. Challenge and creativity

I recently heard a story about a young man who dreamed of being rich. He carried a small notepad in his pocket and jotted down any ideas he encountered that he might use to start a business. He never rejected any thought that crossed his mind, however irrational or unrealistic it might seem at the time. Passing by a supermarket one day, he noticed all the discarded cardboard boxes, so he noted: '*Collect and sell cardboard boxes*'. Days passed, with more ideas accumulating in his notebook, but he still did not have a clue about which specific one to act on.

One morning, he was sitting with some friends discussing the approaching season of date fruit collection. One of his friends remarked that every year, the quantity of dates collected was so huge that it caused a shortage of cardboard boxes. "*Then a single box is sold for as much as five riyals,*" the friend added. Our young man jumped up in excitement; he finally saw his chance. He started collecting a million cardboard boxes to sell to the date merchants at the price of one riyal each. The project was a great success, and he became a millionaire overnight.

Don't underestimate your ideas, even if they might seem small or insignificant. All revolutionary actions and inventions started with a simple idea. Be creative, and always set new challenges. Working on improving your situation through innovation, keeping yourself challenged and creating new opportunities are crucial ingredients in your formula for success. Remember the Qur'anic verse:

﴿فَإِذَا فَرَغْتَ فَٱنصَبْ ۝٧﴾ [الشَّرح: ٧]

﴾Therefore, when you are free [from your immediate task] still labour hard.﴿ *(Qur'an 94: 7)*

Of course, don't forget to couple this with the following verse, the one holding your True Secret:

﴿وَإِلَىٰ رَبِّكَ فَٱرْغَب ۝٨﴾ [الشَّرح: ٨]

﴾And to Allah [alone] turn [all your intentions and hopes and] your supplications.﴿ *(Qur'an 94: 8)*

Take a moment to... welcome creativity

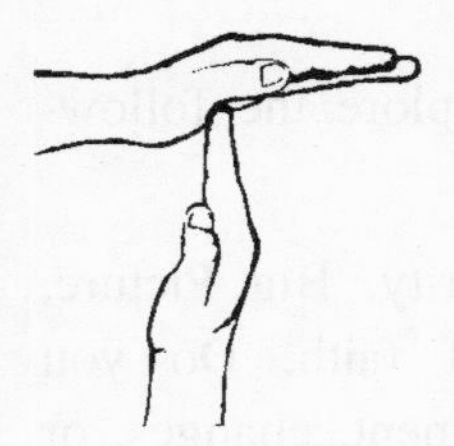

- Brainstorm ideas — all that you can possibly think of — that bring more creativity to everyday life. You can involve your children in this brainstorming activity. It can be really fun. I performed this exercise with my eight-year-old daughter, and here are some ideas that we came up with: learn a new skill, read commentary explaining the Qur'an and apply it in your life, read a new book every week, learn something new every day, take a walk smelling the fresh air, draw out your feelings, never sleep after the dawn prayer, remember to renew your intention before any action, keep an idea journal, feed a bird or a stray cat, call a friend or a distant relative whom you have not contacted for a long time, cook a new dish, plant some seeds or sprouts, buy some flowers, burn incense in your house, collect shells from the beach, watch the sunset, visit a museum, visit an orphanage, take a bubble bath, invite some friends over with no fancy preparations...
- Try some of your ideas this week.

We will take a short break here to assess our progress so far by doing another IPC (In Process Control), focusing this time on your inner resources.

Take a moment to... IPC and assess your resources

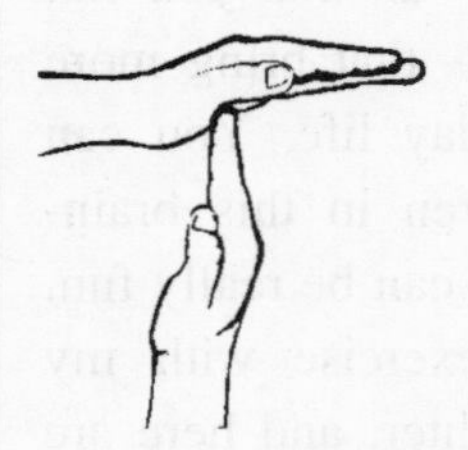

- In your journal, explore the following:

Your beliefs: sincerity, Big Picture, intentions, level of faith. Do you notice any improvement, changes, or additions? Do you need help? (More righteous friends and company, more spiritual nutrients, more effort in purification of the heart...)

Your inner strength and self-esteem: Is it better? Stronger? Not yet? Are you working on it? Are you experiencing occasional bouts of doubt? (It is totally normal to do so. I still do.) How are you dealing with them? Are you still remembering to say your daily dhikr? (You may need to write down phrases of dhikr in your journal. Write specific ones that feel special to you.)

Challenges and creativity: What new challenges are appearing now or have been introduced into your life during the past few weeks? Do you feel more creative (in every aspect of your life, in performing your normal life chores)? More empowered? More inspired by the world and the people around you? Did you add new challenging goals to your daily and monthly plans? Evaluate your goals and plans. Are they the right size, or do you need to push yourself further?

Outer resources

1. Reading

The first verse of the Qur'an that was revealed to Prophet Muhammad (ﷺ) says, 'Read!':

﴿ٱقۡرَأۡ بِٱسۡمِ رَبِّكَ ٱلَّذِى خَلَقَ ۝ خَلَقَ ٱلۡإِنسَٰنَ مِنۡ عَلَقٍ ۝ ٱقۡرَأۡ وَرَبُّكَ ٱلۡأَكۡرَمُ ۝ ٱلَّذِى عَلَّمَ بِٱلۡقَلَمِ ۝ عَلَّمَ ٱلۡإِنسَٰنَ مَا لَمۡ يَعۡلَمۡ ۝﴾   [العَلَق: ١-٥]

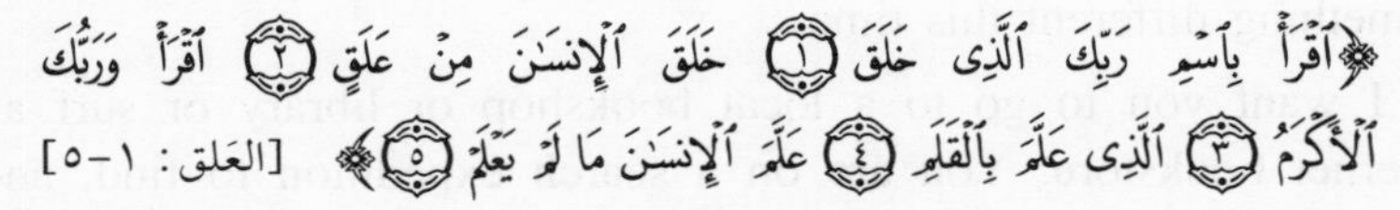

❮Read! In the name of your Creator, Who has created [all that exists], has created the human from a clot [a piece of thick coagulated blood]. Read! And your Creator is the Most Generous, Who has taught [writing] by the pen, has taught humankind that which it did not know.❯   *(Qur'an 96: 1-5)*

Reading is the most important source of learning. It is an invaluable activity that should never be neglected or underestimated. With the advancement of technology, the presence of television and radio and the widespread use of internet facilities, we and our children are getting further and further away from books. Our excuses are endless; the most famous, of course, is that we have no time. Well, there is no excuse. Reading is an order from Allah (ﷻ). We are ordered to read, so read in all fields. Read in order to learn, assimilate, teach, spread knowledge and add to it.

The first step that early Muslims took in building their great civilization, after firmly establishing their religion and faith, was reading. They read and translated all the knowledge available at their time. They learned and put their knowledge into practice, then they added a great deal to science and literature and shared their knowledge and discoveries with the whole world.

You are probably reading a lot already. You read the newspapers, your work-related documents and your children's reports. You may also be reading some weekly magazines or some of the endless information on the internet. I will ask you to do something different this time.

I want you to go to a local bookshop or library or surf an internet bookstore. You are on a search expedition to find, and then purchase or borrow, a book. It has to be an actual physical book, not an e-book. I want you to hold it in your hands, write notes in the margins and highlight useful ideas (or take notes on a small post-it notepad, if it is a library book).

You have probably read hundreds of books, magazines and newspapers in your lifetime. How did you choose them? Maybe they were part of your school, faculty or work curriculum. Maybe they were recommended by someone or were in the field of your expertise. This time, I am asking you to take a different approach in choosing your book. Let the book choose you. Walk through the aisles of a bookshop or surf different book categories on the internet. Give yourself enough time, and let your heart choose for you. Keep your inner intuitive feelings alert. Is there any subject that you always dreamed of learning about, but never had the time, or from which you were discouraged for some reason or another? Is there a special field of interest that you set aside to pursue your career or family life?

Look at new topics, and then pick a book that looks interesting or that is in a field which is totally new to you, one that piques your curiosity. It can be anything from science, computers, math, literature, journalism, cooking, nutrition, medicine, fashion, or interior design... Follow your first thought, your instinct; don't second-guess yourself. Don't think about the use of your chosen book right now; just let your heart choose and let your intuition guide you.

I still do this book hunt from time to time. This is one of my 'apples'. I started this practice around ten years ago when I was working as a teaching assistant in the faculty of Pharmacy. I had preset career goals to be a pharmacist who becomes a university professor one day. At that time, I was starting my master's degree in pharmaceutics, specializing in dosage form design.

While walking through the aisles of the Cairo International Book Fair, my feelings led me to two books: *Nurturing Yourself and Others* and *Seven Steps to a New You.* These were totally alien to my conventional medical mentality and practice at the time, but I followed my inner guidance and bought them. They were my first encounter with the topic of holistic living. Although I did not make an immediate career shift just yet, these books opened my eyes — and my heart — to a new field that I wanted to explore. It was five years later, after thorough investigation and more studying, that I permanently left the faculty of Pharmacy to specialize in natural health and holistic well-being, something I would never have imagined doing at the time I bought my first books on the subject.

Try this... a book hunt

- Choose your book (or rather, let your book choose you). Enjoy reading it, and don't rush for any kind of 'results' just yet; things will unfold with time. Just keep your eyes and heart open to see what the book will bring out of you!

If you find the book boring or uninteresting, don't reject the whole field just yet. You might try another book that discusses the same subject from a different point of view. Dig deeper, write your feelings about the book (whether positive or negative) and record whatever ideas or thoughts came along with your readings.

You can always get a book on another subject, or choose more than one field to explore, if you feel like it. Just keep experimenting, and repeat the process whenever you are finished with your current book. Let reading become a life practice. Always have a new book on hand, and carry it with you to read when you find any spare time.

Take a moment to... think about your library

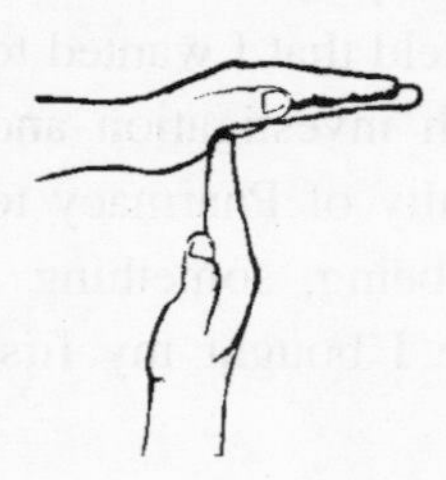

- Review the library that you have collected over the years. Are you satisfied with it? What was your most recent addition?
- After practicing 'book hunts' for some time, re-evaluate your library and your reading progress. Are you reading more books than ever? If not, reconsider the type of books you are reading. Not interesting enough? Not enough time? Remember, no excuses!
- Always add to your library.

2. Learning

Islam stresses the importance of learning for all human beings. In the Qur'an, Allah (ﷻ) instructed Prophet Muhammad (ﷺ):

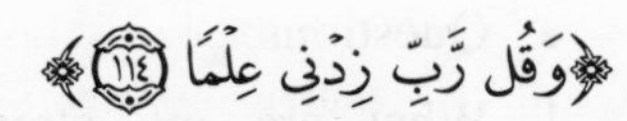
[طه: ١١٤]

﴾And say: Allah, increase me in knowledge [*rabbi zidni 'ilman*].﴿ *(Qur'an 20: 114)*

To urge us to seek knowledge, Prophet Muhammad (ﷺ) promised us that there are rewards for learning, rewards both in this life and in the hereafter: «When a person passes away, his or her deeds are halted except for three of them: an ongoing charity, useful knowledge, and pious offspring who pray for him or her.» (Muslim)

Seeking new knowledge, especially in challenging fields and a variety of subjects, encourages the brain to reach higher capacities and performance levels and develops within an individual incentive, attention and perseverance.[60]

Try this... Self-knowledge Feedback

- The first step in acquiring knowledge is gaining self-knowledge. Do you really know yourself?

  This is a teamwork exercise. It is best performed with a group of family members or close friends, people who know you and can help you discover more about yourself.

- For each person in the group, have one paper with his or her name at the top and the following questions, written with enough space after them for other members of the group to write answers. Pass the papers around the group so that each person has a chance to write about every other group member.

60 Winston

- Questions:

1. What are my strengths, potentials, good traits and talents? What do I do best?

2. How do you think I can be more effective and useful to those around me?

- Rules:

1. Don't sneak a look at the paper with your name on it until everyone has finished.

2. Don't interrupt anyone while he or she is writing the answers.

3. Write only positive assets; this is not the place for negative feedback.

Try this... investigate your learning style

- There are many sites on the internet that help you to check your learning style and find out whether you are left- or right-brain oriented. Are you a visual, auditory or tactile learner? Check it out.

- Read about the different types of intelligence and find out your intelligence strengths.

This information will help you in your choice of books and resources, directing your attention to the fields of knowledge most interesting to you.

Thinking

Another very important source of knowledge is our own thinking. Engaging our minds in regular creative thinking and problem solving activities widens our perspectives and gives us new experiences from which we can learn.

Thinking activities for reaching appropriate solutions and results should be dealt with step by step:

1. Define your goal

First, there must be a useful objective sought by the thinking process, a definite goal to be reached; otherwise, thinking will be a meaningless waste of time and effort.[61] You have to clearly define your purpose and the overall result you want to achieve.

We can see the importance of this first step — defining our purpose — in the attitude of the early Muslims after their migration from Makkah to Madinah. Their ultimate goal was to build a strong Islamic nation, from which they would be able to spread the teachings of Islam around the world. This was the true purpose of the migration, so they started building their city, improving their economy and raising their families to have a safe and sound base from which to launch their activities. Meanwhile their ultimate goal remained sharply focused in their minds. They continued to increase their knowledge about their religion, and they began sending messengers to the Roman Empire, Persia and Egypt to spread news of the goodness of the Islamic faith.

Imam al-Ghazâli, in his book *Al-Ihyâ'*, relates the story of a king who heard about the skill of the Chinese and the Romans in painting and using dyes. He organized a contest in which each

---

61 De Bono

group was supposed to present its best piece of art. He ordered that a huge metal tray be brought for the competition. A curtain was set in the middle of it to hide each side from the other contestants, and each group began its work. The Romans brought the most refined dyes and colours and started painting an exquisite design, while the Chinese kept polishing their side of the tray until it sparkled and shone like a mirror.

When the Romans finished their work, the Chinese claimed that they also had finished, and the king ordered the curtain removed. The Roman side held a fantastically beautiful, colourful design, but to everyone's surprise, the Chinese side acted like a mirror and reflected the same stunning design, with the addition of a crystal-like shine and sparkles.

Well, if the final goal here was to impress the king with wise and innovative ideas, then the Chinese surely did the job. However, if the goal was to prove that their work was skilful and artistic, then the Chinese failed miserably.

This tale shows the importance of having the final goal engraved in our minds all the time. The same final outcome can be an amazing success or a total failure, depending on what results are expected or needed.[62]

2. Gather information

At this stage, you need to gather information, learn more about your problem, and explore all aspects of, and around, the situation. According to Ibn al-Qayyim al-Jawziyah, the acquired knowledge and facts are the means that help the thinking process. In this

---

62 Al-Ghazâli used this story to compare the polishing and refining the Chinese did to the purification process a pious believer does to his or her heart so that it reflects all the beauty of its surroundings.

stage, all factors involved in the situation — all possibilities, shortcomings, advantages, disadvantages and consequences — have to be properly appraised and acknowledged. Be creative; brainstorm to generate and compile as many ideas as you can, with no constraints or limitations. Record everything.[63]

In the Qur'an, Allah (ﷻ) gives us guidelines for building a scientific mind:[64]

- Reflect:

﴿وَهُوَ ٱلَّذِى مَدَّ ٱلْأَرْضَ وَجَعَلَ فِيهَا رَوَٰسِىَ وَأَنْهَٰرًا ۖ وَمِن كُلِّ ٱلثَّمَرَٰتِ جَعَلَ فِيهَا زَوْجَيْنِ ٱثْنَيْنِ ۖ يُغْشِى ٱلَّيْلَ ٱلنَّهَارَ ۚ إِنَّ فِى ذَٰلِكَ لَءَايَٰتٍ لِّقَوْمٍ يَتَفَكَّرُونَ ۝٣﴾ [الرّعد: ٣]

﴾And it is He [Allah] Who spread out the earth, and placed therein firm mountains and rivers, and of every kind of fruit He made *zawjayn ithnayn* [two in pairs — may mean two kinds or it may mean of two sorts, such as black and white, sweet and sour, small and big, and so on]. He brings the night as a cover over the day. Verily, in these things, there are signs [proofs, evidences, and lessons] for people who reflect.﴿

(Qur'an 13: 3)

- Base your knowledge on facts:

﴿قُلْ هَاتُوا۟ بُرْهَٰنَكُمْ إِن كُنتُمْ صَٰدِقِينَ ۝١١١﴾ [البَقَرة: ١١١]

﴾Say: Bring forth your proofs, if you are truthful.﴿

(Qur'an 27: 64)

63 De Bono

64 Al-Qaraḍâwi, *The Sunnah: A Source of Civilization*

• Use scientific methods to collect information:

When the Prophet (ﷺ) and his Companions (may Allah be pleased with them) first migrated to Madinah, he asked his Companions to take a count of every Muslim in the city. He used the statistics to gather the information needed to build his new society.

• Ask for the opinions of people who have experience in the field:

﴿وَإِذَا جَآءَهُمْ أَمْرٌ مِّنَ ٱلْأَمْنِ أَوِ ٱلْخَوْفِ أَذَاعُواْ بِهِۦ وَلَوْ رَدُّوهُ إِلَى ٱلرَّسُولِ وَإِلَىٰٓ أُوْلِى ٱلْأَمْرِ مِنْهُمْ لَعَلِمَهُ ٱلَّذِينَ يَسْتَنۢبِطُونَهُۥ مِنْهُمْ ... ﴿٨٣﴾﴾

[النّساء : ٨٣]

﴾When there comes to them some matter touching [public] safety or fear, they make it known [among the common people]. If only they had referred it to the Messenger or to those charged with authority among them, the proper investigators would have understood it from them [directly]...﴿

(Qur'an 4: 83)

• Check the sources of your information:

﴿وَإِنَّ ٱلظَّنَّ لَا يُغْنِى مِنَ ٱلْحَقِّ شَيْـًٔا ﴿٢٨﴾﴾ [النّجم : ٢٨]

﴾And verily, a guess is no substitute for the truth.﴿

(Qur'an 53: 28)

• Generate your own novel ideas to try to solve problems:

Islam encourages creativity, flexibility and innovation in dealing with life's problems. There is an interesting example of this from the Battle of the Trench, when the Arab tribes gathered to fight the Muslims in Madinah. It seemed impossible for the Muslims to face the huge number of fighters in the opposing army, but Salmân al-Fârisi (رضي الله عنه) came up with a creative idea to build a trench around their city so that the opposing army would be unable to reach them. This tactic was unknown among the Arabs of that time.

Allah (سبحانه وتعالى) also warns us about mere copying or stagnation and about subordination to concepts that go against the precepts of Islam:

﴿وَإِذَا قِيلَ لَهُمُ ٱتَّبِعُوا۟ مَآ أَنزَلَ ٱللَّهُ قَالُوا۟ بَلْ نَتَّبِعُ مَآ أَلْفَيْنَا عَلَيْهِ ءَابَآءَنَآ ۗ أَوَلَوْ كَانَ ءَابَآؤُهُمْ لَا يَعْقِلُونَ شَيْـًٔا وَلَا يَهْتَدُونَ ﴿١٧٠﴾﴾ [البقرة: ١٧٠]

﴾They say: Nay! We shall follow what we found our fathers following. [Would they do that!] Even though their fathers did not understand anything nor were they guided?﴿

(Qur'an 2: 170)

At this stage of gathering information, the more ideas you have, the better. Greater numbers of choices broaden your thinking and generate more alternatives and options to consider. Just carefully analyze each possibility before proceeding with your final conclusion or plan.

3. Devise your plan

Now you are ready to devise your plan, while keeping in mind the purpose of the overall thinking process and, above all, your main mission and goal in life as a Muslim. Check your intention, and be sincere in your thoughts and actions.

In the Qur'an, Allah (سبحانه وتعالى) showed us how Prophet Joseph (عليه السلام) devised and implemented a long-term plan that saved a whole nation from starvation:

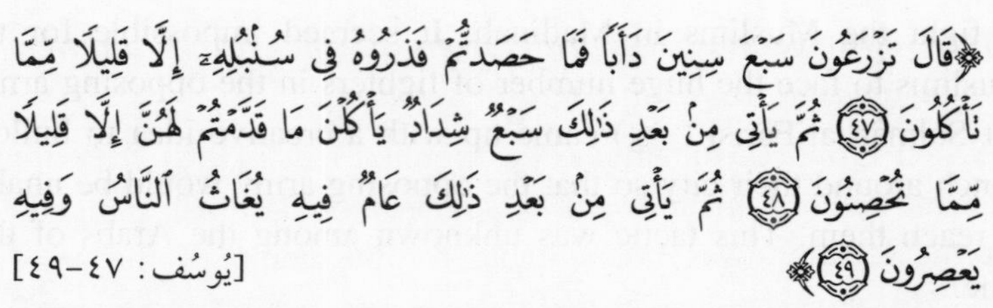

﴿[Joseph] said: For seven consecutive years, you shall sow as usual and that [harvest] which you reap you shall leave in its ears, [all] except a little of it which you may eat. Then after that will come seven hard [years], which will devour what you have laid by in advance for them, [all] except a little of that which you have guarded [and stored]. Then will come a year in which people will have abundant rain and in which they will press [wine and oil].﴾ *(Qur'an 12: 47-49)*

4. Consult with others

Once you have collected your information, studied and analyzed different possibilities and prepared your plan, consult your partners or associates:

﴿... وَشَاوِرْهُمْ فِي ٱلْأَمْرِ ... ﴿١٥٩﴾﴾ [آل عِمران: ١٥٩]

﴿...And consult them in the affairs...﴾ *(Qur'an 3: 159)*

This is a very important step. Consultation helps to strengthen bonds among partners, increase loyalty, and most of all generate beneficial and creative ideas. Prophet Muhammad (ﷺ) used to consult his Companions. Recall the incident during the famous Battle of Badr when the Muslim army camped close to the water at Badr.[65] One of the Prophet's Companions, al-Hubâb ibn al-Mundhir (رضي الله عنه), asked him: "*O Messenger of Allah, is this a place that Allah has ordered you to occupy, so that we can*

---

[65] As-Sibâ'ie

neither advance nor withdraw from it, or is it a matter of opinion, consultation, and military tactics?"

When Prophet Muhammad (ﷺ) replied that it was not a divine order but rather a matter open to suggestion, al-Ḥubâb pointed out that the location was not suitable for the camp of the Muslim army. He suggested a safer and more convenient camping site. The Prophet (ﷺ) accepted his suggestion, which turned out to be one of the important factors in the Muslims' victory in this critical battle.

Notice here that al-Ḥubâb had his priorities straight. He had the final goal clear in his mind, and that is apparent by his first question: "*Is this a place that Allah has ordered you to occupy, so that we can neither advance nor withdraw from it?*" The pleasure of Allah (ﷻ) is the ultimate goal of every Muslim.

5. Implement

After consultation, the fifth and final step is to implement your plan and entrust your affairs to Allah's hands:

﴿فَإِذَا عَزَمْتَ فَتَوَكَّلْ عَلَى ٱللَّهِ ۚ إِنَّ ٱللَّهَ يُحِبُّ ٱلْمُتَوَكِّلِينَ ﴿١٥٩﴾﴾ [آل عِمرَان: ١٥٩]

﴿Then when you have taken a decision, put your trust in Allah. Certainly, Allah loves those who put their trust [in Him].﴾

(Qur'an 3: 159)

Also, beware of making unrealistic plans or leaving promises unfulfilled:

﴿يَٰٓأَيُّهَا ٱلَّذِينَ ءَامَنُوا۟ لِمَ تَقُولُونَ مَا لَا تَفْعَلُونَ ﴿٢﴾ كَبُرَ مَقْتًا عِندَ ٱللَّهِ أَن تَقُولُوا۟ مَا لَا تَفْعَلُونَ ﴿٣﴾﴾ [الصَّف: ٢-٣]

﴿O you who believe! Why do you say that which you do not do? Most hateful it is with Allah that you say that which you do not do.﴾ *(Qur'an 61: 2-3)*

Take a moment to... brainstorm

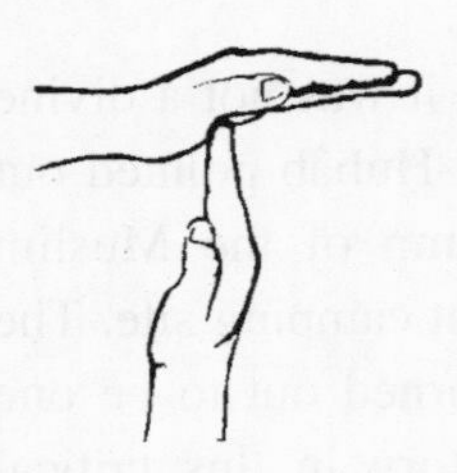

- Arrange a meeting with your friends or family for a brainstorming session. Get a large piece of poster-board. At the top of it, write the specified goal or purpose of your meeting. It might be to reinforce family ties, improve the children's behaviour, or plan an interesting summer holiday. Make sure that everyone's intentions and sincerity are in order, and then allow each person a turn to say and record the first idea that comes through his or her mind.

- Allow all family members to participate, even young children, and never ridicule or belittle any ideas, however strange they might seem.

- When you run out of ideas, discuss the proposed suggestions and choose the most suitable. Then devise a plan to realize your goal.

- Consult all attendees. Let each one choose an active role in the project, and start implementing your plan right away.

3. Experiencing what you learn

Spread your knowledge

In his book, *The 7 Habits of Highly Effective People*, Steven Covey insists on the importance of continuously teaching others what you learn. Teaching, even before applying the knowledge yourself, makes you assimilate, understand and remember any information better.

You do not have to be a professional teacher to spread your knowledge. You never know who will benefit or how others will benefit from what you say. Take care, though. There is a great difference between teaching and preaching. People tend to accept information received in a friendly, unforced manner.

At the start of my career as a teaching assistant, I taught pharmaceutical calculations and physical pharmacy to first-year students. The material was pretty tough, and the calculations, logarithms and statistics involved were lengthy and sometimes complicated. I used to stay up a long portion of the night, practicing different methods to explain the information most effectively, but what helped me the most in improving my teaching methods was actually teaching the material. The more I taught the lessons and received feedback from my students, the more I improved my teaching skills.

The same goes for any new skill or information; the more you willingly give away, the more you receive in return. Most importantly, the benefits of teaching your knowledge to others extend from this life to the afterlife inshallah, provided of course that you closely watch your True Secret. Our Prophet (ﷺ) said: «When a person passes away, his or her deeds are halted except for three of them: an ongoing charity, useful knowledge, and pious offspring who pray for him or her.» (Muslim)

Try this... share your knowledge

- Find someone to teach. It can be a friend, a neighbour, a family member, your child, or the neighbour's children. Sharing your knowledge engraves it in your long-term memory and makes it grow and flourish. It inspires more ideas and adds to your creativity.

Take a professional step

When Zaynab opened her pharmacy in a suburb of Cairo, she was shocked by the incredibly deteriorated state of the residents. Poverty, pitiable health conditions, poor hygiene, ignorance and illiteracy were common features of the area. Zaynab considered raising charity funds to help these people, but on second thought, she asked herself, "*Then what?*" They needed much more than one-time help or handouts.

With the assistance of friends, Zaynab started raising money to build facilities in the area. They opened a nursery and repaired the mosque. They started building schools and workshops for teaching carpentry, sewing and other trades to young residents to help them support themselves and their families. She also organized and conducted many trips, events and lectures teaching Islamic moral values as well as some basic life skills and hygiene. Her small project flourished into a well-organized NGO (non-governmental organization), which attracted more volunteers and more funds and influenced and helped hundreds of people.

Widening your circle of influence and taking professional steps are ways to help your ideas grow and to give you more stamina and energy. You become motivated by the many people surrounding you, and you inspire others to join in as well. Think BIG. Always ask yourself: "*How can I improve the situation?*" Take professional action.

Try this...

- Browse the internet or your local newspapers for any events, workshops, or sessions related to your goal(s).

- Make a list of these places and gather as much detail as you need about them.

- Make a commitment to attend at least one event this coming month. You need to broaden your spectrum and see what others in the same field are accomplishing. You might also meet some interesting people at the event and start a social group related to your field of interest.

Lâmâ, a friend of mine, is a pharmacist who chose long ago to be a stay-at-home mother. When her children got older, she had lots of free time and was growing bored. She decided to take her passion for cooking to a professional level by offering cooking classes from the comfort of her own home. Before starting, Lâmâ studied the demands of her market very carefully. Among her Arabic-speaking acquaintances, there was no real need for her service, so she shifted her attention to expatriates. She remembered a Japanese lady, a co-worker of her husband, who had shown real interest in Middle Eastern cuisine while dining at her home one night. Lâmâ called her and offered her services, and soon she had her first customer. Slowly but steadily, Lâmâ's customers grew in number as she proved her talent and quality of service.

Sarah is another wonderful example. She is the teenage daughter of a friend of mine. Sarah is a highly skilled artist, so she decided to offer drawing and painting classes for young school children. Children loved her because she talked to them in their language, and she laughed and played with them while teaching them the art of seeing, feeling, and expressing beauty.

You can always take your ideas, dreams, or passions one step further. Expand your boundaries and always challenge your potential.

Take a moment to...

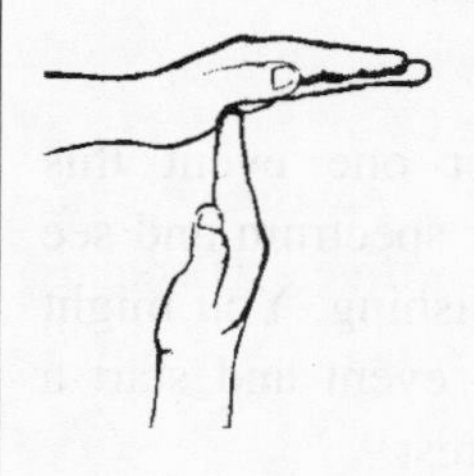

- Take a professional step towards your dream. Attend a workshop or take live or online courses. If you already have enough information and knowledge, start learning how to apply it professionally (study the market, open a small business...)

4. Time management

What does an hour mean to you?

Every hour, hundreds of people are born, and hundreds of others die. Every hour witnesses hundreds of new inventions and discoveries that alter the world we live in. In just one hour, whole civilizations crumble and new dynasties emerge. In one hour, our earth changes position around the sun and our entire solar system moves a great distance within its galaxy. What is an hour for you? What does it mean? What is its value?

It is not uncommon to feel that time is speeding by. Many people complain that although they have so much to do, nothing seems to get done. You may sometimes wish for a twenty-seven hour day or an eight-day week, but believe me, even if this wish were granted, you would still run short of time. Remember the concept of responsibility: look for solutions within yourself, not out there somewhere else. Stop complaining and start taking responsibility for your own time.

Islam teaches us the importance of managing our time wisely. Time in Islam is a very valuable resource, and our Prophet (ﷺ) warns us to avoid wasting it: «There are two blessings whose reward many people lose: good health and free time.» (Bukhari)

Time management is a very broad topic. In this book, I will try to lay out just the main framework for getting the most out of your time. My time management tips can be summarized in three words, or the simple acronym POP:

Plan
Organize
Prioritize

1. Planning

We discussed planning earlier in this chapter, and if you have been doing the exercises, you have already started planning your days, weeks, months and year. Once you include planning in your everyday life, it will become a habit. It will simplify your life and help you organize it, saving you much of the time that used to be wasted. Planning gets the clutter out of your mind. Now that you have your plans on paper, you can concentrate on getting things done, **one step at a time**.

2. Organizing your time

Nothing wastes more time than multi-tasking. It gives you the feeling that you are always busy doing something, but you have few complete accomplishments at the end. Nothing seems to really get done. Of course, by multi-tasking here, I do not mean organized activities that you can do simultaneously to make better use of your time, like listening to the verses of the Qur'an that you are trying to memorize while you are cooking, or putting your laundry in the washing machine while you prepare dinner. These actions actually make better use of your time.

Let me illustrate what I do mean by multi-tasking, using this example of a time when I am planning to go to the supermarket... I head for the kitchen to fetch my shopping list, which is hanging on the refrigerator. I do a quick inventory around the house. I need to add more things to my list. Where's the pencil? Got it. Oh, it's blunt, must go to the office to sharpen it. Better leave a pencil sharpener in the kitchen as well. I have to remember to add that to my shopping list. In the office, I see the laptop. I forgot to check my e-mail today. Let me see... A message from the college. This needs an urgent reply, and it won't take a minute. I write the reply, see a couple of funny messages, check Facebook. Oh, why was I here again? Where is that pencil sharpener? Got it. Back to the kitchen. The telephone rings, and it's a friend of mine. Do I have to answer it? It will only take a few minutes, a quick chat. Now, what was I doing again? Oh! Back to the shopping list. I wanted to add things to it, but now I have forgotten what it is that I need. Let me repeat the inventory. Oh, I remember. Write them down. Go to the bedroom to get dressed. Choose a dress. What's this spot? I have to take this dress to the dry cleaner. Oh, this reminds me of the laundry. Let me quickly put the dirty clothes in the washing machine. The laundry soap is nearly finished. Have to add it to my list. Where is my list? Here it is; I left it in the bedroom. Why is my son always leaving his pants on the floor? Pick them up. Into his wardrobe. This wardrobe is a mess! Let me arrange it quickly. Done. Now to the supermarket. Oh, I forgot to cook the rice for the children's lunch. It's one o'clock already! Maybe I'll go to the supermarket another day. Back to the kitchen...

Okay, now what did I really accomplish that day? Nothing. Did I rest? No. I was very busy all day, but what advancements did I make towards the goals I want to achieve?

This happens when we do not organize our thoughts and plans. This is what I mean by multi-tasking. It helps if you write a daily to-do list and proceed with it one step at a time, without allowing interruptions. If new tasks arise, just add them to your list and proceed with the one task at hand until you are done with it. Our brains usually cannot concentrate on more than one task at a time.

Be prepared to **make good use of time gaps**. Even with the most accurate and detailed planning, you cannot control each minute of your time. There is time wasted in traffic, while waiting for the kids at the school, in the doctor's clinic... Make use of every minute you can. You can listen to audio books or catch up on the news while waiting in traffic. You can practice your dhikr while cooking or walking or shopping in the supermarket. I always carry a book along when I am going to a place where I may have to wait for someone. I also make use of these time gaps to memorize some Qur'an or work on my cross-stitching or embroidery projects. Just make use of every minute of your life. Time is too precious to waste.

At the same time, don't forget to **give your brain a rest**. In our modern 'civilized' world, technological advancement has made it very easy for us to 'save time'. We have a food processor, dishwasher, dough maker, clothes dryer, vacuum cleaner, wireless internet connection... Now we are doing very little physical labour; we are working with our brains.

This brain needs a break, though. It needs time for reflection, for daydreaming, for silence. It needs to minimize its conscious, logical, analytical side to leave room for imagination and creativity, for dreaming and meditating, for grace and reflection. We are not giving our brains this chance. Our grandmothers were chatting, thinking, meditating and saying dhikr while cooking, kneading dough and washing the laundry. They were sharing ideas, support and news while washing the dishes and sweeping the floors. They were giving the brain a rest, or rather a boost, and renewing its powers.

This is why it is important to practice your twenty minutes of morning and evening remembrance of Allah (ﷻ). This regular activity renews your brain power and boosts your creativity. Try practicing a handicraft activity like knitting, baking, painting, or weeding the garden... and ENJOY your time while doing the physical work. Play with your children, run, walk along with them and read to them. This is not time wasted; this is a more beneficial use of the time that you usually consider to be wasted. You have to do these tasks anyway, so why not get the best out of them? Why not use them to restore balance to your brain and reduce your stress level?

3. Prioritize

Here is an illustration of my house of priorities:

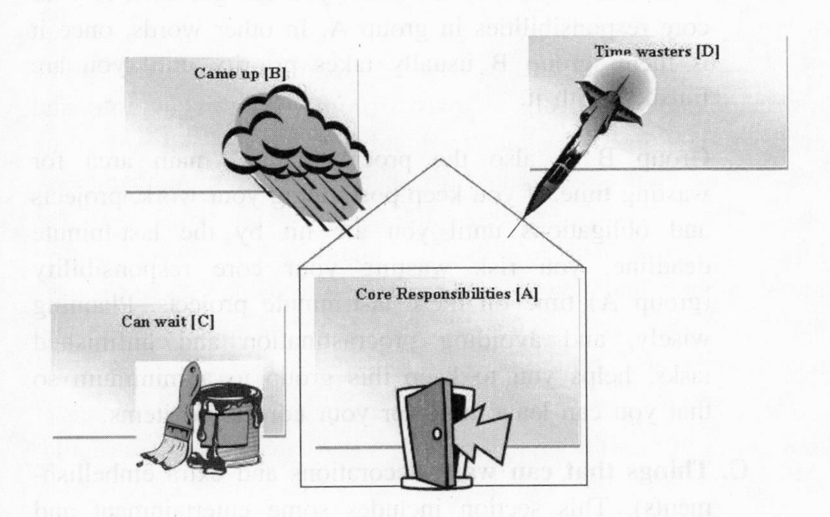

You can classify your daily tasks into four categories:

A. Core responsibilities and daily routine (the body of your house). This group includes your job, family responsibilities, religious obligations (daily prayers and Friday congregational prayers, for instance), housework and other items on your daily to-do list. This section consumes most of your time and energy, and it should be given primary attention and priority.

B. Things that come up (clouds and rain). This group contains emergencies and important things that may arise suddenly, requiring your immediate attention, like an accident, a flat tire, a bout of the flu... things that interrupt your scheduled tasks for a period of time. Group B situations require you to shift your attention to them and deal with them before you can get back to normal life. Hopefully, items in this group are exceptions, and when they are done, you can get back to your core responsibilities in group A. In other words, once it is there, group B usually takes priority until you are finished with it.

Group B is also the procrastinators' main area for wasting time. If you keep postponing your work, projects and obligations until you are hit by the last-minute deadline, you risk wasting your core responsibility (group A) time on these last-minute projects. Planning wisely, and avoiding procrastination and unfinished tasks, helps you to keep this group to a minimum so that you can leave time for your core to-do items.

C. **Things that can wait** (decorations and extra embellishments). This section includes some entertainment and luxuries that are nice to have but are not essential: chatting on the phone, meeting friends, attending a party or a breakfast gathering, shopping... Group C is essential to have in your life, but it is not urgent and is not an everyday necessity.

You must make decisions about things in this group. For example, if a friend calls to chat while you are studying or working on an important project, do you speak with her? If an invitation to a morning gathering happens to fall on your work day, do you go? You must learn to say *no* when it is appropriate. Nicely and politely rejecting some tempting offers will gradually set your boundaries.

D. Time wasters (the missiles that can wreck your house). Group D includes things that should be totally avoided and removed from your daily schedule; they are pure time wasters with few or no benefits whatsoever. If you do not hold your objectives, your long-term plans, and your True Secret constantly before your eyes, you risk falling into the group D trap.

Taking a moment to set your intention before each and every action you perform helps you determine where you stand. Some rest and entertainment could be intended to revive your spirit, restore your energy, and reinforce family or friendship ties. These fall into group C and could include things like taking a walk on the beach, taking a nap, or going out with friends and family. There is no harm in those — unless you overdo them — if you review and adjust your intention in advance.

Other group D activities have no link at all with our Big Picture. These are pure time wasters, like surfing the internet with no objective, reading junk mail, or watching hours of useless TV commercials and programs. If you cannot find any reasonable intention for an action and cannot link it to your Big Picture and True Secret, then remove it from your life immediately.

Other time wasters are things that you do not need to perform yourself. You need to delegate some assignments to your children, your spouse, your employees and others. For instance, you do not have to make your children's beds every morning or set the table for dinner. Your children should assume some of these responsibilities according to their ages and abilities. Review your daily routine and see what assignments you can delegate. Start right away.

Two Ps to avoid

1. Procrastination

As I recalled earlier, procrastination makes you waste your time on things that you have unnecessarily made into group B emergencies. Procrastination adds stress and anxiety to your life and reduces productivity.

If you know that you are a procrastinator, you need to deal first with the causes of this habit. Do you postpone dealing with problems and difficulties because you wish they might just disappear on their own? Or are your reasons more about fear of failure, or maybe laziness? Find the root cause and deal with it. You may need to work on your self-esteem, energy level, better planning strategies and your avoidance of unfinished tasks.

2. Perfectionism

Wanting things to be perfect might seem like a nice thing. Why avoid it? Well, perfectionism is not always a good thing. I am not asking you to compromise on the quality of your performance. I encourage you to be excellent in whatever you do. I just want you to determine whether your longing for perfectionism is the reason behind procrastination and reduced accomplishments.

I love having friends over for tea or dinner. I like socializing and spending quality time gathering the extended family and children together, but I don't do that every week. Why? Because I am a perfectionist, and these social events cause me stress and distract me from my major goals. When I have people over, the house needs to be impeccably clean, the bathrooms sparkling, the table set with the best china, and the food a homemade menu of five-star dishes. When I first read about the drawbacks of perfectionism, I could see that the description fit me perfectly. Perfectionism is unrealistic. Why not have family and friends over for a home delivery pizza or a quick pasta and salad dinner? What's the problem with having some children's toys lying here and there? Kids have to play. My friends all have children, and they will understand that.

Two important concepts remain special for Muslims

1. Determination

Working for the benefit of humanity and the earth is an Islamic obligation. It is part of our mission in this life. Knowing deep inside that we are ordered by Allah (ﷻ) to act as vicegerents on earth, and that we will be held accountable for our actions and highly rewarded for the good in them, inshallah, gives us the stamina and the determination to strive in this cause. Our Prophet Muhammad (ﷺ) taught: «No person's feet will be able to move [on the Day of Judgement] until he is asked about his life and how he spent it, his knowledge and what he did with it, his wealth and where he earned it and how he spent it, and his body and how he used it.» (a sound or reliable hadith recorded by at-Tirmidhi)

How do you spend your life, every minute, every second of your time? Is your time in this life fruitful, as it is required to be, or is it void and barren?

Allah (ﷻ) says:

﴿سَابِقُوٓاْ إِلَىٰ مَغۡفِرَةٖ مِّن رَّبِّكُمۡ وَجَنَّةٍ عَرۡضُهَا كَعَرۡضِ ٱلسَّمَآءِ وَٱلۡأَرۡضِ أُعِدَّتۡ لِلَّذِينَ ءَامَنُواْ بِٱللَّهِ وَرُسُلِهِۦۚ ذَٰلِكَ فَضۡلُ ٱللَّهِ يُؤۡتِيهِ مَن يَشَآءُۚ وَٱللَّهُ ذُو ٱلۡفَضۡلِ ٱلۡعَظِيمِ ٢١﴾ [الحديد: ٢١]

﴾Race with one another for forgiveness from your Lord and the garden of paradise, the breadth of which is as the breadth of the heavens and the earth, which is in store for those who believe in Allah and His Messengers. Such is the bounty of Allah, which He bestows on whom He wills, and Allah is of Infinite Bounty.﴿ *(Qur'an 57: 21)*

This verse describes our life as a race, a noble race to do good deeds and attain the pleasure of Allah (ﷻ).

2. Blessing

The second concept that I consider really unique for Muslims is the blessing Allah (ﷻ) bestows on us when we are on the right track, when we hold tight to our Islamic values and teachings.

Last year, there was too much going on in my life. I was engaged in too many activities at the same time; I was moving to a new house, writing my dissertation proposal for a doctorate degree, working on a new book, writing a children's novel, giving workshops on holistic living, and continuing to memorize Qur'an with my teacher at the mosque. That was, of course, in addition to being a wife and mother of two. I could feel that this work was too much for me to handle, so I decided I must compromise with some things. After going through all of my written plans, though, I could not decide which activities to give up. They all seemed very important. Still, I had to give up something, since there did not seem to be any way that I could accomplish them all.

After deep thinking, I made the tragic mistake of postponing my Qur'an classes. "*I'll resume after I finish with my Ph.D.,*" I said. "*I'm very slow at memorizing; it takes too much time.*" I convinced myself that I could just read from my Qur'an every day, that there was no need for the Qur'an classes that semester. Guess what? That turned out to be the least fruitful semester of my whole life. I finished nothing! No Ph.D. dissertation, no new books. I did not finish organizing my new house and did not prepare for my workshops the way I wanted to.

It was not the Qur'an classes that were wasting my time. They were actually the activity that was adding blessing to my hours! I contacted my Qur'an teacher and discussed with her a more flexible schedule. As soon as I got back to my memorization, the pieces of my life fell into place again. Subḥân Allâh! I sent in my Ph.D. proposal, finished the preliminary draft of my book, arranged a more professional workshop and settled into my new home.

Some sceptics might consider it coincidence or just the feeling of guilt about abandoning my classes that was responsible for my low productivity at the time, but I feel that it was because I lacked the blessing from Allah (ﷻ) that came from memorizing the Qur'an. When you hold on to your True Secret, put your priorities straight and work to the best of your abilities, you definitely feel the effects in your life.

Take a moment to...

look at how you spend your time

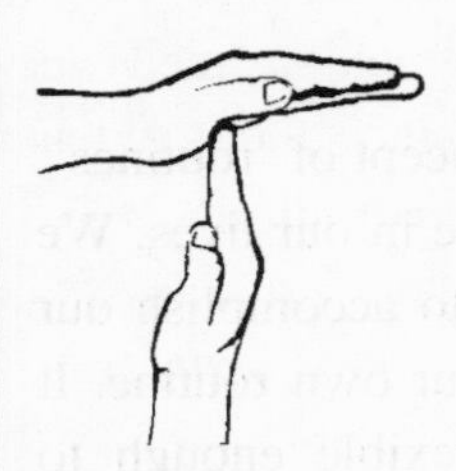

- This week, carry a small notepad with you everywhere you go. For at least three or four days, write down your activities. Do not judge or alter anything. Just behave normally and take note of everything you spend time on. Pay special attention to noting your time gaps and time wasters.

- After you are done, review your notes. Where are you in your house of priorities?

- Delete group D from your life, minimize group C, prioritize and plan your core responsibilities in group A, and leave group B only for emergencies. Make a commitment to yourself to avoid procrastination and unnecessary perfectionism.

- Review your time wasters.

- Set times for your responsibilities and your own personal work. You need time for planning, learning, reading, and progressing on your mission and path. You do not have to take this out of the time you have set aside for your children, home responsibilities or working hours in your office. (We are talking responsibilities and priorities, remember.) Instead, take it from the time lags and the time wasters, such as junk mail, TV and useless shopping. If necessary, wake up one hour earlier or go to sleep one hour later. Avoid interruptions during your dedicated time; set your boundaries. Respect the rights of others, and they will willingly grant yours.

Take a moment to...
set up your own routine

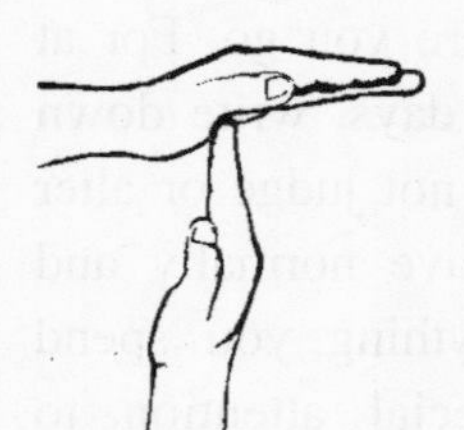

Most of us hate the concept of 'routines'. Still, we need some routine in our lives. We need some kind of order to accomplish our goals. You have to set your own routine. It should be specific but flexible enough to accommodate any unexpected changes from group B. You need specified times for your important daily actions like prayer, dhikr, exercise and journaling; you need regular sleep and eating patterns; you need to fulfil your primary responsibilities as a student, parent, employer or employee; you need some 'me' time for rest and replenishing; and most of all, you need to include enough time for your goals and plans. You can make a daily routine or, preferably, set a weekly pattern to accommodate all your weekly classes, shopping, support group meeting times (more on this later), and so on.

For example, I wake up for the dawn prayer, say my morning dhikr, then wake my children up to pray and prepare for school. After they are gone, I take a walk, write for ten minutes in my journal, memorize Qur'an and do some basic housekeeping (make the bed, put laundry in the washing machine). Then I sit at my desk doing my work (writing, studying, preparing workshops) until it is time for the noon prayer. After the prayer, it is time for housework, cooking, or running errands until the kids arrive home from school.

Afternoon is my time with my children. I help them with homework and studying, if needed, or I sit and chat with them. I do not engage in any of my own intellectual activities because I am not good at concentrating on more than one thing at a time. I prefer to give my children my full attention in the afternoons. If I have time while they are studying, I bake a cake, draw, or stitch.

Now that I know my basic routine, I need to write it out to make it very clear and specific:

5:30 a.m. wake up, pray...

7:00 a.m. take kids to bus

7:30-7:45 walk

8:00-9:00 start laundry, journaling...

9:00-1:00 my working time

1:00 p.m. noon prayer

Tuesday, 10:00 a.m.: workshop session

Wednesday, 10:00 a.m.: Qur'an class

Friday: family time

Saturday: weekly supermarket shopping, other errands...

With your routine, you are able to make yourself more self-disciplined. You need to set your own rules. For example, to make it convenient for you to make the best use of your time, you might consider these tips and hints:

- Watch no television unless it is useful information.
- Read a story to your children or chat with them every day at bedtime.
- Carry a book in your bag or car.
- Carry an idea pad in your bag or pocket.

You might try to make a map or a diagram of your daily routine. If you make it colourful and appealing, you will like looking at it to renew your sense of purpose and re-energize your soul.

Remember, it is a routine, but it is not cast in stone. You can always apply some flexibility or creativity when you need to.

5. Social support

"*The environment that creates winners is almost always made of winners... people who are contented and curious, open and vital, who trust life and respect themselves.*" Barbara Sher in *Wishcraft*.

In your journey towards success and fulfilment, you need company. This is also stressed in Islam, as so much importance is placed on congregational, group and community activities.

Our grandmothers did not need to study economics to know how to perfectly handle their home budgets. They did not need to join cooking classes to be excellent chefs, nor did they need to attend haute couture and embroidery lessons to make their own wedding gowns. What was their secret?

- Practice and building experience
- Mentoring from those who were already experienced and skilled
- Groups and teamwork

As a young child, it was amazing for me to see how the ladies in the family gathered in my grandmother's house to prepare a feast, bake cookies or sew clothes for the young ones before the *Eids* (the two annual Islamic celebrations that occur at the end of Ramadan and at the culmination of the Hajj). You need information for your new project or assistance in your work? Easy. My aunt has a friend who works with a woman whose husband's brother happens to be an expert in the exact field that you want. There was always a long list of acquaintances, contacts, friends, relatives, or even foreigners, who were willing to offer their expertise, skills, information, or financial and moral support. Everyone seemed to know someone who could somehow be linked to a person that could satisfy any need of yours that might come up. All you had to do was ask your family and friends. They were always there for support.

Nowadays it is harder to find such a support system, but it is not impossible. Start by strengthening your family ties and your relationships with friends, neighbours and co-workers. Widen your circle, but always remember your True Secret. You gather friends and family so that you can support them as they support you, for the sake of Allah (ﷻ), not for any worldly gains (although this will come as a 'side effect'). Give without waiting for a reward, build bridges and re-link severed ties while keeping your motives and intentions pure and sincere.

The choice of companionship is very important. Some scholars listed five main characteristics of good friends:

1. When you see them, you remember Allah (ﷻ).
2. Their state of being points to the path of Allah (ﷻ).
3. Their knowledge adds to your knowledge and understanding.
4. They remind you when you are unmindful or inattentive.
5. They help you when they see you remembering Allah (ﷻ) by your thoughts and actions.

Take some time to... form a support group

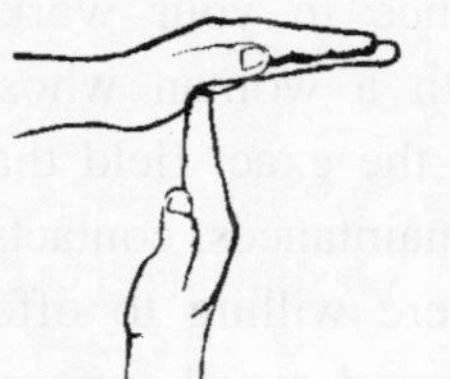

- List five people whom you feel safe talking to about your life dreams and long-term plans — people who have always been supportive.
- List five people who share the same passions or hobbies and would be interested in forming a working group or idea-sharing group with you. Can't find anyone? Join a workshop or book club, or surf the internet for groups already in your area. Someone may soon appear in your life, or maybe someone is already there and you did not notice. Keep your eyes open.

• Plan a weekly or biweekly meeting to discuss your plans and achievements. The session should be fun, so that you look forward to it. It should include at least two people but not have more than five people, to avoid wasting time. The session should have a leader or a facilitator to organize the meeting and keep it focused. It should be well planned, with time for each of you to state your achievements and plans, show your work and listen to comments and suggestions from the others. All attendees should participate; you should be encouraging each other, pointing out accomplishments as well as weaknesses, and suggesting how to deal with these weaknesses.

A typical session will include the following for each person:

❖ Checking on your True Secret.

❖ Reviewing your intention and endorsing your commitment.

❖ Checking your progress, feelings and self-esteem. Did you achieve all your intended goals for the week? Any obstacles?

❖ Brainstorming ideas, plans and future achievements.

❖ Setting next week's schedule, plans and goals.

❖ Forming a list of ideas or plans to work on until the next meeting.

❖ Having some social time with appetizers or refreshments.

❖ Setting a time for the next meeting.

6. Holistic balance (health and energy)

The main idea of holistic living is the acknowledgment that there is much more to the human being than just a physical body.

Our body is the casing, the outer packaging that should of course be kept safe and intact to protect the main core, the real thing.

Body, heart, mind, and soul: all four areas of our existence should be given prime attention. It is all about balance.

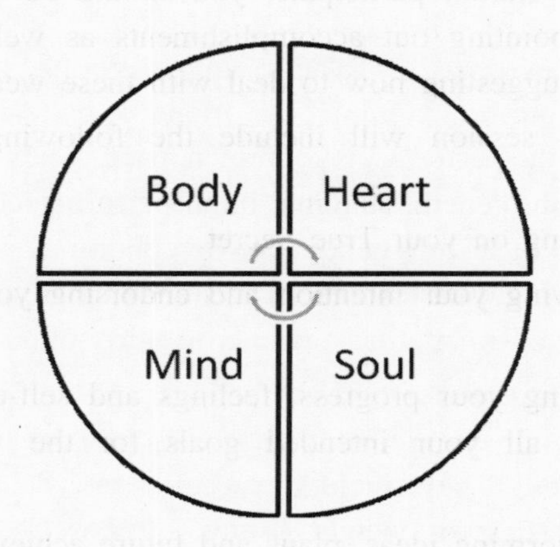

So far, we have been mainly discussing the health of the soul (connection with your Creator, your Big Picture and True Secret), the mind (reading, knowledge and learning) and the heart (pure intentions, social support, self-confidence and inner resources). In this section, I will focus on physical health.

A healthy body

There is a massive amount of advice that could be given on how to keep your body healthy. I will just focus on the two most important areas:

1. Exercise

In this modern era, most of us suffer from a sedentary lifestyle. Most of our jobs do not require much physical effort. Even managing our houses, transportation and common entertainments are low in physical exertion. Still, our bodies need physical activity, and this is the reason that we must practice some form of daily exercise.

There are three types of exercises that are equally essential for your health:

- **Aerobic exercise** — These are exercises like walking, jogging, bicycling, swimming, or friendly ball games... easy exercises that you perform at your own pace. They are essential for cardiac health, general stamina, brain performance, and weight control. To get their full benefits, two conditions should apply: regular practice, at least three or four times a week, and an extended period of time, at least twenty to thirty minutes each time.

- **Strength exercise** — These are muscle-building exercises. They increase your energy, firm your muscles and pump calcium into your bones. They include more 'serious' training, like running, gymnastics, or weight lifting... intense activity that is performed over a short period of time. They are especially essential for teenagers since their bones and muscles grow quickly and are shaped at this time of life. They are also essential for adults, especially women, to minimize bone loss later in life. These exercises are best performed with a coach or in a gym (although this is not a must) and at least once a week.

- **Stretching** — These are slow paced, calm exercises that, besides developing muscle and joint flexibility, help in reducing stress. They should be performed several times per day. Just a few adjusted postures for five or ten minutes are very beneficial in the long run.

Try this... exercise!

- Integrate one variety of each of the three types of exercises into your week. Schedule it in! Experiment with new exercises, new routines and new 'buddy' systems until you find something suitable for you. Then stick to it and add variations over time to keep it interesting and fun.

2. Healthy food choices

The most valuable advice concerning food choices is in these holy words:

﴿وَكُلُوا۟ وَٱشْرَبُوا۟ وَلَا تُسْرِفُوٓا۟ ۚ إِنَّهُۥ لَا يُحِبُّ ٱلْمُسْرِفِينَ ﴿٣١﴾﴾ [الأعراف: ٣١]

﴾And eat and drink but do not waste by extravagance. Certainly He [Allah] does not like those who waste by extravagance.﴿ *(Qur'an 7: 31)*

Basically, eat what you want from good quality food that is *halal* (permissible in Islamic law), but don't overdo it.

Again, advice about nutrition can fill a whole book on its own, so I'll just suggest a brief food replacement plan that may help you make some healthy adjustments to your dietary habits. The plan involves making a commitment to one change each week, while continuing to follow the changes you made during all previous weeks. It is summarized in the following table:

Food replacement plan

Weeks	Old habit	New habit
First Switch to whole grains		
	Replace white flour, pasta and white rice with fibre-rich whole flour, whole grain pasta and brown rice. Experiment with new whole grains and cereals like wheat, barley and oat.	
Second Introduce more vegetables and fruits		
	Vegetables and fruits are rich in vitamins, minerals, fibres and phytonutrients.[66] Eat more salads, and replace high calorie desserts with fruits. Learn new soup recipes. Integrate mixed vegetables into rice, pasta and meat dishes.	
Third Reduce red meat consumption		
	Eat fish twice a week, and twice a week, introduce proteins from plant origins such as legumes, beans or lentils. When you eat meat, choose the lean parts. Eat more poultry, and reduce your portion size.	
Fourth Reduce salt intake		

66 Beneficial nutrients from plant origin that help, among many other things, to fight cancer and protect the cardiovascular and bowel systems

	Although salt (sodium chloride) is an essential body mineral, excess salt is extremely harmful to our cardiovascular systems. We already receive enough salt from fresh vegetables, from some grains, and from the salt added during cooking and processing the food, so there is no need for extra table salt. To add flavor to your food, use spices, which are very rich in phytonutrients and anti-cancer agents. The choices are endless: turmeric, cumin, ginger, basil, peppermint, thyme, rosemary, cardamom, cinnamon, mustard, dill… Experiment.	
Fifth Cut down on coffee and soft drinks, consume more milk and dairy products		
	We all know about the addictive and stress-inducing effects of coffee and, needless to say, the harmful effects of soft drinks. Milk and dairy products, on the other hand, are often missing from our menus. They are the most effective sources of calcium, as well as being good sources of many other nutrients and vitamins.	
Sixth Avoid artificial sweeteners, read the labels		
	Avoid artificial chemicals of all kinds: colours, preservatives, flavouring agents… Read the labels on the food carefully. Avoid any item which contains ingredients that you do not understand or that your grandmother would not have recognized thirty years ago. Try making your own homemade desserts.	
Seven Choose fats wisely		
	Replace saturated fats (ghee, margarine, butter, animal fats) with plant-based unsaturated fats (olive oil, linseed oils, vegetable oils)	

Try this...

- Adopt healthy food choices for the whole family. Simple changes can make a big difference in your health and energy levels.

Take a moment to... reflect on balance in your life

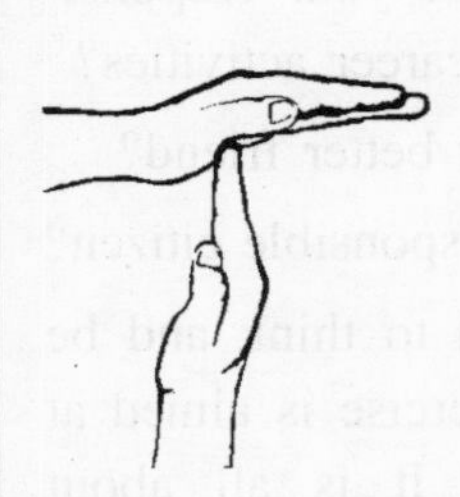

- Remember the list of responsibilities that you recorded in your journal at the start of your journey? Make a page in your journal for each item on your list and write each responsibility at the top of the page.

- For each page, think of ten ways to take care of this responsibility and write the ideas down.

  For example:

Muslim: — How can you fulfil your responsibilities as a Muslim? (By setting a good example, purifying your heart and tongue, and saying your prayers with full devotion.)

Spouse — What do you need to do to boost your relationship with your spouse?

Parent — As a parent, what are your responsibilities towards your children? How can you meet them?

Son/daughter — How can you improve your relations with your parents and fulfil their rights?

Career — How you can take care of your responsibilities as vicegerent on earth through your career activities?

Friend — How can you be a good or better friend?

Citizen — What can you do to be a responsible citizen?

Ten seems like a lot, I know. You need to think and be creative a little here. Get it all out. This exercise is aimed at helping you balance your responsibilities. It is all about balance! As you proceed with it, you will notice that you are working on the four sides of your being: your body, heart, mind and soul.

After you are done with your lists, revise them and review the equilibrium, or lack of it, in your life. Are you giving every responsibility its due attention and effort? Are you leading a balanced life, taking care of your body, heart, mind and soul? Where do you need to make alterations or improvements?

Take a moment to...

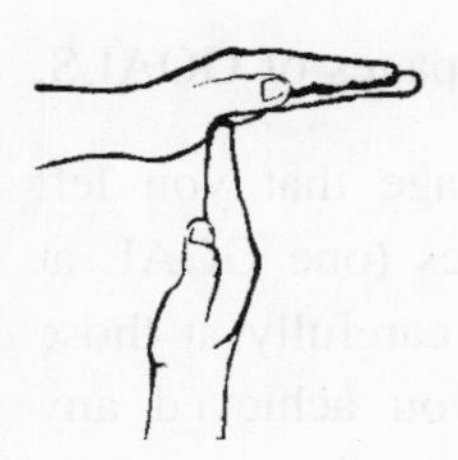

- Review your whole life by classifying it into:
  - ❖ Body (health, exercise, food choice...)
  - ❖ Mind (knowledge, readings...)
  - ❖ Heart (emotional and social life)
  - ❖ Soul (prayers, dhikr, True Secret...)

Check where you need more emphasis in your life. Which sector needs more attention? Are you more interested in the needs of one sector than another?

Take a moment to... gather your resources

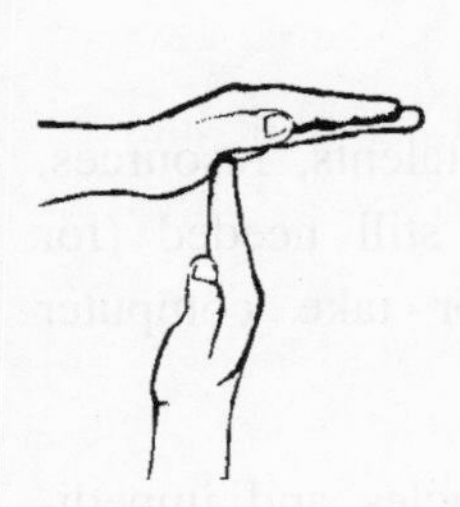

- Inner Resources:
  1. Mindfulness and focus
  2. Gratitude
  3. Satisfaction
  4. Belief
  5. Inner strength
  6. Challenge and creativity

Outer resources:

1. Reading
2. Learning
3. Applying what you learn
4. Time management
5. Social support
6. Holistic balance

Take a moment to...
take practical steps towards your GOALS

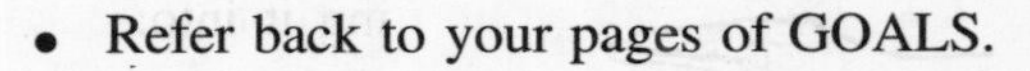

- Refer back to your pages of GOALS.

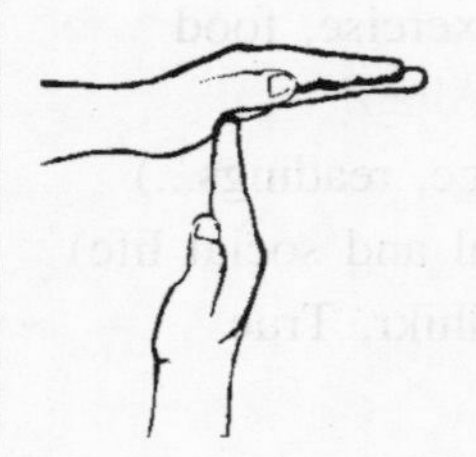

- Open the empty page that you left after your milestones (one GOAL at a time). Now look carefully at those milestones. Have you achieved any of them? Does any milestone seem closer, more possible? Do you feel any different now about your milestones (more enthusiastic, frustrated, depressed, more informed, needing more information, still confused....)?

- For each GOAL, draw a table with three columns:
  1. In the first column, list helping factors (what you already have — you can find those in your powers and potentials list).
  2. In the second column, list skills, talents, resources, training and experiences that are still needed (for example, to study the market or take computer courses).
  3. In the third column, list the obstacles and impediments that you are likely to encounter along your path (money, work studio, legal issues...). Remember the list you devised in the perfect day exercise.

- Write it all down; don't just think about it. This helps direct your attention and focus and helps you assess your progress along the way.

- Decide which GOAL you are going to work on first. (You may be able to deal with more than one at a time.)
- Reconsider your intention. Check on your True Secret and make sure that your plans are consistent with your ultimate goal in life: the pleasure of Allah (ﷻ)!
- Take your table along to the next meeting with your support group. Brainstorm for solutions to your obstacles, missing skills and needed resources. Analyze all the ideas and solutions that you gather. Consider your options and start taking action right away.

7. Fulfilment

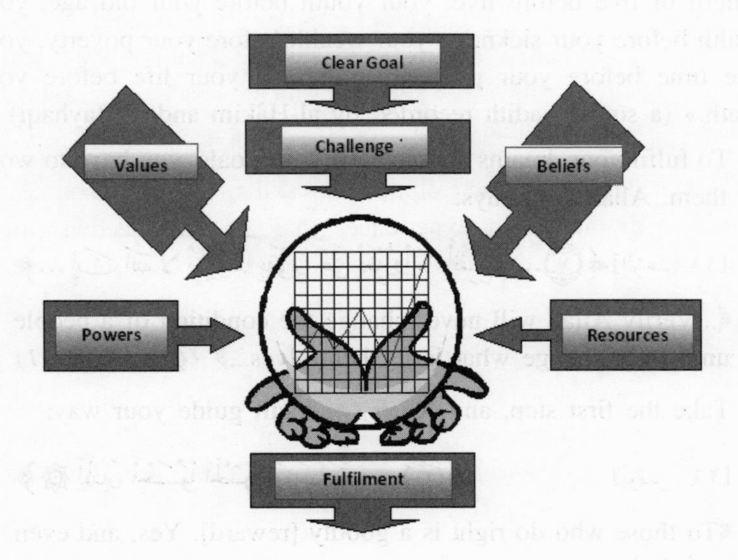

I live in Dubai — I moved there six years ago — and I spend one month each year in my home country, Egypt. My husband and

I decided not to sell our car back home since it is very useful during the vacation. My husband, a mechanical engineer who is extremely fond of cars, spends the last week of our vacation changing the oil, adjusting the tires, polishing, cleaning, greasing... ensuring that the car is in perfect shape before he leaves it in the specially rented garage. The next year, when he is reunited with his precious car again, it breaks his heart. The tires are flat, the oil needs changing again, and the battery has died. "*What a waste of time and effort!*" I exclaim (only to myself, of course).

Our talents and potentials are just like this car. If you leave them unused, they rust and age. Using them is the only way to keep them in good shape.

Our Prophet (ﷺ) gave us the most beneficial advice: «Take benefit of five before five: your youth before your old age, your health before your sickness, your wealth before your poverty, your free time before your preoccupation, and your life before your death.» (a sound hadith recorded by al-Ḥâkim and al-Bayhaqi)

To fulfil your dreams and achieve your goals, you have to work on them. Allah (سبحانه وتعالى) says:

﴿... إِنَّ ٱللَّهَ لَا يُغَيِّرُ مَا بِقَوْمٍ حَتَّىٰ يُغَيِّرُوا۟ مَا بِأَنفُسِهِمْ ... ﴿١١﴾﴾ [الرّعد: ١١]

﴿...Verily Allah will never change the condition of a people until they change what is in themselves...﴾ *(Qur'an 13: 11)*

Take the first step, and Allah (سبحانه وتعالى) will guide your way:

﴿۞ لِّلَّذِينَ أَحْسَنُوا۟ ٱلْحُسْنَىٰ وَزِيَادَةٌ ... ﴿٢٦﴾﴾ [يُونس: ٢٦]

﴿To those who do right is a goodly [reward]. Yes, and even more!...﴾ *(Qur'an 10: 26)*

﴿هَلْ جَزَآءُ ٱلْإِحْسَـٰنِ إِلَّا ٱلْإِحْسَـٰنُ ﴿٦٠﴾﴾ [الرَّحمٰن: ٦٠]

﴾Is there any reward for good other than good?!﴿

(Qur'an 55: 60)

Start by defining what you can change about your situation. As Stephen Covey puts it in *The 7 Habits of Highly Effective Families*, define your 'circle of influence'. Then assess your abilities. Be positive, creative, content and optimistic. By assuming responsibility for your situation, by stopping the blame, accusations and complaints, you will find the required stamina and the driving force to actually do something about your concerns. You should do this with any issues that you are facing:

- Health concerns — beware of the 'Why me?' attitude
- Marriage problems — do not say: '*My partner is the one to blame!*'
- Economic instabilities — avoid anger, depression, helplessness and the 'Why me?' attitude
- Children's bad behaviour — stop shouting and blaming them: '*They never listen to me!*'

When you recognize that there are changes you can make to change the state of your affairs, then you change your world view and you can start carrying your own responsibility and making real improvements in your life.

My young son had a bad temper. He got angry at the slightest of matters and sometimes started yelling and hitting his younger sister. At first, I used to respond by shouting and grounding him, but it only made things worse. One day, I realized that it was not fair to blame him for his bad temper since I suffer from a pretty bad temper myself, so I decided to be more 'responsible'. I told him that I know how hard it is to control our anger when we get frustrated by other's behaviours, and I confessed that I could not punish him anymore because I was making the same mistake.

"*Instead,*" I added. "*We will try to help each other fix our behaviour.*"

I explained to him what Prophet Muhammad (ﷺ) said about strength: «He (ﷺ) asked: Who do you count as strong among you? The Companions said: The one who throws people down (during fights). He (ﷺ) said: No, the strong one is the one who controls his temper when he gets angry.» (Muslim)

Then, I proposed a contest to see who was the strongest member of our family. My son designed what we decided to call a 'strengthometer'.

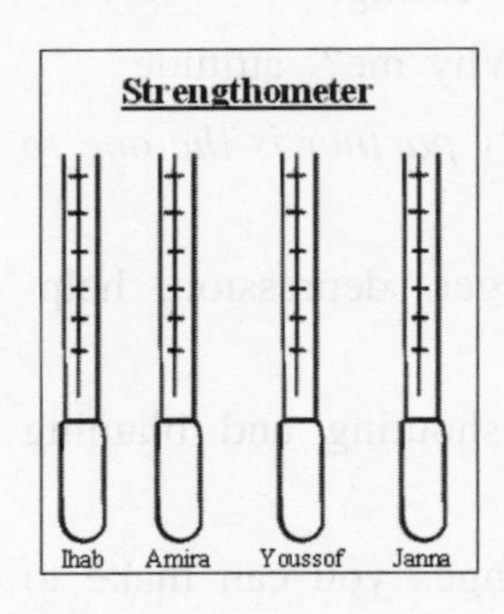

He created one for each member of the family, printed them, and stuck the papers on the refrigerator. Every time one of us succeeded in controlling his or her temper, we shaded one mark higher on the designed meter. The one who reached the top of the strengthometer first would get a present. Both of my kids were very excited about the idea, and the whole family got involved in the contest. It worked very well, better and faster than even I expected, and both my son and I soon showed a remarkable improvement in anger management.

Fulfilment means that you concentrate on your circle of influence, on what you can actually do. Now you are focused on action, not on wishes and dreams. You have concerns, but that does not distract you from dealing with only what you have the power to change yourself.

Meanwhile, you allow your concerns and your circle of influence to exist within your bigger circle of appreciation. Inside your circle of appreciation, you appreciate the actual process rather than fretting about your challenges and problems. You take pleasure in the journey of action and achievements, not worrying about the results. You enjoy the process, not the product. You feel grateful for all that life brings you. You learn from mistakes and setbacks while never giving up. Thomas Edison once said, "*The greatest weakness lies in giving up. The most certain way to succeed is always to try just one more time*."[67]

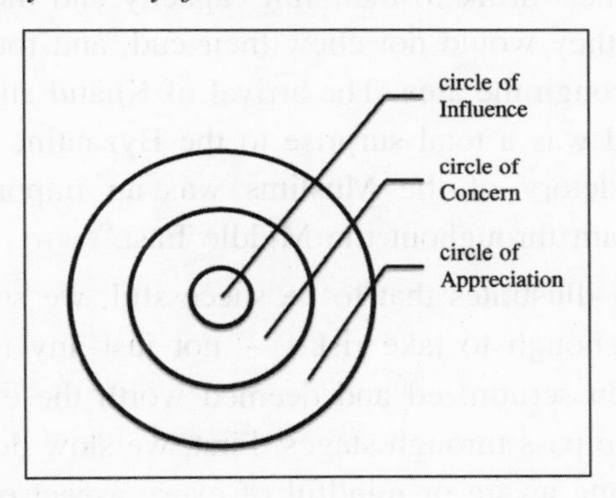

Take calculated risks

During the caliphate of Abu Bakr (رضي الله عنه), the Islamic empire was expanding greatly. When the Muslim army in Syria experienced some problems, orders were sent to the great fighter and commander Khâlid ibn al-Waleed (رضي الله عنه) to come urgently to join the army in Syria and lead them in the conquests.

Khâlid was in Iraq at the time, and the only known way to Syria was through a long southern route called the Dumat al-Jandal trail. It would take a great deal of time to traverse it, and that was a luxury the Muslims did not have, since the Byzantine army was already threatening the Muslim troops in Syria. Khâlid considered another option. There was a dangerous desert route, via

---

[67] http://quotationsbook.com

Palmyra to the north. It was a shorter journey, but one that involved crossing a waterless desert and totally unknown territory.

Khâlid decided to take the risk and cross the desert. It was worth it, he thought, since it was a risk that could save the Muslim army and open the route for spreading Islam to the world. Khâlid ordered the soldiers to take as much water as they could carry, made the camels drink to their full capacity and then bound their jaws so that they would not chew their cud, and found a guide to lead them through the area. The arrival of Khâlid and his troops at the battlefield was a total surprise to the Byzantine army, and the subsequent victory of the Muslims was an important factor in spreading Islam throughout the Middle East.[68]

This story illustrates that to be successful, we sometimes have to be brave enough to take risks — not just any risks, but risks that have been scrutinized and deemed worth the effort. To fulfil our dream, we pass through stages. First, we slow down or stop so that we become aware or mindful of every aspect of the situation around us. This is followed by thinking, studying, learning, comparing options available to us and making choices. Then we accept a new challenge, decide to act on it, and take some calculated risks. This courage to take action is what I call 'crossing the desert', an essential stage before finally achieving our dream.

---

[68] As-Sarjâni, R. راغب السرجاني. n.d. http://www.islamstory.com

Do you know what a black hole is?

A black hole is a region of space where the gravitational field is so powerful that nothing, including light, can escape its pull. Objects can fall into it, but nothing can come out of it. It is called 'black' because it absorbs all the light that hits it, reflecting nothing.

Being absent-minded, or living life as if we are operating on autopilot, kills human creativity. Autopilot living is like this black hole, with a ruthless gravity that pulls everything towards its centre.

Living in ignorance, being unaware, not adding to our knowledge and avoiding risks and challenges will definitely kill our dreams. This sucks light out of our lives just like a black hole. We need challenges and risks to thrive, and we need to fulfil those calculated risks one step at a time to add life to our days, rather than just adding days to our lives.

There is no such thing as complete failure

"*The person who never made a mistake never tried anything new.*" Albert Einstein[69]

I remember hearing about a four-year-old girl's interview to get into kindergarten. The interviewer asked her about a letter of the alphabet that she did not recognize. The little girl replied immediately: "*You don't expect me to know everything, do you? If I knew everything, why would I go to school in the first place?*"

Do not allow failure to cause you to quit. It is not what happens that matters in the long run; what matters is how you choose to respond to it. Always try again and again.

---

69 http://quotationsbook.com

Sir Roger Gilbert Bannister is a former athlete from the U.K.; he is best known as the first man in history to run a mile in less than four minutes. At the 1952 Olympics, Bannister finished fourth out of the medallists. Although he set a British record in the process, he felt disappointed and unhappy. Considering his performance at the Olympics a failure, Bannister spent two months considering whether to give up running. In the end, he decided on a new goal: to be the first man to run a mile in under four minutes. Accordingly, he intensified his training.

'Experts' in sports at the time claimed that it was humanly impossible to run a mile in less than four minutes. Nevertheless, this mistaken assertion was debunked by Bannister, who achieved his goal and set a new record. This historic event took place on May 6, 1954.

But guess what? Just forty-six days later, Bannister's new record was broken by his Australian rival, John Landy. Once it had been shown to be possible, many others followed who could run a four-minute mile.[70]

What is impossible is what we perceive as impossible. All that Bannister did was to prove that running a mile in less than four minutes was actually feasible. He changed people's mindset and shifted their long-held paradigm, their wrong belief that hindered their performance.

Be committed

Fulfilment also involves commitment. Commitment means having perseverance, devoting yourself to something and sticking to your choice.

---

[70] http://en.wikipedia.org/wiki/Roger_Bannister

It takes commitment to finish what you have started. How many times do we start great things only to eventually lose our resoluteness and see our goal or dream fade away? To succeed, you have to care about what you are doing and continually renew your intention, motivation and dedication to it. Always strive to do more than what is minimally expected, even if it will take more time and effort. Doing things right will give you a good feeling about yourself. Prophet Muhammad (ﷺ) said: «Allah (ﷻ) likes that when one of you does a job, he does it right (and excels in it).» (a reliable hadith recorded by aṭ-Ṭabarani)

Take a moment to...

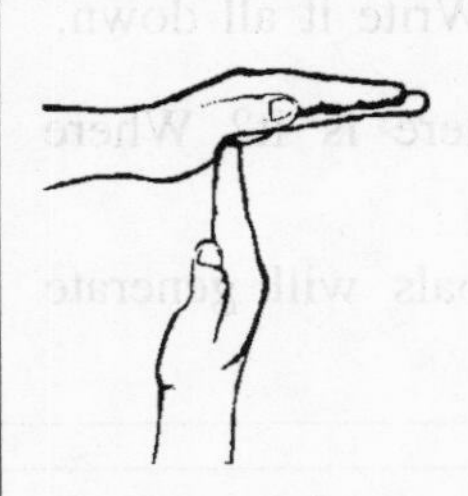

- Remember some important task that you failed to achieve.
- If you had another chance, is there anything you would have done differently? Would you have changed the way you reacted?

Take a moment to... redefine your goal

- Right now, renew your commitment. State your life goal specifically and succinctly.
- My goal/dream is...
- My intention is...
- The resources and skills I need to acquire are...
- The time frame I expect for achievement is... (between one and five years)
- The milestones that I will meet on my path, that will show me that I am on the right track, are...

Go over what you wrote when you meet with your support group. What do they think? How can they help you?

Try this... test your level of commitment

- Think about what this dream means to you. To what extent are you willing to struggle and sacrifice to achieve this goal?
- Are you really committed to it? Why? What are your motives? What is your intention? Write it all down.
- Remember your True Secret. Where is it? Where does it fit in your latest plans?

Renewing your commitment to your goals will generate power in you.

Take a moment to... cross the desert

- Sit comfortably, relax, and take a few deep breaths.

Think:

- Are you ready to cross the desert? To dig your treasure out?
- What are you waiting for?

In your journal, write about your fears and obstacles.

Write down the empowering affirmations and dhikr that you chose. Write them down, don't just say them. Write them again and again until you feel that they have become engraved in your mind and soul. Here are some of mine:

﴿إِنَّمَآ أَمْرُهُۥٓ إِذَآ أَرَادَ شَيْـًٔا أَن يَقُولَ لَهُۥ كُن فَيَكُونُ ﴿٨٢﴾﴾ [يس : ٨٢]

﴿Verily, His Command, when He intends a thing, is only that He says to it: Be! And it is!﴾ *(Qur'an 36: 82)*

﴿وَمَن يَتَوَكَّلْ عَلَى ٱللَّهِ فَهُوَ حَسْبُهُۥٓ ۚ إِنَّ ٱللَّهَ بَٰلِغُ أَمْرِهِۦ ۚ قَدْ جَعَلَ ٱللَّهُ لِكُلِّ شَىْءٍ قَدْرًا ﴿٣﴾﴾ [الطّلاق : ٣]

﴿And whoever puts his trust in Allah, then He will suffice him. Verily, Allah will accomplish His purpose. Indeed, Allah has set a measure for all things.﴾ *(Qur'an 65: 3)*

﴿أَلَيْسَ ٱللَّهُ بِكَافٍ عَبْدَهُۥ ۖ وَيُخَوِّفُونَكَ بِٱلَّذِينَ مِن دُونِهِۦ ۚ ... ﴿٣٦﴾﴾ [الزُّمَر : ٣٦]

﴿Is not Allah Sufficient for His slave? Yet they try to frighten you with those [whom they worship] besides Him!...﴾ *(Qur'an 39: 36)*

﴿يُثَبِّتُ ٱللَّهُ ٱلَّذِينَ ءَامَنُوا۟ بِٱلْقَوْلِ ٱلثَّابِتِ فِى ٱلْحَيَوٰةِ ٱلدُّنْيَا وَفِى ٱلْءَاخِرَةِ ۖ ... ﴿٢٧﴾﴾ [إبراهيم : ٢٧]

﴿Allah will establish in strength those who believe, with the word that stands firm in this world and in the hereafter...﴾ *(Qur'an 14: 27)*

Take the next step! Make a commitment to do something **this week** that takes you **one step** closer to your dream.

Try this... voluntary late night prayer

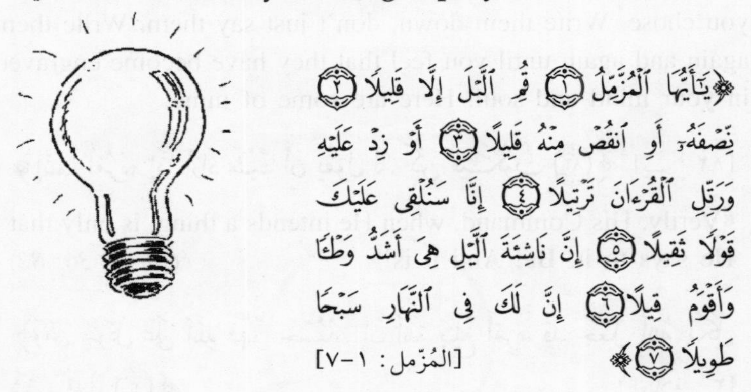

﴿يَـٰٓأَيُّهَا ٱلْمُزَّمِّلُ ١ قُمِ ٱلَّيْلَ إِلَّا قَلِيلًا ٢
نِّصْفَهُۥٓ أَوِ ٱنقُصْ مِنْهُ قَلِيلًا ٣ أَوْ زِدْ عَلَيْهِ
وَرَتِّلِ ٱلْقُرْءَانَ تَرْتِيلًا ٤ إِنَّا سَنُلْقِى عَلَيْكَ
قَوْلًا ثَقِيلًا ٥ إِنَّ نَاشِئَةَ ٱلَّيْلِ هِىَ أَشَدُّ وَطْـًٔا
وَأَقْوَمُ قِيلًا ٦ إِنَّ لَكَ فِى ٱلنَّهَارِ سَبْحًا
طَوِيلًا ٧﴾ [المُزّمل: ١-٧]

﴿O you who wraps himself [in clothing], arise [to pray] the night, except for a little, half of it or a little less than that, or a little more; and recite the Qur'an in a slow, pleasant tone and style. Verily, We will send down to you a weighty word [with obligations and laws]. Indeed, the rising by night [for prayers] is hard and most potent and good for governing oneself and most suitable for [understanding] the Word [of Allah]. Verily, there is for you by day prolonged occupation with ordinary duties.﴾ *(Qur'an 73: 1-7)*

Night prayer is truly a blessing for the person who offers it. It gives a person wonderful stamina and an incomparable boost of energy for work and fulfilment of one's goals. You cannot understand it until you experience it yourself. Try it for this whole week, and always remember your True Secret: sincerely make your intention for praying to be only to worship Allah (ﷻ) and please Him.

8. Surrender to the will of Allah

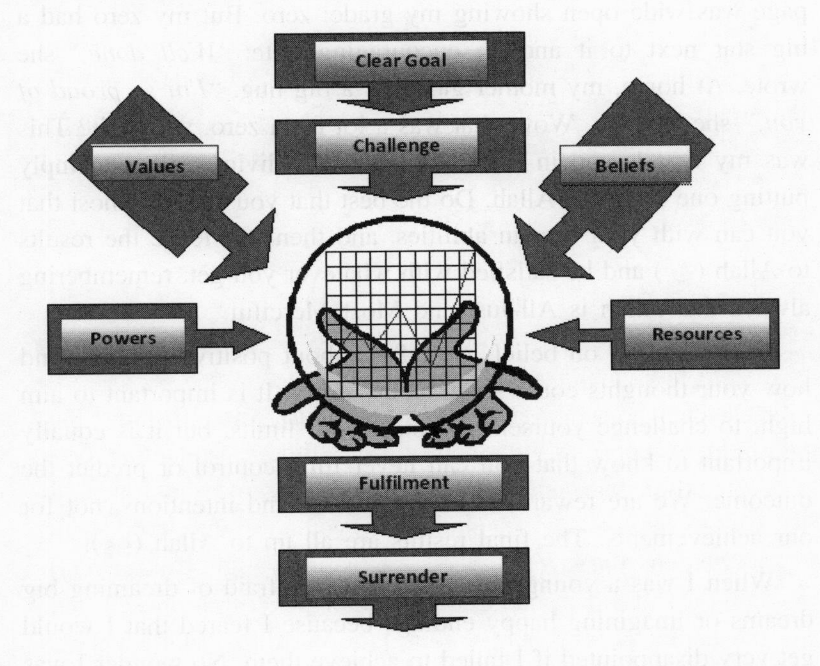

I have always hated spelling. I cannot write one proper sentence without at least one or two spelling mistakes. I think that whoever invented this computer spell-checker is a genius. (I don't know how I could have written this book without it.)

In fifth grade, I had a very strict teacher who graded our spelling tests using minuses. If you made ten mistakes, you got a zero; thirteen errors, you had a minus three; fifteen wrong, minus five; and so on. My grades ranged from -20 to -5. One time, I decided to really make an extra effort. I spent the whole week reading, writing, copying and practicing my spelling with all the books I could lay my hands on. On the day of the test, I truly tried my best.

At the end of the day, the teacher handed me my notebook. The page was wide open showing my grade: zero. But my zero had a big star next to it and an encouraging note: '*Well done,*' she wrote. At home, my mother gave me a big hug. "*I'm so proud of you,*" she told me. Wow, that was a lot for a zero, wasn't it? This was my first lesson in surrendering to the divine will, or simply putting one's trust in Allah. Do the best that you can, the most that you can with your human abilities, and then just leave the results to Allah (﷾) and be satisfied with whatever you get, remembering always that Allah is All-Just and Most Merciful.

In the section on belief, we talked about positive thinking and how your thoughts could shape your reality. It is important to aim high, to challenge yourself and push your limits, but it is equally important to know that you can never fully control or predict the outcome. We are rewarded for our actions and intentions, not for our achievements. The final results are all up to Allah (﷾).

When I was a young girl, I was always afraid of dreaming big dreams or imagining happy endings because I feared that I would get very disappointed if I failed to achieve them. No wonder I was never chosen for the lead role in school plays and I never participated in class competitions or sports or art contests. When you feel you cannot, your subconscious mind works from this premise and simply carries it out.

There is a very critical balance that needs to be sought here. Be optimistic, hold positive thoughts, be sure of your success and achievements, trust yourself and your abilities, and be powerful... BUT don't be arrogant. Be grateful to Allah (﷾) for any success you achieve. Expect to succeed and fulfil your wishes, goals and dreams... BUT don't get disappointed or depressed if things do not turn out exactly as you wished. You never really know what is best for you.

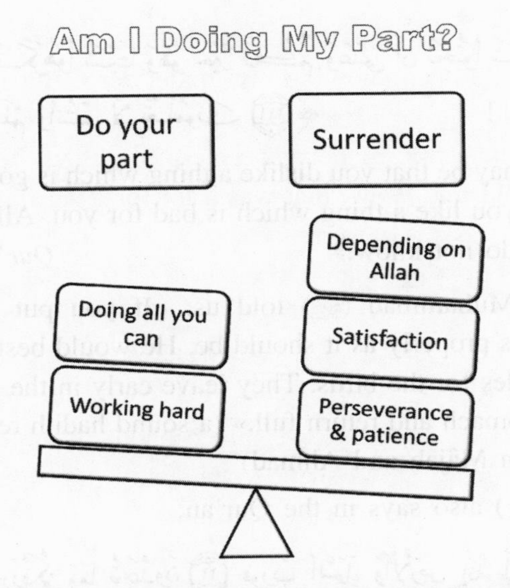

Sometimes the little setbacks and obstacles that we encounter on our path are lessons from Allah (ﷻ) to give us strength and wisdom. Calamities and afflictions are part of our big life test. Contained within them are valuable guidance and wisdom. Sickness and loss are favours from Allah (ﷻ) that wipe away our sins, so that we return to Him (ﷻ) with a pure, loving heart.

Reliance on Allah (ﷻ) means entrusting your affairs to Him and believing in Him fully, in His all-encompassing power and wisdom and in His kindness and mercy. Surrendering to the will of Allah (ﷻ) does not mean giving up actions and efforts. On the contrary, Muslims ought to work, seek knowledge and adopt the most praiseworthy means of attaining a successful and prosperous life, but a stage comes in life when all that is humanly possible has been done, and the results cannot be anticipated. At that time, you leave everything to Allah (ﷻ) and make your will agree with the divine will. Only Allah (ﷻ) knows what the final outcome is to be, and He says in the Qur'an:

﴿وَعَسَىٰٓ أَن تَكۡرَهُواْ شَيۡـٔٗا وَهُوَ خَيۡرٞ لَّكُمۡۖ وَعَسَىٰٓ أَن تُحِبُّواْ شَيۡـٔٗا وَهُوَ شَرّٞ لَّكُمۡۚ وَٱللَّهُ يَعۡلَمُ وَأَنتُمۡ لَا تَعۡلَمُونَ ٢١٦﴾ [البقرة: ٢١٦]

﴾And it may be that you dislike a thing which is good for you and that you like a thing which is bad for you. Allah knows, but you do not know.﴿ *(Qur'an 2: 216)*

Prophet Muhammad (ﷺ) told us: «If you put your trust in Allah (ﷻ) as properly as it should be, He would bestow upon you as He provides for the birds. They leave early in the morning with an empty stomach and return full.» (a sound hadith recorded by at-Tirmidhi, Ibn Mâjah and Aḥmad)

Allah (ﷻ) also says in the Qur'an:

﴿وَفِي ٱلسَّمَآءِ رِزۡقُكُمۡ وَمَا تُوعَدُونَ ٢٢ فَوَرَبِّ ٱلسَّمَآءِ وَٱلۡأَرۡضِ إِنَّهُۥ لَحَقّٞ مِّثۡلَ مَآ أَنَّكُمۡ تَنطِقُونَ ٢٣﴾ [الذّاريات: ٢٢-٢٣]

﴾And in the heaven is your provision and that which you are promised. Then, by the Owner of the sky and the earth, it is the truth [what has been promised to you], just as it is the truth that you can speak.﴿ *(Qur'an 51: 22-23)*

Surrendering to Allah (ﷻ) involves two important features:[71]

- Maintaining your patience and forbearance under all circumstances, without getting stressed, worried or depressed.
- Remaining content and satisfied with whatever is destined for you and making your will conform to the divine will with total acceptance, trust and faith.

Only with true reliance on Allah (ﷻ) can you achieve peace of mind. If you work, strive and apply all worldly means, Allah (ﷻ)

---

71 Al-Ghazâli, *The Book of Religious Learning*

will reward your efforts with His might and strength. This is His divine promise:

﴿وَمَن يَتَوَكَّلْ عَلَى ٱللَّهِ فَهُوَ حَسْبُهُۥٓ ۚ إِنَّ ٱللَّهَ بَٰلِغُ أَمْرِهِۦ ۚ قَدْ جَعَلَ ٱللَّهُ لِكُلِّ شَىْءٍ قَدْرًا ﴿٣﴾﴾ [الطّلاق: ٣]

﴿And whoever puts his trust in Allah, then He will suffice for him. Verily, Allah will accomplish His purpose. Indeed Allah has set a measure for all things.﴾ *(Qur'an 65: 3)*

There is an important lesson in the story of Prophet Moses (ﷺ), when Allah (ﷻ) ordered him to leave Egypt:

﴿فَأَسْرِ بِعِبَادِى لَيْلًا إِنَّكُم مُّتَّبَعُونَ ﴿٢٣﴾﴾ [الدّخان: ٢٣]

﴿Allah said: Depart you with My slaves by night. Surely, you will be pursued.﴾ *(Qur'an 44: 23)*

Moses (ﷺ) obeyed Allah's command and departed with the Israelites, fleeing Pharaoh and his people. Pharaoh followed them with a huge army until he reached them at sunrise. The Red Sea was now in front of Moses (ﷺ) and the Israelites, and Pharaoh's army was behind them.[72] The Israelites felt helpless and said to Moses (ﷺ):

﴿إِنَّا لَمُدْرَكُونَ ﴿٦١﴾﴾ [الشُّعَراء: ٦١]

﴿We are sure to be overtaken.﴾ *(Qur'an 26: 61)*

Moses (ﷺ), on the other hand, was confident and calm. He replied:

﴿قَالَ كَلَّآ ۖ إِنَّ مَعِىَ رَبِّى سَيَهْدِينِ ﴿٦٢﴾﴾ [الشُّعَراء: ٦٢]

---

72 Ibn Katheer

﴿Nay! Verily, my Lord is with me. He will guide me.﴾ *(Qur'an 26: 62)*

Moses' people perceived only the worldly means and the material facts; that is why they felt helpless and powerless in this dire situation. They failed to rely on Allah (ﷻ) and surrender to His power and might. On the opposite side, we see Moses' behaviour. His total surrender to the will and command of Allah gave him strength and reassurance. He trusted that Allah (ﷻ) would never fail his faithful Messenger, as Allah (ﷻ) told him and his brother Haroon from the beginning:

﴿قَالَ لَا تَخَافَآ إِنَّنِي مَعَكُمَآ أَسۡمَعُ وَأَرَىٰ ٤٦﴾ [طه: ٤٦]

﴿He [Allah] said: Fear not! Verily, I am with you both, hearing and seeing.﴾ *(Qur'an 20: 46)*

The salvation of Moses (عليه السلام) and the Israelites came in the most amazing miracle:

﴿فَأَوۡحَيۡنَآ إِلَىٰ مُوسَىٰٓ أَنِ ٱضۡرِب بِّعَصَاكَ ٱلۡبَحۡرَۖ فَٱنفَلَقَ فَكَانَ كُلُّ فِرۡقٖ كَٱلطَّوۡدِ ٱلۡعَظِيمِ ٦٣ وَأَزۡلَفۡنَا ثَمَّ ٱلۡأٓخَرِينَ ٦٤ وَأَنجَيۡنَا مُوسَىٰ وَمَن مَّعَهُۥٓ أَجۡمَعِينَ ٦٥ ثُمَّ أَغۡرَقۡنَا ٱلۡأٓخَرِينَ ٦٦ إِنَّ فِي ذَٰلِكَ لَأٓيَةٗۖ وَمَا كَانَ أَكۡثَرُهُم مُّؤۡمِنِينَ ٦٧ وَإِنَّ رَبَّكَ لَهُوَ ٱلۡعَزِيزُ ٱلرَّحِيمُ ٦٨﴾ [الشُّعَرَاء: ٦٣-٦٨]

﴿Then We inspired Moses [saying]: Strike the sea with your stick. And it parted, and each separate part [of that sea water] became like the huge, firm mass of a mountain. Then We brought the others [Pharaoh's party] near to that place. And We saved Moses and all those with him. Then We drowned the others. Verily, in this is indeed a sign [or a proof], yet most of them are not believers. And verily, your Lord, He is truly the All-Mighty, the Most Merciful.﴾ *(Qur'an 26: 63-68)*

Another great lesson in surrender to the divine will is that of Prophet Muhammad's migration from Makkah to Madinah. The Prophet (ﷺ) devised a secret plan to steal away from the polytheists of the Quraysh, who did not want to see him succeed. The Prophet's cousin 'Ali ibn Abi Ṭâlib (رضي الله عنه) slept in his bed while he left the house to meet with Abu Bakr (رضي الله عنه), who was to be his companion on the journey. Abu Bakr had prepared the mounts for the trip and hired a guide who was well-acquainted with the unusual routes through the Arabian desert. Abu Bakr's daughters 'Â'ishah (رضي الله عنها) and Asmâ' (رضي الله عنها) were responsible for the preparation and the delivery of food for the journey. His son 'Abdullah (رضي الله عنه) was charged with following the plans and plots of the Quraysh and delivering the news to his father and the Prophet (ﷺ) in their hiding place, the cave of Thawr. Every detail was well planned, and all that was humanly possible was done.

The Quraysh set out in search of the Prophet (ﷺ), and they reached the mouth of the cave.[73] Abu Bakr said: "*By Allah, O Messenger of Allah, if one of them looks down at his feet, he will see us!*" The Prophet's answer was: «O Abu Bakr, what do you think of two when Allah is the third one with them?» (Bukhari)

This is a clear lesson in surrendering to the divine will and relying on Allah (سبحانه وتعالى), as well as a lesson in sincerity and total trust and submission. When you have done your best, leave the end results to Allah (سبحانه وتعالى). He is the All-Preserving, the Ever Near, the Answerer, the Director of All Affairs, the Trustee and the All-Sufficient.

---

73 As-Sibâ'ie

Take a moment to... check your progress — do your part

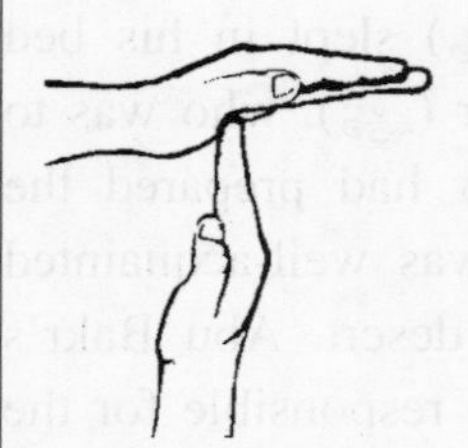

- What have you achieved so far?
- Visualize your GOALS and brainstorm about them and your milestones every night before you go to bed. In the morning, write down any ideas or thoughts in your journal.

Take a moment to... deal with helplessness

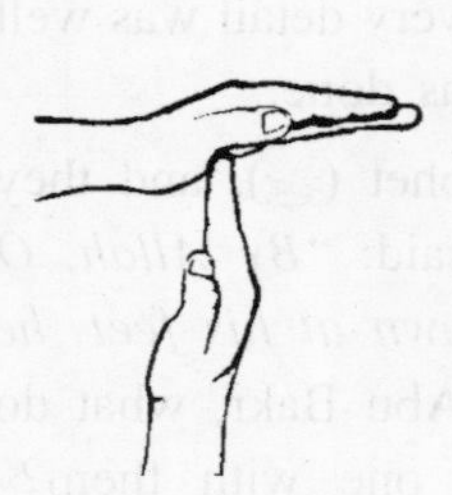

- Think for a moment: did you ever feel helpless? What was the reason behind this feeling?
- Reflect on this verse:

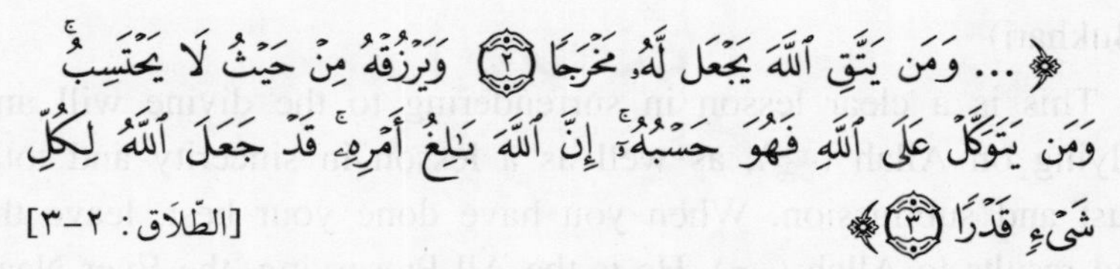

﴿... وَمَن يَتَّقِ ٱللَّهَ يَجْعَل لَّهُۥ مَخْرَجًا ﴿٢﴾ وَيَرْزُقْهُ مِنْ حَيْثُ لَا يَحْتَسِبُ ۚ وَمَن يَتَوَكَّلْ عَلَى ٱللَّهِ فَهُوَ حَسْبُهُۥٓ ۚ إِنَّ ٱللَّهَ بَٰلِغُ أَمْرِهِۦ ۚ قَدْ جَعَلَ ٱللَّهُ لِكُلِّ شَىْءٍ قَدْرًا ﴿٣﴾﴾ [الطلاق: ٢-٣]

﴾...And whoever fears Allah and keeps his duty to Him, He will make a way for him to get out [from every difficulty], and He will provide for him from [sources] he never could imagine. And whoever puts his trust in Allah, then He will suffice for him. Verily, Allah will accomplish His purpose. Indeed, Allah has set a measure for all things.﴿

(Qur'an 65: 2-3)

- Now copy this verse in your journal. Write it three, four or more times until you fully feel it in your heart.
- Use this verse in your daily prayers this week. Reflect on its meanings, feel complete awe, and surrender to your Creator.
- When you know that you are doing all that is in your human power, let go of the results.

9. Flexibility

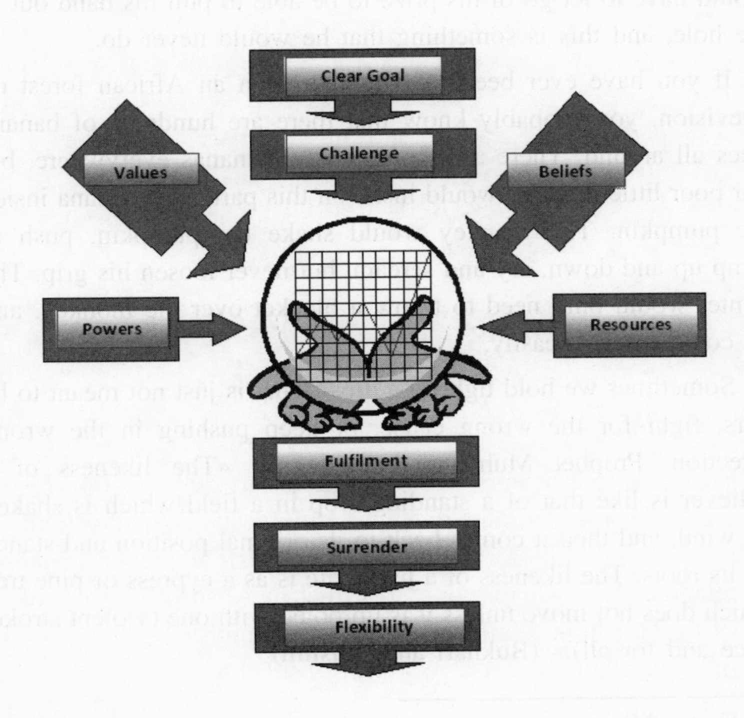

I read an interesting story about how people in Africa used to catch monkeys.[74] A hunter would get a large pumpkin, make a small hole in it, and take it to the area where he wanted to catch his prey. He would hold the pumpkin high in the air so that all the monkeys could see it, then put it on the ground and tie it very well so that they could not move it away. Next, the hunter held a ripe banana up in the air so that the monkeys could see it. He took the banana and put it inside the pumpkin through the small hole he had made earlier. Then he just walked away, hid behind a tree and waited. One curious monkey would soon approach the pumpkin, put his tiny hand in the hole and hold the banana. Trying to take the fruit out, the monkey's hand would inevitably get stuck. He would have to let go of his prize to be able to pull his hand out of the hole, and this is something that he would never do.

If you have ever been to Africa or seen an African forest on television, you probably know that there are hundreds of banana trees all around. There are thousands of bananas everywhere, but our poor little monkey would insist on this particular banana inside the pumpkin. The monkey would shake the pumpkin, push it, jump up and down, cry and scream, but never loosen his grip. The hunter would only need to throw a blanket over the monkey, and he could catch it easily.

Sometimes we hold tight to a dream that is just not meant to be ours, fight for the wrong cause, or keep pushing in the wrong direction. Prophet Muhammad (ﷺ) said: «The likeness of a believer is like that of a standing crop in a field which is shaken by wind, and then it comes back to its original position and stands on its roots. The likeness of a hypocrite is as a cypress or pine tree which does not move unless it is uprooted with one (violent stroke, once and for all).» (Bukhari and Muslim)

---

74 Sloat and Doane

In a similar hadith, he (ﷺ) said: «The parable of the believer is that of a fresh tender plant. From whatever direction the wind comes, it bends it, but when the wind becomes quiet, it becomes straight again. Similarly, a believer is afflicted with calamities [but, like the fresh plant, he regains his normal state soon after Allah (ﷻ) removes the difficulties].» (Bukhari)

You see, first you have to accept your situation with all its unpleasant surprises. Then you have to adjust yourself to the divine will. Only then will you be able to assess your options wisely and be flexible in confronting life with tolerance and endurance.

We have to be flexible enough to figure out the 'deliverance options', or the various ways — maybe some unexpected — that the Owner of the Universe uses to provide support for us. Allah says:

﴿فَعَسَىٰٓ أَن تَكْرَهُوا۟ شَيْـًٔا وَيَجْعَلَ ٱللَّهُ فِيهِ خَيْرًا كَثِيرًا ١٩﴾

[النّساء: ١٩]

﴿It may be that you dislike a thing and Allah brings through it a great deal of good.﴾ *(Qur'an 4: 19)*

﴿وَعَسَىٰٓ أَن تَكْرَهُوا۟ شَيْـًٔا وَهُوَ خَيْرٌ لَّكُمْ ۖ وَعَسَىٰٓ أَن تُحِبُّوا۟ شَيْـًٔا وَهُوَ شَرٌّ لَّكُمْ ۗ وَٱللَّهُ يَعْلَمُ وَأَنتُمْ لَا تَعْلَمُونَ ٢١٦﴾

[البقرة: ٢١٦]

﴿It may be that you dislike a thing which is good for you and that you like a thing which is bad for you. Allah knows, but you do not know.﴾ *(Qur'an 2: 216)*

How do you like your TEA?

Remember what you learned earlier about the ABC system and how your endorsed beliefs can change your whole perception of a situation? Similarly, you can think of the idea as TEA: a Trigger, an Endorsed belief, and an Action.

- You are confronted with a Trigger.
- You work on your Endorsed belief, which can change your perception.
- Thus, you can adapt and control your chosen Action.

Your approach to any situation is mainly determined by your way of thinking — or rather, your endorsed beliefs (E). These beliefs affect your decisions, your actions and your subsequent emotional state.

For instance, I keep getting bad grades on spelling tests (Trigger-T). If my beliefs (Endorsed beliefs-E) are that I am a failure, I cannot do better, and this is a gift that I do not have, then my subsequent action (Action-A) will be to give up. The consequences are, of course, more bad grades and feelings of depression. On the other hand, I could choose to believe that I would be able to do better if I put my heart into it (E). My subsequent action would thus change. I would work harder and try to improve (A), and the consequences would be much better. Being flexible in the way we approach any situation can improve our perception and thus our subsequent actions.

Let's look at another example. If you have too much work to do (T), you may perceive your situation as stressful and overwhelming (E), but if you are flexible enough to change your approach, it will be easier for you to adapt. You could focus on the final rewards of your hard work, such as the appreciation that you expect to receive from your boss, a promotion, or maybe some time off at the end; you could change your frustration into feelings of motivation and challenge (adjusted E). By changing any aspect of your inner world, you generate high quality options (A) to change the results that you come up with in the end.

Take a moment to...

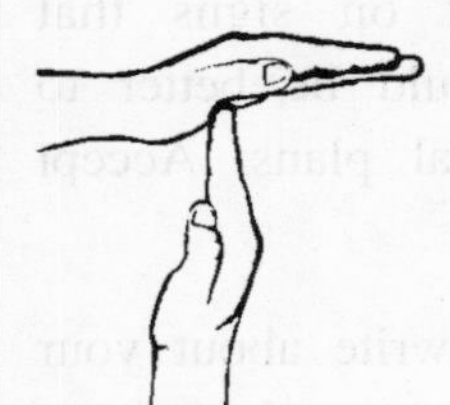

- Reflect on Allah's promise:

﴿إِنَّا لَنَنصُرُ رُسُلَنَا وَٱلَّذِينَ ءَامَنُوا۟ فِى ٱلْحَيَوٰةِ ٱلدُّنْيَا وَيَوْمَ يَقُومُ ٱلْأَشْهَـٰدُ ﴿٥١﴾﴾ [غافر: ٥١]

﴿Verily, We will indeed help [and make victorious] Our Messengers and those who believe, [both] in this world's life and on the Day when the witnesses will stand forth [the Day of Resurrection].﴾ *(Qur'an 40: 51)*

- Now remember that the promised victory does not have to come in the way that we want or expect. Being flexible helps us to acknowledge and appreciate all of the ways in which Allah (ﷻ) supports us.
- Also remember that even if the 'success' we were hoping for was not fully achieved, we still received a reward for every action we took along the way. Allah (ﷻ) will not let our reward be lost:

﴿إِنَّا لَا نُضِيعُ أَجْرَ مَنْ أَحْسَنَ عَمَلًا ﴿٣٠﴾﴾ [الكهف: ٣٠]

﴿Verily, as for those who believe and work righteousness, We shall not suffer to perish the reward of any who do a [single] righteous deed.﴾ *(Qur'an 18: 30)*

Take a moment to...

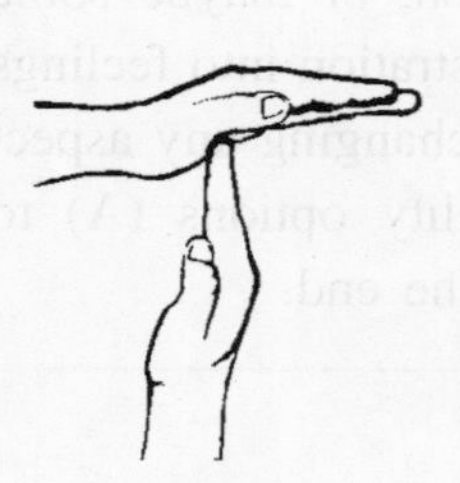

- Go back and read your GOALS page(s) and your milestones. Are you on the exact track that you envisioned?
- Reflect on signs in your life encouraging you to follow the path that you chose, and reflect on signs that suggest that it would be better to make some adjustments to your original plans. Accept Allah's gifts and direction.
- Open your journal to a new page and write about your feelings about your goals, as well as any deviations, variation, redirection, new ideas, new gifts and signposts that you have encountered along your way.
- Revisit your GOALS and milestones page. Do you want to add any new ones, new ideas, or new plans? If so, write them down.

10. Accountability

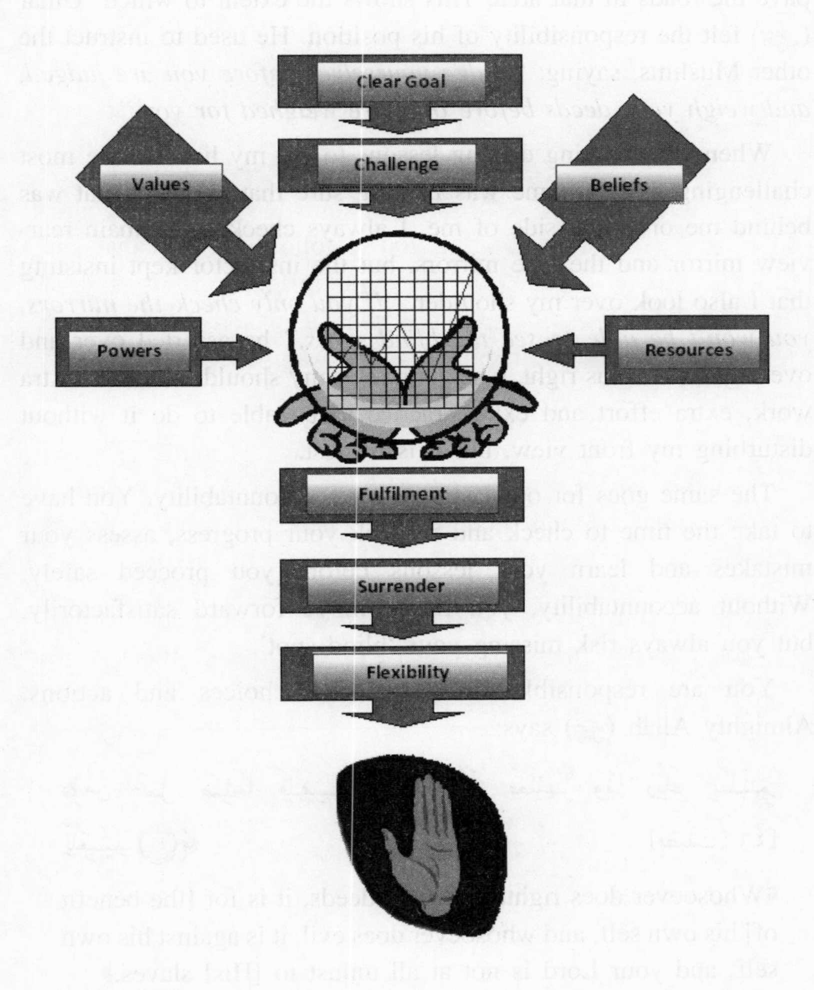

Responsibility entails accountability both in this world and in the hereafter. When 'Umar ibn al-Khaṭṭâb (رضي الله عنه) was the caliph, he once said that he was afraid that if a mule fell in the mountain roads of Iraq and broke his legs, Allah (ﷻ) might ask him why he did not pave the roads in that area. This shows the extent to which 'Umar (رضي الله عنه) felt the responsibility of his position. He used to instruct the other Muslims, saying: "*Judge yourselves before you are judged, and weigh your deeds before they are weighed for you.*"

When I was taking driving lessons to get my license, the most challenging thing for me was making sure that I knew what was behind me or to the side of me. I always checked the main rear-view mirror and the side mirrors, but the instructor kept insisting that I also look over my shoulder. "*If you only check the mirrors, you won't be able to see the blind spots,*" he asserted over and over again. He was right. Checking over my shoulders entails extra work, extra effort and extra practice to be able to do it without disturbing my front view, but it is a must.

The same goes for our last step here: accountability. You have to take the time to check and recheck your progress, assess your mistakes and learn your lessons before you proceed safely. Without accountability, you might move forward satisfactorily, but you always risk missing your 'blind spot'.

You are responsible for your own choices and actions. Almighty Allah (ﷻ) says:

﴿مَّنْ عَمِلَ صَٰلِحًا فَلِنَفْسِهِۦ ۖ وَمَنْ أَسَآءَ فَعَلَيْهَا ۗ وَمَا رَبُّكَ بِظَلَّٰمٍ لِّلْعَبِيدِ ﴿٤٦﴾﴾ [فُصّلت: ٤٦]

﴾Whosoever does righteous good deeds, it is for [the benefit of] his own self, and whosoever does evil, it is against his own self; and your Lord is not at all unjust to [His] slaves.﴿

(Qur'an 41: 46)

﴿إِنْ أَحْسَنتُمْ أَحْسَنتُمْ لِأَنفُسِكُمْ ۖ وَإِنْ أَسَأْتُمْ فَلَهَا ... ﴿٧﴾﴾ [الإسراء: ٧]

﴾[And We said]: If you do good, you do good for your own selves, and if you do evil [you do it] against yourselves...﴿
(Qur'an 17: 7)

Take a moment to...

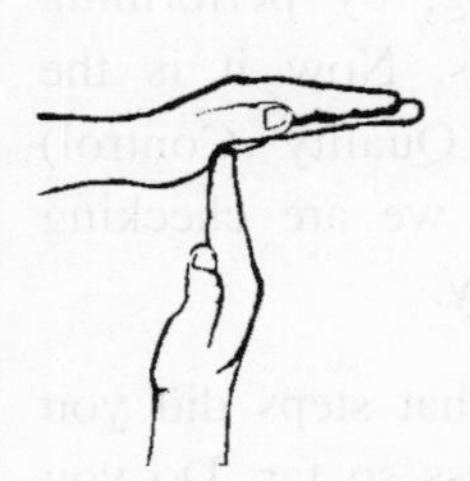

- List five steps forward (emotional or material ones) that you have achieved towards your dream, even if they are baby steps.
- List the five best nurturing actions ('apples') that you did for yourself during this course. Do you think you deserve a reward now that you have finished the program?
- Evaluate your progress.
- List five main commitments that you promised yourself. (You may or may not have fulfilled them yet.) Renew them. Commit to work on them for the next six months.

Reminder:

- Are you still performing your Conscience Exam?
- Do you always remember your True Secret and your dhikr, your remembrance of Allah (ﷻ)?
- Are you still seeing the Big Picture, the purpose of your existence?

Align yourself to your right path!

Take a moment to... see what we have done

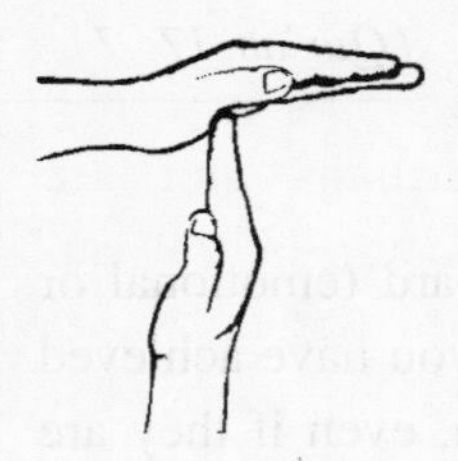

- During the course of this chapter, you have been assessing your progress and monitoring the changes that you are undergoing, by performing regular IPC checks. Now it is the time for a QC (Quality Control) check. Notice that we are checking quality, not quantity.

- Look at the GOALS that you chose. What steps did you take towards them? Evaluate your progress so far. Do you need to add more challenges? More GOALS?

- In your journal, explore:

  ❖ Your feelings, your awareness of your daily chores

  ❖ Your outlook on life and others around you (more/less optimistic, compassionate, forgiving...)

  ❖ Enthusiasm

  ❖ Self-esteem

  ❖ Goals

  ❖ Faith

  ❖ Values

  ❖ Priorities

  ❖ Intention and True Secret

  ❖ Gratitude

  ❖ Are you saying dhikr regularly? How many times did you pray the late night prayer this week?

Take a moment to...
redefine your responsibilities

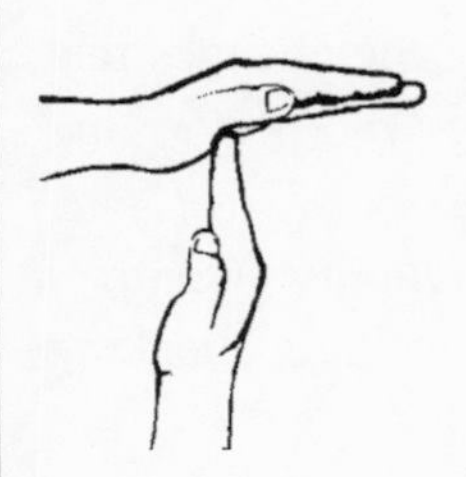

- Remember that our Prophet (ﷺ) said: «You are all guardians and are responsible for those under your care.» (Bukhari)

- Review the definition of your responsibilities that you wrote at the start of this chapter: your role around the house, at work, in college, with your family and friends... How do you see it now? Are there any additions or alterations in those responsibilities or in the way that you will plan to carry them out?

- Assess your progress.
- Check your intention.

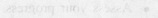

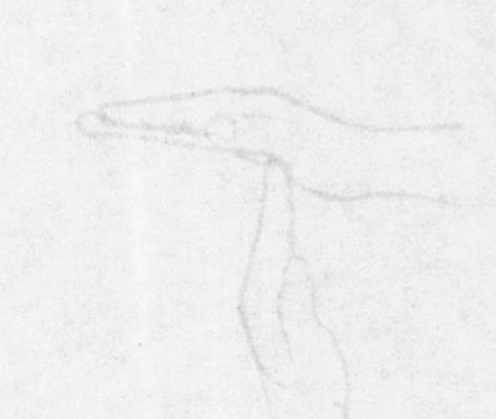

Chapter III
Helpers along the Way

Helpers along the Way

Do you think it is easy?

Being sincere to Allah (ﷻ) in every act and thought is far from easy. It is a lifelong struggle against one's self and worldly distractions. It is a challenging task requiring our continuous effort to be in control over the base desires of our own selves. It is also considered in Islam to be a sacred type of *jihad* (struggle or striving in the way of Allah), as Prophet Muhammad (ﷺ) said: «A *mujâhid* (one who strives in the way of Allah) is one who engages in jihad against his own self in obeying Allah (ﷻ).» (a sound hadith recorded by al-Albâni)

Purifying our intention so that every act is only for the sake of Allah (ﷻ) is very difficult. We are human after all; we seek a comfortable life, wealth and success. Who among us does not enjoy receiving praise and compliments now and then? Who does not feel pain for losing a worldly possession or falling ill, even when we are struggling to be grateful and satisfied for all of the other blessings Allah has bestowed on us? Allah (ﷻ) says about human beings:

﴿وَإِذَآ أَنْعَمْنَا عَلَى ٱلْإِنسَٰنِ أَعْرَضَ وَنَـَٔا بِجَانِبِهِۦ وَإِذَا مَسَّهُ ٱلشَّرُّ فَذُو دُعَآءٍ عَرِيضٍ ﴿٥١﴾﴾ [فصّلت: ٥١]

﴾And when We show favour to man, he withdraws and turns away; but when evil touches him, then he has recourse to long supplications.﴿ *(Qur'an 41: 51)*

By nature, the human being is inclined to forget. When we get used to our blessings, when we feel comfortable and satisfied, we sometimes forget to thank Allah (ﷻ). We fail to perceive the true source of our good fortune. At other times, we get distracted by life's demands and daily hassles and stray away from our true purpose in life, from the meaning of our creation:

﴿وَمَا خَلَقْتُ ٱلْجِنَّ وَٱلْإِنسَ إِلَّا لِيَعْبُدُونِ ۝٥٦﴾ [الذّاريات: ٥٦]

﴿And I [Allah] created the jinns and humans only so they could worship Me [alone].﴾ *(Qur'an 51: 56)*

That is why we constantly need helpers along the way — reminders and guidelines to keep us focused — so that we can adjust our path when we stray from the straight path of Allah (ﷻ). In this chapter, I will suggest some tools to help keep you focused on what is truly important in life, to help you adjust your intention and check your sincerity.

Supplication

Supplication is one of the surest remedies for the soul. When you supplicate to Allah (ﷻ) and feel the closeness and connection to your Creator, you gain a tremendous boost of spiritual enlightenment.

Supplication is a direct connection between you and Allah (ﷻ). It fills your heart with humility, devotion, sincere love and longing. It relieves sadness and strengthens your faith. Allah (ﷻ) says:

﴿۞ يَٰٓأَيُّهَا ٱلنَّاسُ أَنتُمُ ٱلْفُقَرَآءُ إِلَى ٱللَّهِ وَٱللَّهُ هُوَ ٱلْغَنِىُّ ٱلْحَمِيدُ ۝١٥﴾

[فاطِر: ١٥]

﴿O people! It is you who stand in need of Allah, but Allah is

rich [free of all wants and needs], worthy of all praise.﴾
(Qur'an 35: 15)

When we are used to making regular supplications, when we make this act of worship an integral part of our everyday lives, then we feel the blessing of Allah (ﷻ) in our lives, and we experience His closeness, His guidance and His mercy. A man came to the Prophet Muhammad (ﷺ) one day and asked him: "*Is Allah far away, so we should call out to Him, or is He close by, so we should whisper to Him?*" Allah (ﷻ) Himself answered the man's question[75] in a verse of the Qur'an:

﴿وَإِذَا سَأَلَكَ عِبَادِي عَنِّي فَإِنِّي قَرِيبٌ أُجِيبُ دَعْوَةَ ٱلدَّاعِ إِذَا دَعَانِ فَلْيَسْتَجِيبُوا۟ لِي وَلْيُؤْمِنُوا۟ بِي لَعَلَّهُمْ يَرْشُدُونَ ﴿١٨٦﴾﴾ [البقرة: ١٨٦]

﴾And when My slaves ask you [O Muhammad] concerning Me, then [answer them], I am indeed near [to them by My knowledge]. I respond to the invocations of the supplicant when he calls on Me [without any mediator or intercessor]. So let them obey Me and believe in Me, so that they may be led aright.﴿ *(Qur'an 2: 186)*

The answer came straight from Allah (ﷻ). This is a clear proof of His closeness and of how much He cares. Allah (ﷻ) also promises us that He always answers our calls:

﴿وَقَالَ رَبُّكُمُ ٱدْعُونِىٓ أَسْتَجِبْ لَكُمْ ... ﴿٦٠﴾﴾ [غافر: ٦٠]

﴾And your Lord said: Invoke Me; I will respond to you...﴿
(Qur'an 40: 60)

Prophet Muhammad (ﷺ) taught us: «No Muslim invokes (Allah) with a supplication, without Allah (ﷻ) answering it in one of the following three ways: He promptly answers his supplication

---

75 Khaled, *The Worshiping Acts of the Believer*

(by giving him what he asks for), or He delays it for him until (He gives it as a reward to him in) the hereafter, or He keeps him away from an equivalent evil.» (a sound hadith recorded by al-Ḥâkim)

Our Prophet (ﷺ) also said: «Allah (ﷻ) is ever generous, and if a servant raises his hands to Him (in supplication), He hates to return them empty.» (a sound or reliable hadith, or close to it, recorded by at-Tirmidhi and Abu Dâwood)

However, we should never be impatient for the answer, as the Messenger of Allah (ﷺ) said: «One's supplication will be granted if he is not impatient.» (Bukhari and Muslim)

Have complete faith in Allah (ﷻ) and believe that He wills only what is best for you. The Prophet (ﷺ) told us that He will eventually answer your prayers and grant your wishes: «Supplicate to Allah (ﷻ) and be certain that it will be answered.» (at-Tirmidhi and al-Ḥâkim; al-Albâni graded it as reliable)

Show awe, submissiveness, and humility to your Creator. The Messenger of Allah (ﷺ) cautioned: «Know that Allah (ﷻ) does not accept supplication from a negligent, inattentive heart.» (at-Tirmidhi and al-Ḥâkim; al-Albâni graded it as reliable)

Thus, we must always be sincere in our supplications. As part of our supplications, we should ask Allah (ﷻ) to help us practice our True Secret: sincerity.

Divine remembrance (dhikr Allah)

Dhikr is a beautiful type of meditation that increases your concentration and helps you focus on the important meaning of your existence. It redirects your thoughts and feelings to the true purpose of your creation. It strengthens your heart and soul and dissipates your worries.

Prophet Muhammad (ﷺ) taught us hundreds of phrases of dhikr to use in everyday life. There are expressions for remembering Allah (ﷻ) when we wake up, go to sleep, enter a marketplace, get dressed, go in or out of the home, eat and drink, and so on. There is also dhikr to be practiced every day after the dawn and mid-afternoon prayers to calm us down, centre our awareness and adjust our priorities.

A man once came to Prophet Muhammad (ﷺ) and asked him to specify an Islamic act of worship that it was especially important to cling to. The Prophet (ﷺ) said: «Keep your tongue moist from (repeating) dhikr Allah.» (at-Tirmidhi; al-Albâni graded it as sound)

In addition, Allah (ﷻ) taught us in the Qur'an to perform our dhikr in abundance:

﴿وَٱذْكُرُوا۟ ٱللَّهَ كَثِيرًا لَّعَلَّكُمْ تُفْلِحُونَ ﴿٤٥﴾﴾ [الأنفال: ٤٥]

﴿And remember the Name of Allah much [both with tongue and mind], so that you may be successful.﴾ *(Qur'an 8: 45)*

﴿يَٰٓأَيُّهَا ٱلَّذِينَ ءَامَنُوا۟ ٱذْكُرُوا۟ ٱللَّهَ ذِكْرًا كَثِيرًا ﴿٤١﴾﴾ [الأحزاب: ٤١]

﴿O you who believe! Remember Allah often and much.﴾ *(Qur'an 33: 41)*

As its name implies, 'divine remembrance' helps us to always remember our Big Picture, our ultimate goal in life. It directs us towards mindful living, and it helps us to become aware of the little touches, blessings and gifts that cross our path, through faithful and conscious connection to the great source of these gifts, Allah (ﷻ).

Because of its value, it is imperative to include time in your busy daily schedule for divine remembrance. Start with five or ten minutes twice a day. Never underestimate the value of these precious minutes. Don't let life rush by and distract you, because Allah (ﷻ) warns us in the Qur'an:

﴿يَٰٓأَيُّهَا ٱلَّذِينَ ءَامَنُواْ لَا تُلۡهِكُمۡ أَمۡوَٰلُكُمۡ وَلَآ أَوۡلَٰدُكُمۡ عَن ذِكۡرِ ٱللَّهِۚ وَمَن يَفۡعَلۡ ذَٰلِكَ فَأُوْلَٰٓئِكَ هُمُ ٱلۡخَٰسِرُونَ ٩﴾ [المنافقون: ٩]

﴿O you who believe! Let neither your property nor your children divert you from the remembrance of Allah. Whoever does that, then they are the losers.﴾ *(Qur'an 63: 9)*

Recite your dhikr aloud or repeat it silently. In either case, feel the meaning behind every word and let the valuable lessons sink into your heart and soul, remembering these words of Allah (ﷻ):

﴿فَٱذۡكُرُونِيٓ أَذۡكُرۡكُمۡ ... ١٥٢﴾ [البَقَرَة: ١٥٢]

﴿Therefore, remember Me; I will remember you...﴾ *(Qur'an 2: 152)*

By practicing your dhikr daily, you will soon reap its remarkable benefits in your life, whether on your physical body, on your heart and emotions, or on your spiritual well-being:

﴿أَلَا بِذِكۡرِ ٱللَّهِ تَطۡمَئِنُّ ٱلۡقُلُوبُ ٢٨﴾ [الرَّعد: ٢٨]

﴿Verily, in the remembrance of Allah do hearts find rest [and satisfaction].﴾ *(Qur'an 13: 28)*

Acts of worship

All acts of worship, whether obligatory or recommended, drive you closer to Allah (ﷻ). Our Prophet Muhammad (ﷺ) taught us: «Allah the Almighty has said: Whoever shows enmity to a friend of Mine, I shall be at war with him. My servant does not draw near to Me with anything more loved by Me than the religious duties I have imposed upon him, and My servant continues to draw near to Me with supererogatory works so that I shall love him. When I love him, I am his hearing with which he hears, his sight with which he sees, his hand with which he strikes, and his foot with which he walks. Were he to ask (something) of Me, I would surely give it to him; and were he to ask Me for refuge, I would surely grant him it. I do not hesitate about anything as much as I hesitate about (seizing) the soul of My faithful servant; he hates death and I hate hurting him.» (Bukhari)

Ablution

Ablution is an act of purification of both the body and soul. It aims first at removing any physical dirt from the body or clothing.

﴿يَٰٓأَيُّهَا ٱلَّذِينَ ءَامَنُوٓاْ إِذَا قُمۡتُمۡ إِلَى ٱلصَّلَوٰةِ فَٱغۡسِلُواْ وُجُوهَكُمۡ وَأَيۡدِيَكُمۡ إِلَى ٱلۡمَرَافِقِ وَٱمۡسَحُواْ بِرُءُوسِكُمۡ وَأَرۡجُلَكُمۡ إِلَى ٱلۡكَعۡبَيۡنِۚ ... ٦﴾ [المائدة: ٦]

﴾O you who believe! When you intend to offer the prayer, wash your faces and your hands [and forearms] up to the elbows, rub [by passing wet hands over] your heads, and [wash] your feet up to the ankles...﴿ *(Qur'an 5: 6)*

Yet ablution is far from being merely a physical act. It drives away evil thoughts, clears the mind and prepares one to concentrate on the glorification and worship of Allah (ﷻ). Prophet Muhammad (ﷺ) told us that ablution also washes away sins, purifying and cleansing the soul: «If the Muslim performs ablution and washes his face, any offence he overlooked with his eyes will come out with the water; and when he washes his hands, any assault he committed with his hands will come out with the water; and when he washes his feet, any misdeed to which he walked with his feet will come out with the water, until he concludes (the ablution) free from sins.» (Muslim and at-Tirmidhi)

Our Prophet (ﷺ) taught us how ablution helps control anger and rage. He (ﷺ) said: «Anger is from the devil, the devil was created from fire, and only water extinguishes fire. Therefore, if one of you becomes angry, let him perform ablution.» (a reliable hadith recorded by Aḥmad and Abu Dâwood)

Today, the amazing calming effect of water has been scientifically proven and is used all over the world as treatment. Many psychologists advise patients suffering from anxiety, stress, fits of rage or panic attacks to use water therapy.

Prayer

Our five obligatory daily prayers are recurrent reminders that make us aware of our thoughts and actions and help us to regularly adjust our intention, focus on the Big Picture and correct any minor deviation or unintentional straying away from the straight path. Our prayers are spread over our day, from dawn until it is time to retire for the night, to keep our connection with Allah (ﷻ) strong throughout the day and thus to supply our souls with an infinite source of energy. In addition, the reward for prayer does not occur only during the actual performance of it. Prophet Muhammad (ﷺ) informed us: «You are in prayer for as long as you are waiting for it.» (Bukhari)

For the early Muslims, the time they spent praying served to calm, console and reassure their souls. Prophet Muhammad (ﷺ) used to say to Bilâl (رضي الله عنه), his Companion who was responsible for calling the people to gather for prayer: «O Bilâl, give the call to prayer, and bring comfort to my heart.» (a sound hadith recorded by Abu Dâwood)

Allah (ﷻ) taught us in the Qur'an to seek help through prayers during tough times when we are facing life's struggles:

﴿يَٰٓأَيُّهَا ٱلَّذِينَ ءَامَنُواْ ٱسْتَعِينُواْ بِٱلصَّبْرِ وَٱلصَّلَوٰةِۚ إِنَّ ٱللَّهَ مَعَ ٱلصَّٰبِرِينَ ﴿١٥٣﴾﴾

[البقرة: ١٥٣]

﴾O you who believe! Seek help in patience and prayer. Truly Allah is with the patient ones.﴿ *(Qur'an 2: 153)*

Late Night prayer

Late night prayer is not obligatory for Muslims, yet it offers many spiritual and physical benefits. In the Qur'an, Allah (ﷻ) stresses the importance of this sacred prayer to help us through difficult tasks and challenges in life:

﴿قُمِ ٱلَّيْلَ إِلَّا قَلِيلًا ﴿٢﴾ نِّصْفَهُۥٓ أَوِ ٱنقُصْ مِنْهُ قَلِيلًا ﴿٣﴾ أَوْ زِدْ عَلَيْهِ وَرَتِّلِ ٱلْقُرْءَانَ تَرْتِيلًا ﴿٤﴾ إِنَّا سَنُلْقِى عَلَيْكَ قَوْلًا ثَقِيلًا ﴿٥﴾ إِنَّ نَاشِئَةَ ٱلَّيْلِ هِىَ أَشَدُّ وَطْـًٔا وَأَقْوَمُ قِيلًا ﴿٦﴾﴾

[المُزّمل: ٢-٦]

﴾Stand [to pray] all night, except for a little, half of it or a little less than that, or a little more; and recite the Qur'an in a slow, pleasant tone and style. Verily, We will send down to you a weighty Word [with obligations and laws]. Indeed, the rising by night [for prayers] is hard and most potent and good for governing oneself and most suitable for [understanding] the Word [of Allah].﴿ *(Qur'an 73: 2-6)*

Obligatory charity (zakât) and non-obligatory charity

Prophet Muhammad (ﷺ) cautioned us: «Do not tighten your purse, or Allah (ﷻ) will withhold His blessings from you.» (Bukhari)

Acts of charity are powerful lessons in detachment from material life. Although Muslims are required to work and strive for success and prosperity, they should not become obsessed or overly fascinated with any worldly possessions.

Allah (ﷻ) warns us:

﴿إِنَّمَآ أَمْوَٰلُكُمْ وَأَوْلَٰدُكُمْ فِتْنَةٌ وَٱللَّهُ عِندَهُۥٓ أَجْرٌ عَظِيمٌ ﴿١٥﴾﴾

[التغابن: ١٥]

﴿Your wealth and your children are only a trial, whereas Allah, with Him is a great reward [in paradise].﴾ *(Qur'an 64: 15)*

Performing acts of charity also teaches us contentment and humility. It feeds the soul with love and devotion and adjusts a Muslim's priorities in life, always directing his or her efforts to higher and more sacred goals.

The obligation of paying zakât to the needy is an act of devotion aiming at purifying one's soul as well as purifying one's wealth. Allah says in the Qur'an:

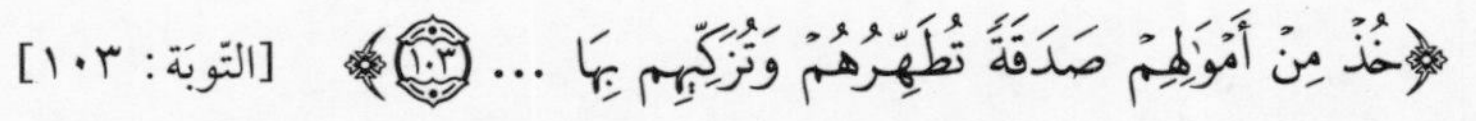
﴿خُذْ مِنْ أَمْوَٰلِهِمْ صَدَقَةً تُطَهِّرُهُمْ وَتُزَكِّيهِم بِهَا ... ﴿١٠٣﴾﴾ [التوبة: ١٠٣]

﴿Take alms from their wealth in order to purify them and sanctify them with it...﴾ *(Qur'an 9: 103)*

Fasting

Almighty Allah (ﷻ) says in His noble Book:

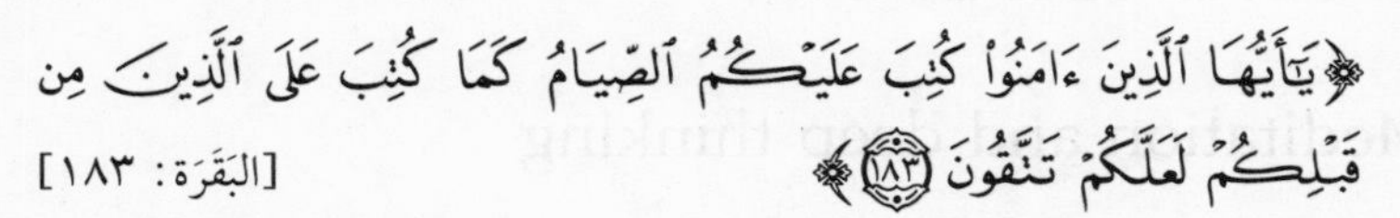

﴿يَا أَيُّهَا الَّذِينَ آمَنُوا كُتِبَ عَلَيْكُمُ الصِّيَامُ كَمَا كُتِبَ عَلَى الَّذِينَ مِن قَبْلِكُمْ لَعَلَّكُمْ تَتَّقُونَ ﴿١٨٣﴾﴾
[البقرة: ١٨٣]

﴾O you who believe! Fasting is prescribed for you as it was prescribed for those before you, that you may attain piety [and God-consciousness].﴿ *(Qur'an 2: 183)*

In instructing us how to fast, Prophet Muhammad (ﷺ) taught us: «Whoever does not abandon false speech, acting upon that and (acts of) ignorance (and sin), then Allah (ﷻ) has no need of him abandoning his food and drink.» (Bukhari)

From this guidance we can clearly see that the main purpose of fasting is to make us righteous, pious servants of Allah (ﷻ), and to increase in us our love of Allah (ﷻ), our fear of His wrath and our hope in His mercy. Fasting is another food for the soul.

Fasting, whether during the month of Ramadan or at other times throughout the year, is an excellent lesson in sincerity and true devotion to our Creator, since we perform this act only for Him (ﷻ). Prophet Muhammad (ﷺ) informed us that Allah (ﷻ) says: «All of the deeds of human beings are for themselves, except fasting. It is for Me, and I will reward them for it.» (Bukhari and Muslim)

Fasting is a lesson in patience and self-control. It disciplines the body by giving the mind control over physical desires and temptations, thus building strong willpower and effective devotion. Fasting frees the soul from the slavery of earthly cravings. It is another lesson for us in detachment from worldly possessions, so that we can restore our command over our bodies and regain dignity, freedom and total peace with our Creator, with ourselves and with the whole universe.

Meditation and deep thinking

﴿إِنَّ فِى خَلْقِ ٱلسَّمَٰوَٰتِ وَٱلْأَرْضِ وَٱخْتِلَٰفِ ٱلَّيْلِ وَٱلنَّهَارِ لَءَايَٰتٍ لِّأُو۟لِى ٱلْأَلْبَٰبِ ﴿١٩٠﴾ ٱلَّذِينَ يَذْكُرُونَ ٱللَّهَ قِيَٰمًا وَقُعُودًا وَعَلَىٰ جُنُوبِهِمْ وَيَتَفَكَّرُونَ فِى خَلْقِ ٱلسَّمَٰوَٰتِ وَٱلْأَرْضِ رَبَّنَا مَا خَلَقْتَ هَٰذَا بَٰطِلًا سُبْحَٰنَكَ فَقِنَا عَذَابَ ٱلنَّارِ ﴿١٩١﴾﴾ [آل عِمرَان: ١٩٠-١٩١]

﴿Verily, in the creation of the heavens and the earth, and in the alternation of night and day, there are indeed signs for men of understanding, those who remember Allah standing, sitting and lying down on their sides and think deeply about the creation of the heavens and the earth [saying]: Our Lord! You have not created [all] this without purpose. Glory to You! [Exalted are You above all that they associate with You as partners.] Give us salvation from the torment of the hellfire.﴾

(Qur'an 3: 190-191)

Reflecting on the creations of Allah (ﷻ) gives us a feeling of serenity and peace. It fills the soul with relief and surrender to its Omniscient Creator. Pondering on the wonder of Allah's creation assures you that you are in safe hands, well taken care of and well protected.

In addition to having tremendous spiritual benefits, reflection and meditation act as a powerful stress management tool that calms you down, heals your physical body and sharpens your mind.

Take your camera along and go for a walk in the neighbourhood. It does not matter whether you live in a compound, in the countryside, or on a busy street. Walk around while being mindful of your surroundings. Take photos of what you notice, what captures your eyes, good or bad. Think like a child who walks along a street for the first time holding his mother's hand. He cannot stop expressing his excitement about anything and everything he sees: "*WOW — a tree! Wow — a filthy dog! Wow — a yellow flower! Wow — a crumbled down wall!*"

Concentrate on the beauty surrounding you. Search for the beauty in everything around you, in the smile of a child, in the peacefulness of the night, in the flower growing out of a crack in the pavement, in the crunch of a leaf falling from an autumn tree...

Go back to your home, review your photos, choose some and print them out. Stick them in your journal and write about your feelings. What did those images generate in your heart? Look further and try to find the beauty behind each of them. There must be hidden beauty in everything, because Allah (ﷻ) says that He is the One:

﴿ٱلَّذِىٓ أَحْسَنَ كُلَّ شَىْءٍ خَلَقَهُۥ ... ﴿٧﴾﴾ [السَّجدَة: ٧]

﴿Who made all things good which He created...﴾

(Qur'an 32: 7)

Find a lesson, a hidden meaning. Write about it.

Of course you cannot carry your camera along twenty-four hours a day, seven days a week. This is just an exercise to train your mind to notice the beauty in your life, to subconsciously search for it everywhere around you. Soon your eyes will be your faithful camera, and your heart will be your beautiful canvas.

Seeing and feeling the beauty around us fills our hearts with sincere love, certainty, compassion and purity. The beauty of the universe is a continuous reminder of Allah's power, wisdom and mercy. Meditation and deep thinking are our safest ways to find true knowledge and spiritual enlightenment. They are beautiful types of worship that provide food for the soul and a feast for the eyes.

Reciting and memorizing the Qur'an

The Qur'an is the greatest book of all times. It is the word of Allah (ﷻ), the last message from Him to all of humankind. With its unique construction, the Qur'an holds a miraculous power of healing and spiritual transcendence, delivering wisdom and mercy to us:

﴿وَنَزَّلْنَا عَلَيْكَ ٱلْكِتَٰبَ تِبْيَٰنًا لِّكُلِّ شَىْءٍ وَهُدًى وَرَحْمَةً وَبُشْرَىٰ لِلْمُسْلِمِينَ ﴿٨٩﴾﴾ [النحل: ٨٩]

﴾And We have sent down to you the Book [this Qur'an] as an exposition of everything, a guidance, a mercy and glad tidings for those who have submitted themselves [to Allah as Muslims].﴿ *(Qur'an 16: 89)*

﴿... قُلْ هُوَ لِلَّذِينَ ءَامَنُوا۟ هُدًى وَشِفَآءٌ ... ﴿٤٤﴾﴾ [فصّلت: ٤٤]

﴾...Say: It [this Qur'an] is for the believers a guide and a healing...﴿ *(Qur'an 41: 44)*

Reading and memorizing the Qur'an is another powerful reminder of our ultimate goal in life. It teaches us reverence and awe of our Creator, Allah (ﷻ):

﴿لَوْ أَنزَلْنَا هَٰذَا ٱلْقُرْءَانَ عَلَىٰ جَبَلٍ لَّرَأَيْتَهُۥ خَٰشِعًا مُّتَصَدِّعًا مِّنْ خَشْيَةِ ٱللَّهِ وَتِلْكَ ٱلْأَمْثَٰلُ نَضْرِبُهَا لِلنَّاسِ لَعَلَّهُمْ يَتَفَكَّرُونَ ﴿٢١﴾﴾

[الحشر: ٢١]

﴾Had We sent down this Qur'an on a mountain, you would surely have seen it humbling itself and being torn asunder by the fear of Allah. Such are the parables which We put forward to humankind that they may reflect.﴿ *(Qur'an 59: 21)*

It is a guide for our religious practices as well as a guidebook for our whole style of living. If we dig into its meanings, we will find treasures of wisdom and knowledge beyond all expectation. Allah (ﷻ) describes it this way:

﴿كِتَٰبٌ أُحۡكِمَتۡ ءَايَٰتُهُۥ ثُمَّ فُصِّلَتۡ مِن لَّدُنۡ حَكِيمٍ خَبِيرٍ ۝١﴾ [هُود: ١]

﴾[This is] a Book, the verses of which are perfected [in every sphere of knowledge] and then explained in detail from One [Allah] Who is All-Wise and Well-Acquainted [with all things.﴿ *(Qur'an 11: 1)*

Releasing worry

Let me tell you about one of my own experiences with worry: "*Mama, something is wrong with my eye. It hurts!*" cried my son, diverting my attention away from the workers who were bustling around our house, packing our household goods. I looked at Youssof's eye. It was swelling, literally enlarging, inflating like a balloon before my eyes. Its colour was a deep blood red. It looked scary.

It was almost sunset, and the workers were finishing up for the day. Since it was getting late, I could not find any ophthalmologist to see my son. I panicked as I packed the children in the car and drove from one clinic to another. I called another hospital, and they announced, "*The doctor will be leaving in fifteen minutes.*"

"*But I need at least twenty minutes to reach you,*" I pleaded. "*Please ask him to wait. It's an emergency.*"

I was driving like crazy, running over speed bumps without slowing down. "*Slow down Mama — you're scaring me,*" cried my daughter in the back. "*I feel nauseous.*"

"*We're almost there,*" I declared apologetically.

On the way to the hospital, I was murmuring all the prayers and supplications I could think of. When I parked, another glance at Youssof's eye gave me a big sigh of relief. The swelling was already starting to subside. I guessed that perhaps the dust from the packing had triggered an allergic response in his eye.

When we finally walked out of the doctor's clinic, I realized that for the past hour or so, the persistent thoughts and stress about moving and leaving my home had been out of my mind. All my concerns about leaving behind family and friends, deciding what to take with us, searching for a new home, wondering how we would deal with financial challenges... they all just shrank. They seemed so trivial. A deep sense of gratitude enveloped my heart, and I appreciated what a long-forgotten feeling that was.

Sometimes we need a wake-up call to remind us not to worry about everything in our lives, not to panic and fret. Apprehension, anxiety and worry are literally intoxicating our bodies and shielding our vision from our unlimited blessings.

The solution for worry and stress is taught to us repeatedly in the Qur'an and the Sunnah. Allah (ﷻ) teaches us to fear nothing and no one but Allah (ﷻ) and to detach ourselves from materialistic, worldly thoughts. This frees our minds by allowing us to remember that nothing in this life can last forever, and that what may seem today to be an unsolvable problem will soon pass and fade away:

﴿ٱعْلَمُوٓا۟ أَنَّمَا ٱلْحَيَوٰةُ ٱلدُّنْيَا لَعِبٌ وَلَهْوٌ وَزِينَةٌ وَتَفَاخُرٌۢ بَيْنَكُمْ وَتَكَاثُرٌ فِى ٱلْأَمْوَٰلِ وَٱلْأَوْلَٰدِ ۖ كَمَثَلِ غَيْثٍ أَعْجَبَ ٱلْكُفَّارَ نَبَاتُهُۥ ثُمَّ يَهِيجُ فَتَرَىٰهُ مُصْفَرًّا ثُمَّ يَكُونُ حُطَٰمًا ... ﴿٢٠﴾﴾ [الحديد: ٢٠]

﴿Know that the life of this world is only play and amusement, pomp and mutual boasting among you, and rivalry in respect of wealth and children, as the likeness of vegetation after rain. Its growth is pleasing to the tiller, but afterwards it dries up and you see it turning yellow. Then it becomes straw...﴾

(Qur'an 57: 20)

We have to concentrate on what is truly important, on our True Secret and our Big Picture. We have to be totally sincere and devoted to Allah (ﷻ) and strive to attain His pleasure and approval. Prophet Muhammad (ﷺ) said: «Whoever's main concern is this worldly existence, Allah will unravel his efforts and bring his poverty between his eyes, and what will reach him from this world is only what is predestined for him. Whoever's intention is the hereafter, Allah will strengthen his efforts and put wealth and prosperity into his heart, and the world will be driven to him.» (al-Albâni, who said its narrators are reliable)

The Messenger of Allah (ﷺ) also said: «Whoever makes his concern only one (that of the hereafter), Allah (ﷻ) will make him content with (his share in this) worldly life; but whoever is surmounted by worries, Allah will not bother in which worldly valley he might perish.» (a sound or reliable hadith recorded by al-Ḥâkim)

I once read an interesting story about a professor who began his class by holding up a glass with some water in it. He asked the students, "*How much do you think this glass weighs?*" "*Fifty grams!...One hundred grams!...One hundred twenty-five grams!*" the students answered. "*I really don't know. We'd have to weigh it,*" said the professor, "*but my question is: what would happen if I held it up like this for a few minutes?*" "*Nothing,*" the students said. "*Okay, what would happen if I held it up like this for an hour?*" the professor asked. "*Your arm would begin to ache,*" said one of the students. "*You're right. Now what would happen if I held it for a day?*" "*Your arm could go numb. You might have severe muscle stress and paralysis and have to go to the hospital for sure!*" ventured another student, and all the students laughed. "*Very good, but during all this, did the weight of the glass change?*" asked the professor. "*No.*" "*Then what caused the arm ache and the muscle stress?*" The students were puzzled. "*What should I do now to relieve the pain*?" asked the professor again. "*Put the glass down!*" said one of the students. "*Exactly!*" said the professor.

Life's problems are something like this. Hold the weight of them in your head for a few minutes, and you seem okay. Think of them for a long time, and you begin to ache. Hold them even longer, and they begin to paralyze you until you are not able to do anything. It is important to think of the problems in your life, but it is even more important to 'put them down' at the end of every day before you go to sleep. That way, you can release the stress. You wake up the next day fresh and strong and ready to handle any issue or challenge that comes your way.

Take a moment to...

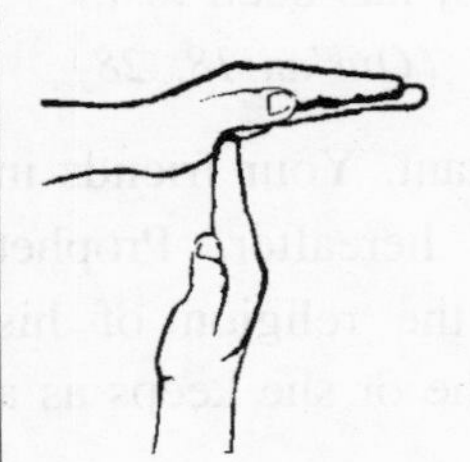

- Memorize this supplication to use when you are afflicted by distress: «O Allah, I seek Your mercy. Do not make me reliant on my own self even for an instant, and lead all my affairs to success. There is none worthy of worship other than You. [*Allâhumma raḥmataka arjoo, fa lâ takalni ilâ nafsi tarfata 'ayn, wa aṣlih lee sha'ni kullah, lâ ilâha illâ anta.*]» (Abu Dâwood and Aḥmad; al-Albâni graded it as sound)

Social support

It was narrated that some noble men from the dominant tribe of Quraysh told the Prophet Muhammad (ﷺ) that if he wanted them to follow his faith and become Muslims, he must no longer allow poor believers and slaves to attend the same meetings as them. The Prophet (ﷺ), in his desire for them to believe in the new religion, briefly considered their demand, but Allah (ﷻ) sent down these verses to announce the true values of the Islamic nation:

﴿وَٱصْبِرْ نَفْسَكَ مَعَ ٱلَّذِينَ يَدْعُونَ رَبَّهُم بِٱلْغَدَوٰةِ وَٱلْعَشِيِّ يُرِيدُونَ وَجْهَهُۥ ۖ وَلَا تَعْدُ عَيْنَاكَ عَنْهُمْ تُرِيدُ زِينَةَ ٱلْحَيَوٰةِ ٱلدُّنْيَا ۖ وَلَا تُطِعْ مَنْ أَغْفَلْنَا قَلْبَهُۥ عَن ذِكْرِنَا وَٱتَّبَعَ هَوَىٰهُ وَكَانَ أَمْرُهُۥ فُرُطًا ﴿٢٨﴾﴾ [الكهف: ٢٨]

﴿And keep yourself [O Muhammad] patiently with those who call on Allah [such as your Companions who remember Allah with glorification, praising Him in prayers and other righteous deeds] morning and afternoon, seeking His Face, and do not let your eyes overlook them, desiring the pomp and glitter of the life of the world. Do not obey him whose heart We have made heedless of Our remembrance, one who follows his own lusts and whose affair [in the form of deeds] has been lost.》

(Qur'an 18: 28)

The company that you keep is very important. Your friends in this world will be your company in the hereafter. Prophet Muhammad (ﷺ) said: «A person is upon the religion of his friend, so let every one of you look to whom he or she keeps as a friend.» (al-Albâni, who said it is reliable)

Allah (ﷻ) says:

﴿وَسِيقَ ٱلَّذِينَ كَفَرُوٓاْ إِلَىٰ جَهَنَّمَ زُمَرًاۖ ... ﴿٧١﴾﴾ [الزُّمَر : ٧١]

《And those who disbelieved will be driven to hell in groups...》

(Qur'an 39: 71)

﴿وَسِيقَ ٱلَّذِينَ ٱتَّقَوۡاْ رَبَّهُمۡ إِلَى ٱلۡجَنَّةِ زُمَرًاۖ ... ﴿٧٣﴾﴾ [الزُّمَر : ٧٣]

《And those who kept their duty to their Lord will be led to paradise in groups...》 *(Qur'an 39: 73)*

Our Prophet (ﷺ) told us a story that demonstrates the significance of putting ourselves in good situations and surroundings, among righteous and virtuous people: «Once, from among those who were before you, there was a man who had murdered ninety-nine people. Then (feeling the gravity of his sin) he set out asking for the most knowledgeable person on earth. He came upon a monk and told him that he had murdered ninety-nine people and asked whether his repentance could be accepted. The monk replied in the negative, and so the man killed him. When he did that, the number of his victims reached one hundred. Then he set out asking for the most knowledgeable person on earth, and he came upon a scholar. The man told him that he had murdered one hundred people and asked whether his repentance could be accepted. The scholar said: Yes, and who can prevent you from your repentance? Go to such and such village where there are people who are worshipping Allah, and worship Allah (ﷻ) with them, and do not return to your homeland, for it is a corrupted land. So he left for it, but death overtook him midway. The angels of mercy and the angels of punishment quarrelled amongst themselves regarding him. The angels of mercy said: He came repentant, directing his heart towards Allah. The angels of punishment said: He never did any good deeds. So an angel came in the form of a human being, and they asked him to judge between them. He said: Measure the distances between his body and the two villages; he would belong to the land to which he is closer. They measured, and he was found to be closer to the village he was aiming for, so the angels of mercy took his soul.» (Muslim)

Our Prophet (ﷺ) also taught us: «The example of a good companion in comparison with a bad one is like that of the musk seller and the blower of the bellows [a blacksmith]. From the first, you would either buy musk or enjoy its good smell, while from the second, you would either burn your clothes or come away having experienced a repugnant odour.» (Bukhari)

In Islamic history, we have many stories of strong friendships in which one friend gave of his or her advice and possessions to help the other better follow the straight path of Allah (ﷻ). An example of such a friendship existed among 'Umar ibn al-Khaṭṭâb, Hishâm ibn al-'Âṣ and 'Ayyâsh ibn Abi Rabee'ah (may Allah be pleased with them), all of whom decided to migrate to Madinah following the Prophet's orders.

At the time of their planned departure, Hishâm was detained, so 'Umar and 'Ayyâsh travelled on alone. Abu Jahl ibn Hishâm and al-Ḥârith ibn Hishâm intercepted them to persuade their cousin,

'Ayyâsh, against the trip. They said to him: "*Your mother has vowed that no comb will touch her head and she will not seek shade from the sun until she sees you.*" 'Ayyâsh felt sorry for his mother and decided to return to Makkah.

'Umar (رضي الله عنه) tried to stop him, saying: "*'Ayyâsh, by Allah, all the people want to do is to lead you astray from your religion, so beware of them. By Allah, if lice bother your mother, she will comb her hair, and if the heat of Makkah becomes unbearable, she will seek shade.*" 'Ayyâsh said: "*I would rather respect my mother's oath, and I have some wealth I want to take from there.*" 'Umar (رضي الله عنه) did not give up; he said to his friend: "*By Allah, you know that I am one of the wealthiest men of Quraysh, and I will give you half of my wealth, just do not go with them.*" When 'Ayyâsh insisted on going back to Makkah, 'Umar (رضي الله عنه) gave him his camel and asked him to stay on her back so that if he suspected anything treacherous, he could easily flee.

As 'Umar (رضي الله عنه) had feared, as soon as 'Ayyâsh started his journey back, Abu Jahl and al-Ḥârith tricked him; they tied him up and took him back to Makkah, where he was put on trial and imprisoned.

Still, 'Umar (رضي الله عنه) never gave up on his friends. Later, Allah (سبحانه وتعالى) revealed this verse:

﴿قُلْ يَٰعِبَادِىَ ٱلَّذِينَ أَسْرَفُوا۟ عَلَىٰٓ أَنفُسِهِمْ لَا تَقْنَطُوا۟ مِن رَّحْمَةِ ٱللَّهِ ۚ إِنَّ ٱللَّهَ يَغْفِرُ ٱلذُّنُوبَ جَمِيعًا ۚ إِنَّهُۥ هُوَ ٱلْغَفُورُ ٱلرَّحِيمُ ﴿٥٣﴾﴾ [الزُّمر : ٥٣]

﴿Say: O My slaves who have transgressed against themselves! Despair not of the mercy of Allah. Verily, Allah forgives all sins. Truly, He is Oft-Forgiving, Most Merciful.﴾

(Qur'an 39: 53)

'Umar (ﷺ) wrote it down and sent it to his friend Hishâm in Makkah. This little note helped to save his friends from disbelief and brought them back to the Muslims.[76]

This remarkable story shows the magnificent feeling of brotherhood that Islam established among Muslims. It shows how a sincere and true friend can save you and guide you to the right path. Our Prophet (ﷺ) stressed this often through many statements like these: «The example of the believers, in their mutual love and mercy, is like the example of a body. If one part feels pain, then all of the body suffers from sleeplessness and fever.» (Bukhari)

«The believer to the believer is like a solid building, one part supporting the other.» (Bukhari)

Family ties

Prophet Muhammad (ﷺ) said: «Whoever desires an increase in their sustenance and age should keep good relations with their kith and kin.» (Bukhari)

Regrettably, the meaning of the family today is shrinking, along with its size. A few years ago, the family did not consist only of children, parents and grandparents; it extended to aunts, uncles and close as well as distant cousins. Family gatherings were held frequently, and all family members were connected deep in their hearts with strong ties. They cared for each other's welfare, asked about the sick, supported the widows, and took care of the orphans and the less fortunate members among them.

In my early childhood, I lived with and enjoyed this connection. I took great pleasure in family gatherings at my grandmother's house, a huge old apartment that was always full of

---

[76] Sallâbi, *'Umar ibn al-Khaṭṭâb: His Life and Times*, and Khâlid, *Good Deeds: So Hasten Towards All That is Good*

friendly and caring faces. Back then, there were no mobile phones, and only the well-off among us had a land line, but no one missed the gatherings, especially at Eid and Ramadan. Everybody knew the needs of the others, rejoiced at their happiness and supported them in their calamities. Our extended family ties were a tremendous source of power and support.

By contrast, nowadays, we have much more sophisticated telecommunications systems, but do we use them to strengthen our family ties or only to support our business deals and work relationships? The support that one can get from his or her own family is irreplaceable.

What we can do is start with ourselves, by connecting our intra-family ties and not giving up if others do not respond positively. The nature of our present life has put a great deal of stress on all of us, so give your family a chance. Our Prophet (ﷺ) said: «The one connecting his womb-related relatives is not he who connects with those who connect with him and severs with those who sever with him. It is he who, when they sever them [the womb-related relations], he connects them.» (Bukhari)

In another hadith, it is reported: «A man once came to the Messenger of Allah (ﷺ) and said: Prophet of Allah, I have relatives with whom I have good relations, but they do not reciprocate. I do good to them, and they repay me with evil. I am gentle with them, but they are rough with me. The Prophet (ﷺ) said: If it is as you say, it is as if you are feeding them hot ashes, but Allah (ﷻ) will remain in your support as long as you persist.» (Muslim)

Prophet Muhammad (ﷺ) also taught us: «May his nose be rubbed in the dust, then may his nose be rubbed in the dust, and then may his nose be rubbed in the dust! The Companions responded: Who, O Messenger of Allah? He replied: Whoever saw his parents in their elderly years and did not enter paradise (through taking good care of them).» (Muslim)

When I was a young girl, I remember the weekly trips I used to take with my grandmother to visit an elderly distant relative of hers. The lady had no children of her own, but she had many nieces and nephews, who did not care about her. Her age and physical condition caused her to be very dependent, and her closest family members considered her a burden that they looked forward to getting rid of. My grandmother arranged a nice place for the woman to live, and she made sure that she received the proper care and the nursing that was required. I used to accompany my grandmother during her regular visits over the years, until the lady passed away. I was still very young back then, but I remember those visits very well. I remember the care and love that I saw in my grandmother's eyes, and I recall the appreciation and gratitude I sensed in the woman's voice. All she was asking for was some sincere affection and compassion, and that is exactly what she was getting, but unfortunately not from her closest family members.

Today, my grandmother is in her nineties. Her feet can no longer support her. Her body is weakened. She needs regular care, affection and love, and this is what she is receiving from all of her children and grandchildren. This is the result of the seed that she planted in the hearts of her children through her fine example, and it is now reaping excellent fruits for her.

In this fast-paced, materialistic world in which we live, we need more than ever to get closer to our families, both the close family and the extended family. We need to have regular family gatherings, and we especially need to involve our children in these gatherings. It is important to let our children meet distant family members and share family experiences, to involve them in helping and caring for the weak, the poor and the needy, and to let them feel the meaning of being responsible. Children have to live the experience and see it before their eyes. Set a good example for them, like you plant a seed, so that one day they will grow up to be dependable and to support the adult members of your family, inshallah.

I also advise planning a regular weekly family time, during which you gather your close family members to tighten your relationship with each other, discuss family matters, teach your children new skills, share experiences and feelings, and show genuine care for one another.[77] Family time generates love, compassion and closeness. It also helps in solving and warding off family problems as well as correcting, or preventing, the wrongful behaviour of any member of the family.

Love

It was Christmas Eve in 1914, during the First World War, and the German and British troops were at the battlefront, down in their trenches waiting for the orders to fight. That night, homesick soldiers started whole-heartedly to sing their Christmas carols. Soldiers from rival sides sang. Their sounds rang high up in the dark sky above them. Each sang in his own language and from his own faith, but the common human longing for peace, for home, for family and for love was in the air. Unexpectedly, the soldiers came out of their trenches, approached each other and united their voices. That night, they shared baked cakes, puddings, candles and cigars. They shared their human side.[78]

We all studied World War I in our history classes at school, and we know very well that the war intensified, killing and

---

77 Covey
78 Baldwin

torturing millions of human beings. You may never have even heard of this peaceful night — a night that united the hearts and feelings of thousands of soldiers along the front lines; a night of pure instinct, that revealed real human nature searching for love and peace; a night that was reported in the letters, diaries, and memoirs of soldiers from both sides; a night that terrified war commanders and world leaders who wanted 'their' war to take place against all human nature and needs. The momentary truce was not given the chance to expand beyond that place. Soldiers from both sides were rapidly transferred to other positions and replaced by fearless troops who perceived the other side as an enemy to be killed, not as equal brothers.

If given the chance, love can spread — love that knows no boundaries of race, beliefs, language or gender, pure love, the pure natural inclination of humans instilled by Allah (ﷻ), which can end the world's misery and conflicts.

Our Prophet (ﷺ) taught us: «By the One who holds my soul in His Hand, you will not believe until you love each other. Shall I tell you about something that if you do it, it will cause you to love one another? Spread the greeting of peace (*as-salâmu 'alaykum,* the Islamic greeting which means 'peace be upon you') among you.» (Muslim, Abu Dâwood and at-Tirmidhi)

Love has special meaning in a Muslim's life. The admiration of nature's beauty, the pure sacred feelings between a man and his wife, and the unconditional love of a parent are reflections of great blessings from Allah (ﷻ); they are a manifestation of His divine names and attributes. This love is a bridge that leads a wise mind to the All-Powerful, All-Compassionate Creator.

For Muslims, love of Allah (ﷻ) comes first. It is the purest and truest kind of affection, the essence of every creation. It is the requirement of faith for the true Muslim, as Allah, the Exalted, the

Almighty says in His noble book:

﴿قُلْ إِن كَانَ ءَابَآؤُكُمْ وَأَبْنَآؤُكُمْ وَإِخْوَٰنُكُمْ وَأَزْوَٰجُكُمْ وَعَشِيرَتُكُمْ وَأَمْوَٰلٌ ٱقْتَرَفْتُمُوهَا وَتِجَٰرَةٌ تَخْشَوْنَ كَسَادَهَا وَمَسَٰكِنُ تَرْضَوْنَهَآ أَحَبَّ إِلَيْكُم مِّنَ ٱللَّهِ وَرَسُولِهِۦ وَجِهَادٍ فِى سَبِيلِهِۦ فَتَرَبَّصُوا۟ حَتَّىٰ يَأْتِىَ ٱللَّهُ بِأَمْرِهِۦ ۗ وَٱللَّهُ لَا يَهْدِى ٱلْقَوْمَ ٱلْفَٰسِقِينَ ﴿٢٤﴾﴾ [التوبة: ٢٤]

﴾Say: If your fathers, your sons, your brothers, your wives, your kindred, the wealth that you have gained, the commerce in which you fear a decline, and the dwellings in which you delight are dearer to you than Allah and His Messenger, and striving hard and fighting in His cause, then wait until Allah brings about His decision [torment]; and Allah does not guide the people who are rebellious [and disobedient to Him].﴿

(Qur'an 9: 24)

Allah (ﷻ) promises us that if we love Him and follow His path, He will love us in return:

﴿قُلْ إِن كُنتُمْ تُحِبُّونَ ٱللَّهَ فَٱتَّبِعُونِى يُحْبِبْكُمُ ٱللَّهُ وَيَغْفِرْ لَكُمْ ذُنُوبَكُمْ ۗ وَٱللَّهُ غَفُورٌ رَّحِيمٌ ﴿٣١﴾﴾ [آل عمران: ٣١]

﴾Say [O Muhammad to the people]: If you [really] love Allah, then follow me [accept Islamic monotheism and follow the Qur'an and the Sunnah]. Allah will love you and forgive you your sins, and Allah is Oft-Forgiving, Most Merciful.﴿

(Qur'an 3: 31)

Imagine how great it would be to earn the love of Allah (ﷻ)!

Our Prophet (ﷺ) is the best example of love and compassion in all spheres of his life, including his personal life with his wives, daughters, grandchildren and other relatives, and his public life, spreading his love and mercy among all human beings.

The Prophet (ﷺ) loved his wives dearly. Even after his wife Khadeejah (ﷺ) died, he continued to love her, mention her virtues, pray for her mercy and honour her friends. He (ﷺ) also used to kiss his grandchildren and play with them. Once he kissed his grandson al-Ḥasan ibn 'Ali (ﷺ) while al-Aqra' ibn Ḥâbis at-Tameem (ﷺ) was sitting beside him. Al-Aqra' said, "*I have ten children, and I have never kissed any one of them.*" Allah's Messenger (ﷺ) cast a look at him and said: «Whoever is not merciful to others will not be treated mercifully.» (Bukhari)

Abu Hurayrah ad-Dawsi (ﷺ) also narrated that the Prophet (ﷺ) once sat in the compound of his daughter Fâṭimah's house and asked about his grandson al-Ḥasan, but Fâṭimah (ﷺ) kept the boy in for a while. Abu Hurayrah thought she was either changing his clothes or giving him a bath. After a while, the boy came out running, and the Prophet (ﷺ) embraced and kissed him and then said: «O Allah! Love him, and love whoever loves him.» (Bukhari)

The Prophet loved his people and supplicated to Allah (ﷺ) for them. He rarely invoked Allah (ﷺ) for the punishment of the disbelievers, even though they fought against him and his followers for years. Instead, he regularly supplicated for their guidance. A very clear example of love and mercy is shown by his behaviour when he conquered Makkah, finally gaining the upper hand over the people who had for so long tortured him and his Companions. According to some of his biographers, the Prophet (ﷺ) asked the people of Makkah: "*What do you think I should do to you?*" They replied: "*O noble brother and generous nephew, we expect nothing but goodness from you.*" He (ﷺ) said: "*I speak to you with the same words that the Prophet Joseph spoke to his brothers (who had seriously wronged him): Go! No reproach on you this day. You are free.*"[79]

---

[79] Al-Mubarakpuri

Love, mercy, compassion and forgiveness are all important Islamic traits. They are not signs of weakness. On the contrary, they are true signs of strength because by loving and forgiving, you cease to be the victim of hatred and anger, and you triumph over your own evil.

We can further develop these characteristics within ourselves by looking for the good in each person. Everyone has to have a good side; we are human after all. Try to identify each person's motivations, understand them, show compassion and find excuses for their mistakes. We are helped in this by remembering the guidance Allah (ﷻ) gives us:

﴿وَجَزَٰٓؤُا۟ سَيِّئَةٍ سَيِّئَةٌ مِّثْلُهَا ۖ فَمَنْ عَفَا وَأَصْلَحَ فَأَجْرُهُۥ عَلَى ٱللَّهِ ۚ ... ﴿٤٠﴾﴾ [الشورى: ٤٠]

﴾And the retribution for an evil act is an evil one like it, but whoever pardons and makes reconciliation — his reward is due from Allah...﴿ *(Qur'an 42: 40)*

Take a moment to...

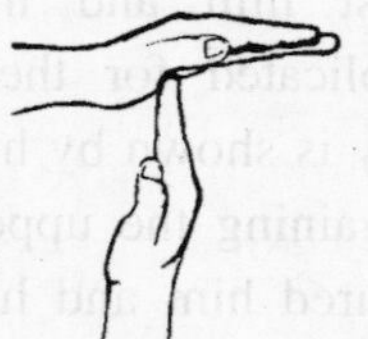

- Reflect on the meaning of love in your life. Are Allah (ﷻ) and His Messenger (ﷺ) dearer to you than all worldly gains and possessions?
- Re-evaluate different kinds of love in your life. Are you sincere in your love for your spouse, your children, your parents, your friends, your neighbours, your nation and your fellow Muslims? Do you love them for the sake of Allah (ﷻ)?
- Remember the Prophet's saying: «Whoever wants to taste the sweetness of faith, let him love a person only for the sake of Allah (ﷻ).» (Aḥmad and al-Ḥâkim; al-Albâni graded it as sound)

Detachment from worldly attractions

Imam al-Ghazâli prescribed detachment as medicine for empowering sincerity.[80] It helps you focus on your main goal and define your priorities.

There is an old tale about a pious Muslim scholar who led a very poor life in a small village in Upper Egypt, entirely detached from the world. He had many students and was totally devoted to teaching them their religion. He never asked for any worldly benefits. One day, a student of his was travelling to Morocco, and the student asked the scholar if he needed anything from there. The scholar replied, "*Just deliver my greetings to my esteemed teacher*," and he gave him the name and address of his teacher in Morocco and told him about how pious, wise and ascetic this teacher was.

The student travelled to the faraway land, where he asked about the teacher and was led to a great palace with huge pillars and tremendous riches. The student was amazed. He delivered the message and asked for any reply. The Moroccan teacher said: "*I pray for your teacher that Allah may help him to get the world out of his heart*."

Having returned to Egypt, the student delivered the message to the scholar. Tears poured from the latter's eyes, wetting his face and beard. The student, surprised by the scholar's reaction, proceeded to tell him about the rich life of his teacher in the western land. The scholar said: "*My son, he managed to get the world out of his heart, so Allah delivered it into his hands; but me, I cannot get it out of my heart just yet*."

Detachment from worldly possessions is not synonymous with being poor. Being detached means that you enjoy your blessings

---

80 Al-Ghazâli, *The Revival of Religious Knoweldge*

and belongings, appreciate all the gifts that constantly appear in your life, and work and strive for success and prosperity, but you do not become attached to these objects to the extent that they become the purpose of your life, nor do you make your pleasure and contentment dependent on them. External possessions can never be used as a measure of your true happiness.

Indeed, the more generous you are, the more prosperous you will become. Detachment is an excellent tool for adjusting your priorities and testing your sincerity. Allah (ﷻ) says:

﴿لِّكَيْلَا تَأْسَوْا عَلَىٰ مَا فَاتَكُمْ وَلَا تَفْرَحُوا بِمَا آتَاكُمْ ۗ وَاللَّهُ لَا يُحِبُّ كُلَّ مُخْتَالٍ فَخُورٍ ﴿٢٣﴾﴾ [الحديد: ٢٣]

﴾In order that you may not grieve for the sake of the things you fail to get, nor rejoice because of that which has been given to you. Allah does not like prideful boasters.﴿ *(Qur'an 57: 23)*

What is life anyway?

The Glorious Qur'an teaches us the true value of this worldly life:

﴿وَاضْرِبْ لَهُم مَّثَلَ الْحَيَاةِ الدُّنْيَا كَمَاءٍ أَنزَلْنَاهُ مِنَ السَّمَاءِ فَاخْتَلَطَ بِهِ نَبَاتُ الْأَرْضِ فَأَصْبَحَ هَشِيمًا تَذْرُوهُ الرِّيَاحُ ۗ وَكَانَ اللَّهُ عَلَىٰ كُلِّ شَيْءٍ مُّقْتَدِرًا ﴿٤٥﴾ الْمَالُ وَالْبَنُونَ زِينَةُ الْحَيَاةِ الدُّنْيَا ۖ وَالْبَاقِيَاتُ الصَّالِحَاتُ خَيْرٌ عِندَ رَبِّكَ ثَوَابًا وَخَيْرٌ أَمَلًا ﴿٤٦﴾﴾ [الكهف: ٤٥-٤٦]

﴾And put forward to them the example of the life of this world. It is like the water [rain] which We send down from the sky, and the vegetation of the earth mingles with it and becomes fresh and green, but [later] it becomes dry twigs, which the winds scatter; and Allah is Able to do everything. Wealth and children are the adornment of the life of this world, but the good righteous deeds [five compulsory prayers, deeds of obedience to Allah, good speech, remembrance of Allah with glorification, praises and thanks, and so on] that last, are better with Allah for rewards and better in respect of hope.﴾

(Qur'an 18: 45-46)

﴿ٱعۡلَمُوٓاْ أَنَّمَا ٱلۡحَيَوٰةُ ٱلدُّنۡيَا لَعِبٞ وَلَهۡوٞ وَزِينَةٞ وَتَفَاخُرُۢ بَيۡنَكُمۡ وَتَكَاثُرٞ فِي ٱلۡأَمۡوَٰلِ وَٱلۡأَوۡلَٰدِۖ كَمَثَلِ غَيۡثٍ أَعۡجَبَ ٱلۡكُفَّارَ نَبَاتُهُۥ ثُمَّ يَهِيجُ فَتَرَىٰهُ مُصۡفَرّٗا ثُمَّ يَكُونُ حُطَٰمٗاۖ وَفِي ٱلۡأٓخِرَةِ عَذَابٞ شَدِيدٞ وَمَغۡفِرَةٞ مِّنَ ٱللَّهِ وَرِضۡوَٰنٞۚ وَمَا ٱلۡحَيَوٰةُ ٱلدُّنۡيَآ إِلَّا مَتَٰعُ ٱلۡغُرُورِ ٢٠﴾ [الحديد: ٢٠]

﴿Know that the life of this world is only play and amusement, pomp and mutual boasting among you, and rivalry in respect of wealth and children, as the likeness of vegetation after rain: the growth of it is pleasing to the tiller; but afterwards it dries up and you see it turning yellow, and then it becomes straw. But in the hereafter [there is] a severe torment [for the disbelievers and evil-doers], and [there is] forgiveness from Allah and [His] good pleasure [for the believers who are good-doers], whereas the life of this world is only a deceiving enjoyment.﴾ *(Qur'an 57: 20)*

In the next verse, Allah (ﷻ) teaches us what is truly important in life, what we should be looking for instead of the fleeting pleasures of this life:

﴿سَابِقُوٓاْ إِلَىٰ مَغۡفِرَةٖ مِّن رَّبِّكُمۡ وَجَنَّةٍ عَرۡضُهَا كَعَرۡضِ ٱلسَّمَآءِ وَٱلۡأَرۡضِ أُعِدَّتۡ لِلَّذِينَ ءَامَنُواْ بِٱللَّهِ وَرُسُلِهِۦۚ ذَٰلِكَ فَضۡلُ ٱللَّهِ يُؤۡتِيهِ مَن يَشَآءُۚ وَٱللَّهُ ذُو ٱلۡفَضۡلِ ٱلۡعَظِيمِ ٢١﴾ [الحديد: ٢١]

﴿Race one with another in hastening towards forgiveness from your Lord [Allah] and towards paradise, the width of which is as the width of heaven and earth, prepared for those who believe in Allah and His Messengers. That is the grace of Allah, which He bestows on whom He pleases, and Allah is the Owner of Great Bounty.❳ *(Qur'an 57: 21)*

Take a moment to... Evaluate your worldly attachments

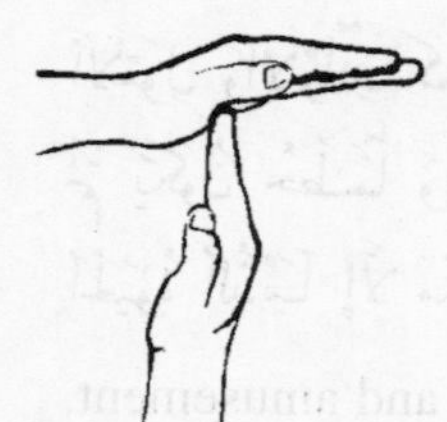

- How important are they in your life?
- Can your True Secret help you detach from them?
- This month, every time you go to the supermarket to buy food, drop a few coins in a charity box. You can give any amount you want; just keep doing it for this whole month while remembering the millions of hungry people around the globe.

Try this... let go of material attachments

A friend of mine, a widow with two demanding children, passed through a time of very difficult financial circumstances. Still, she never felt any worries about money. She once told me her secret:

Whenever I feel financially challenged, I remember the people who are needier than I am. At least I have a decent home, daily food and a supportive family. So I go out right away and give some money in charity, and I get the reward im-

mediately from Allah (ﷻ). It is not the financial reward that I am seeking but the deep feeling of security, peace and satisfaction that I feel in my heart; that is the best of all.

Patience and steadfastness

Allah Almighty (ﷻ) says:

﴿إِنَّمَا يُوَفَّى ٱلصَّـٰبِرُونَ أَجْرَهُم بِغَيْرِ حِسَابٍ ۝١٠﴾ [الزُّمَر: ١٠]

﴾Only those who are steadfast shall receive their rewards in full, without reckoning.﴿ *(Qur'an 39: 10)*

He, the Exalted, also says:

﴿وَٱللَّهُ مَعَ ٱلصَّـٰبِرِينَ ۝٢٤٩﴾ [البَقَرَة: ٢٤٩]

﴾And Allah is with the *ṣâbireen* [those who are patient and steadfast].﴿ *(Qur'an 2: 249)*

We are faced with challenges, stresses and difficulties every day of our lives. This life is not an easy journey, and patience is required at each step along the way. Patience is the driving power that will keep us going.[81] The Qur'an teaches us:

﴿وَٱسْتَعِينُوا۟ بِٱلصَّبْرِ وَٱلصَّلَوٰةِ ۚ وَإِنَّهَا لَكَبِيرَةٌ إِلَّا عَلَى ٱلْخَـٰشِعِينَ ۝٤٥﴾

[البَقَرَة: ٤٥]

﴾And seek help in patience and prayer, and truly it is extremely heavy and hard except for the *khâshi'oon* [the true believers in Allah who obey Allah with full submission, fear His punishment, and believe in His promise of paradise and in His warnings of hell].﴿ *(Qur'an 2: 45)*

81 Carter-Scott

According to al-Ghazâli, there are three kinds of patience:[82]

1. Patience with things that we cannot control, like accidents and natural disasters, physical pain and diseases. The practice of this type of patience leads to contentment of the soul. Prophet Muhammad (ﷺ) said: «The believer's affair is amazing; it is all for the good, and that is not the case with anyone other than a believer. If good times come to him, he is thankful and thus it is good for him; and if bad times befall him, he is patient and thus it is also good for him.» (Muslim)

Allah (ﷻ) says:

﴿وَلَنَبْلُوَنَّكُم بِشَىْءٍ مِّنَ ٱلْخَوْفِ وَٱلْجُوعِ وَنَقْصٍ مِّنَ ٱلْأَمْوَٰلِ وَٱلْأَنفُسِ وَٱلثَّمَرَٰتِ ۗ وَبَشِّرِ ٱلصَّٰبِرِينَ ﴿١٥٥﴾ ٱلَّذِينَ إِذَآ أَصَٰبَتْهُم مُّصِيبَةٌ قَالُوٓا۟ إِنَّا لِلَّهِ وَإِنَّآ إِلَيْهِ رَٰجِعُونَ ﴿١٥٦﴾ أُو۟لَٰٓئِكَ عَلَيْهِمْ صَلَوَٰتٌ مِّن رَّبِّهِمْ وَرَحْمَةٌ ۖ وَأُو۟لَٰٓئِكَ هُمُ ٱلْمُهْتَدُونَ ﴿١٥٧﴾﴾ [البقرة: ١٥٥-١٥٧]

﴿And certainly, We shall test you with something of fear, hunger, loss of wealth, lives and crops, but give glad tidings to the *ṣâbireen* [the patient and steadfast ones], who when afflicted with calamity, say: Truly, to Allah we belong and to Him we shall return. They are those on whom are the blessings [and forgiveness] from Allah, and [they are those who] receive His mercy, and it is they who are the guided ones.﴾

(Qur'an 2: 155-157)

2. Patience at the inclination of evil. This type of patience includes self-control, forbearance by containing one's anger, and the acceptance of one's situation. If bad habits are added to desire or passion, things can really get out of control. To restrain oneself

---

82 Al-Ghazâli, *The Book of Religious Learning*

from sinful deeds, a person must practice patience. Prophet Muhammad (ﷺ) said: «A *mujâhid* (one who strives in Allah's cause) is one who engages in jihad against his own self in obeying Allah (ﷻ), and a *muhâjir* (immigrant) is one who migrates from all crimes and sins.» (al-Albâni graded it as sound)

This type of patience includes patience in the face of people's offences, with forgiveness and forbearance. Prophet Muhammad (ﷺ) instructed us to have patience with other people: «Join the ties with one who severs them from you, give charity to the one who deprives you, and forgive the one who oppresses you.» (al-Albâni graded it as sound)

This is a high degree of patience that requires a lot of training and self-control, but it is true nourishment for the soul and a way to enlightenment and self-purification.

3. Patience, or forbearance, in experiencing pleasure and happiness. When people feel very comfortable and enjoy physical health, safety, property, wealth and the admiration of others, they might throw themselves into these worldly comforts and possessions without control, failing to remember either the source of their blessings or the ultimate purpose of their creation. According to Muslim scholars, this kind of patience is more difficult to practice than the other two types.

Allah (ﷻ) says:

﴿إِنَّمَآ أَمْوَٰلُكُمْ وَأَوْلَـٰدُكُمْ فِتْنَةٌ ۚ وَٱللَّهُ عِندَهُۥٓ أَجْرٌ عَظِيمٌ ﴿١٥﴾﴾

[التغابن : ١٥]

﴾Your wealth and your children are only a trial, whereas Allah, with Him is a great reward [in paradise].﴿ *(Qur'an 64: 15)*

Material possessions are tests that require us to exercise patience in order to prevent them from controlling our lives and to keep us from becoming enslaved by our desires. Again, we are reminded of the importance of detachment. Patience is an essential requirement to keep us detached from worldly passions. Enjoy your youth, your wealth and your children, but do not get too attached to any of them. Do not let them distract you from your true mission in life.

Epilogue

Reading about Islamic history gives us insight into how one person can change the world, how one person's true sincerity can make all the difference. The story of Shaykh 'Abdullah ibn Yaseen is a typical example.[83] You may never have heard of this great man — I only recently did, and I was utterly amazed by his willpower, dedication, commitment and strength. The story begins around 1048 CE (440 AH) in the deep Saharan desert of northwestern Africa, in what is now the country of Senegal.

Among the most powerful Berber groups in the area were the Sanhaja tribes. These tribes had embraced Islam, but over time, they had drifted away from its teachings. They drank alcohol, committed adultery, cheated, stole and fought with each other. The only thing they knew from Islam was the testimony of faith, but they applied none of its meaning to their lives. Yaḥyâ ibn Ibrâheem was the chief of one of the biggest Sanhaja tribes. Although he was a good man with a pure uncorrupted nature, he too was ignorant of the teachings of Islam and thus stood helpless before the corruption in his land.

Trying to seek a solution for the problems plaguing his people, Yaḥyâ decided to perform the hajj pilgrimage to Makkah. On his way back home, he stopped to attend the lessons at the mosque of al-Qayrawân, an important centre of Islamic learning, located in what is today the country of Tunisia. At that time, al-Qayrawân was one of the greatest Muslim cities in North Africa.

---

83 As-Sarjâni

Yaḥyâ learned there that the problem of his people lay in their ignorance of the religion that they professed to espouse. To address this dilemma, one of the scholars of al-Qayrawân, Shaykh 'Abdullah ibn Yaseen, agreed to go to the Sanhaja tribes with Yaḥyâ.

'Abdullah ibn Yaseen was a well-known religious intellectual who had students from all over North Africa. He lived in one of the biggest and most civilized cities of the time, and he enjoyed a great reputation and a great deal of prestige. Still, he decided to put all this aside and travel into the Great Desert to teach the Berber tribes about Islam.

Time passed, with Ibn Yaseen trying his best to preach Islam and correct the ways of the people, but to no avail. As is the case with many reformers, his teaching was rejected, and he was forced to leave the tribes after threats of physical harm.

Still, Ibn Yaseen did not give up. Although he could have just returned to his country, where many students would willingly have come to benefit from his knowledge, he chose the role that most would flee from. He chose the harder road; he chose to stay to lead people to the right path. Ibn Yaseen retired to a deserted region in the Sahara, in the northern part of Senegal. He built a tent there, then sent word to the Sanhaja tribes informing them of his location and telling them that whoever was interested in learning his religion and reaching Allah's straight path could join him there. His invitation appealed to five of the Berber's youth, who soon joined him. This seemingly humble step was the start of what would be the great dynasty of the Moors or Almoravids (known in Arabic as the *Murâbiṭoon*), as we will soon see.

Shaykh 'Abdullah ibn Yaseen taught his followers strict obedience to the Qur'an and the Sunnah of the Prophet (ﷺ), and he enforced a regular system of discipline, justice and organization. He taught them how to apply Islam's teachings to their everyday lives, how to live as true Muslims. He taught them ethics and moral values, along with responsibility, self-discipline and self-reliance.

It did not take long for his students to advance to be scholars and preachers themselves. These students felt a responsibility to spread their knowledge first among their friends and relatives. They went back to their homes and returned with new students, and the cycle continued. Soon one tent was not enough; they added a second, then a third and a fourth. Their number was steadily on the rise, and their organization was getting stronger and sturdier, spreading Islam to the Berber areas of the Sahara and to the African tribes south of the desert. Under Ibn Yaseen's direction, this group, which would be called the Almoravids, began to thrive.

Ibn Yaseen was eventually martyred during an expedition to bring some of the African tribes in line with the Almoravids. He died after eleven years of real struggle for the cause of Islam. At the time of his death, the Almoravids' number had already reached twelve thousand real Muslims who followed and applied the teachings of the Qur'an and Sunnah.

The Almoravid dynasty, which was started by one man's vision, sincerity and dedication, helped spread Islam to most of northern Africa, including the present-day countries of Morocco, the Western Sahara, Mauritania, Gibraltar, Tunisia, Algeria, a great part of what is now Senegal and Mali in the south, and Spain and Portugal to the north.

As this story and many others like it illustrate, you should never underestimate the power of one person. Never underestimate your power! A vision can only be changed to reality when it finds someone to make it his or her true vocation. Such a person then inspires others to find their callings as well. Dreams are realized when they are aligned with your beliefs and convictions and when they are surrendered to the divine will. Thus your vision or dream is as powerful as you want it to be.

This book does not offer a magic recipe for eternal happiness, optimal health or unlimited prosperity. It is a practical prescription for satisfaction in life while seeking the pleasure of Allah (ﷻ). It presents a realistic view of life and helps you recognize the important things, the things that really matter, and thus enables you to set your priorities straight.

We are all in a continuous quest for happiness and health, love and success, and this is exactly what we can find by following our True Secret. By being sincere to Allah (ﷻ) in everything that we say and do, by re-evaluating our intention before considering any life choices — even the smallest, seemingly unimportant ones — we can attain our worldly happiness as well as our eternal bliss.

As I mentioned earlier, being sincere is not always an easy task. It requires patience, continuous practice and lots of help. I hope that you have already gotten your journal and started setting your goals and devising some plans. If not, please start now. Get your notebook and start your journey. Remember that the ultimate goal of all Muslims is to attain the pleasure of Allah (ﷻ), and then define suitable long-term and short-term goals for yourself.

At the same time, work with the helping tools presented in Chapter III: your acts of worship, supplications, dhikr, meditations, social support, family ties, and heart purification tools such as love and detachment. Evaluate your intention and sincerity, and renew your intention each morning and each night before you go to bed.

Be certain that you can make a difference in your life and in the life of our whole Muslim Ummah. Just be sincere in your intention.

Almighty Allah (ﷻ) told His Messenger to say:

﴿أَنَّمَآ إِلَٰهُكُمْ إِلَٰهٌ وَٰحِدٌ فَمَن كَانَ يَرْجُواْ لِقَآءَ رَبِّهِۦ فَلْيَعْمَلْ عَمَلًا صَٰلِحًا وَلَا يُشْرِكْ بِعِبَادَةِ رَبِّهِۦٓ أَحَدًۢا ﴿١١٠﴾﴾ [الكهف: ١١٠]

﴾It has been inspired to me that your God is One [Allah]. So whoever hopes for the meeting with his Lord, let him work righteousness and associate none as a partner in the worship of his Lord.﴿ *(Qur'an 18: 110)*

This fundamental concept in Islam, the true, pure and practical monotheistic faith, is repeated over and over in the Qur'an and the sayings of the Prophet Muhammad (ﷺ): «Allah (ﷻ) said: I am the One, One Who does not stand in need of a partner. If anyone does anything in which he associates anyone else with Me, I shall abandon him with the one whom he associates with Allah (ﷻ).» (Muslim)

Our dear Prophet (ﷺ) also taught us a phrase of dhikr to protect our sincerity:

اللهم انا نعوذ بك من ان نشرك بك شيئا نعلمه و نستغفرك لما لا نعلمه

«O Allah! We seek refuge with You from associating in Your worship any partner that we are aware of, and we ask Your forgiveness for what we are not aware of.» (al-Mundhiri; al-Albâni said it is sound)

Finally, I want to end with the beautiful words that 'Umar ibn al-Khaṭṭâb (ﷺ) said upon entering Jerusalem: "*Allah has honoured you with Islam. If you seek honour elsewhere, you will be humiliated.*"[84]

[84] As-Sarjâni, R. راغب السرجاني. n.d. http://www.islamstory.com

References

Hadith References

Abu Dâwood, Sulaymân as-Sijistâni. *Sunan Abu Dâwood.*

al-Albâni, Muḥammad Nâṣir ad-Deen. *As-Silsilah as-Ṣaḥeeḥah.*

al-Bayhaqi, Aḥmad Ḥusayn. *As-Sunan al-Kubrâ.*

al-Bukhari, Muḥammad Ismâ'eel. *Ṣaḥeeḥ al-Bukhâri.*

al-Ḥâkim, Muḥammad 'Abdullah. *Al-Mustadrak 'alâ aṣ-Ṣaḥeeḥayn.*

Ibn Ḥanbal, Aḥmad Muḥammad. *Musnad Imâm Aḥmad ibn Ḥanbal.*

Ibn Ḥibbân, Abu Ḥâtim Muḥammad. *Ṣaḥeeḥ ibn Ḥibbân.*

Ibn Mâjah, Muḥammad ibn Yazeed. *Sunan ibn Mâjah.*

al-Mundhiri, Zaki ad-Deen 'Abdul 'Adheem. *At-Targheeb wat-Tarheeb.*

Muslim, Abul-Ḥasan ibn al-Ḥajjâj. *Ṣaḥeeḥ Muslim.*

an-Nasâ'i, Aḥmad ibn Shu'ayb. *Sunan an-Nasâ'i.*

at-Tirmidhi, Muḥammad 'Eesâ. *Al-Jâmi' aṣ-Ṣaḥeeḥ.*

Sources in English

Baldwin, Christina. *Storycatcher: Making Sense of Our Lives through the Power and Practice of Stories*. Novato, CA, USA: New World Library, 2005.

Cameron, Julia. *The Artist's Way*. London: Pan Books, 1995.

Carter-Scott, Cherie. *If Life is a Game, These are the Rules*, export ed. New York: Broadway Books, 1999.

Chopra, Deepak. *Quantum Healing: Exploring the Frontiers of Mind/Body Medicine*. New York: Bantam, 1990.

Conwell, Russell H. "Acres of Diamonds." http://www.temple.edu/about/Acres_of_Diamonds.htm (accessed 2009).

Covey, Stephen R. *The 7 Habits of Highly Effective Families*. London: Simon & Schuster, 1999.

De Bono, Edward. *Teach Yourself to Think*. UK: Penguin Books, 1996.

Doane, Darryl and Sloat, Rose D. *Stories They Will Remember*. Massachusetts, USA: Human Resource Development Press, 2005.

Dyer, Wayne W. *You'll See It When You Believe It*. Arrow Books, 1990.

Al-Ghazali, A.M. *The Book of Religious Learning*, vols. I to IV. Trans. F. Karim. Delhi: Islamic Book Service, 2001.

Ibn Katheer, Ismâ'eel. *Stories of the Prophets*. Trans. Husain Maqbool. KSA: International Islamic Publishing House, 2006.

Miller, Emmett E. *Deep Healing: the Essence of Mind/Body Medicine*, 6th printing. USA: Hay House, 2004.

al-Mubarakpuri, Safi-ur-Rahman. *The Sealed Nectar: Biography of the Noble Prophet*. Riyadh: Maktaba Darussalâm, 1995.

Pepper, Dennis. *The Oxford Book of Animal Stories*. London: Oxford, 1994.

al-Qahtâni, Sa'eed 'Ali Wahf. *Fortification of the Muslim: Supplications from the Qur'an and Sunnah*. Cairo: Darussalam, 2004.

Radin, Dean. *Entangled Minds*. New York: Paraview Pocket Books, 2006.

Sallâbi, Ali. M. *'Umar ibn al-Khaṭṭâb: His Life and Times*, vols. 1 & 2. Trans. Nasiruddin al-Khattab. Riyadh: International Islamic Publishing House, 2007.

Santrock, John W. *Psychology 7*, 7th ed. USA: McGraw Hill Companies, 2003.

Schnebly, Lee. *Nurturing Yourself and Others*. Cambridge, MA, USA: Da Capo Press, 2000.

Seligman, Martin. *Authentic Happiness*. London: Nicholas Brealey Publishing, 2005.

Seymour, John and Martin Shervington. *Peak Performance through NLP*. Dorling Kindersley, 2001.

Sher, Barbara. *Wishcraft*, 2nd ed. New York: Ballantine Books, 2004.

as-Sibâ'ie, Mustafâ. *The Life of Prophet Muhammad: Highlights and Lessons*, 2nd English ed. Trans. Nasiruddin al-Khattab. Riyadh: International Islamic Publishing House, 2005.

Subordinate Courts of Singapore. "Vanilla Ice Cream That Puzzled General Motors!" http://app.ejustice.gov.sg/blogs/our_blog/archive/2007/04/19/new-post.aspx (accessed December 2007).

Wikipedia: The Free Encyclopedia. "Arthur Ashe." http://en.wikipedia.org/wiki/Arthur_Ashe (accessed December 2007).

Winston, Robert. *The Human Mind: And How to Make the Most of It*. Bantam Books, 2004.

Zarabozo, Jamaal al-Din. *Purification of the Soul: Concept, Process and Means*. Denver, USA: Al-Basheer, 2002.

Source in French

Solé, Robert. *Le Tarbouche*. France: Editions du Seuil, 1992.

Sources in Arabic

'Abd al-Kâfi, O. (د. عمر عبد الكافي) هذا ديننا. [This is Our Religion]. (Audio recordings) UAE: Markaz ash-Shareet al-Islâmi, 2005 & 2006.

Abu al-'Aṭṭâ, N. K. (نظمي خليل ابو العطا) . المعجزات التربوية لعمر بن عبد العزيز [The Educational Miracles of 'Umar ibn 'Abdul-'Azeez]. Egypt: Dâr as-Salâm, 2005.

al-Ghazâli, A. M. (ابو حامد محمد الغزالي). احياء علوم الدين [The Revival of Religious Knowledge]. Beirut: Dâr al-Ma'rifah, 2004.

al-Ghazali, M. (محمد الغزالي). خلق المسلم [A Muslim's Manners]. Cairo: Dar ar-Rayân lith-Tharât, 1987.

——. جدد حياتك [Renew your life]. 5th ed. Cairo: Nahḍat Miṣr, 2003.

——. الجانب العاطفي من الاسلام [The Emotional Side of Islam]. Egypt: Dâr ash-Shurook, 2006.

al-Jawziyah, Ibn al-Qayyim. (شمس الدين ابن قيم الجوزية) مفتاح دار السعادة [The Key to the House of Happiness]. Beirut: al-Maktabah al-'Aṣriyah, 2003.

Khaled, A. (عمرو خالد). فعل الخير من مجموعة: فاستبقوا الخيرات [Good Deeds: So Hasten Towards All That is Good]. (Tape recording). Cairo: Dâr al-Balâgh, 2003a.

——. عبادات المؤمن [The Worshiping Acts of the Believer]. Cairo: 'Areej, 2003b.

al-Qaraḍâwi, Y. (يوسف القرضاوي). التوكل [Surrender to the Divine Will]. Cairo: ar-Risâlah, 2001.

——. *The Sunnah: A Source of Civilization,* 2nd ed. Cairo: Al-Falah Foundation, 2002.

——. النية و الاخلاص [Intention and sincerity]. 6th ed. Cairo: Wahbah, 2006.

Quṭb, Sayyid. *In the Shade of the Qur'an*, 35th ed. Egypt: ash-Shurooq, 2005.

aṣ-Ṣâbooni, M. A. محمد علي الصابوني صفوة التفاسير. [The Best of Interpretations of the Qur'an]. Beirut: al-Maktabah al-

‘Aṣreeyah, 2005.

Ṣabri, Muḥammad Fatḥi. (محمد فتحي صبري). البيروني [Al-Birooni] Cairo: Dâr al-Fikr al-‘Arabi, 1997.

Sallâbi, Ali. M. (علي محمد محمد الصلابي). التاريخ الاسلامي [Islamic history]. Cairo: Dâr at-Tawzee‘ wan-Nashr al-Islâmiyah, 2006.

as-Sarjâni, R. راغب السرجاني. n.d. http://www.islamstory.com

——. الموسوعة الميسرة في التاريخ الاسلامي [The Simplified Encyclopaedia of Islamic History]. Cairo: Iqrâ’, 2005.

——. http://www.islamstory.com [last accessed in June 2010]

‘Ulwan, ‘Abdullah. *Islam, the Law of Life*. Egypt: Dâr as-Salâm, 2003.

Glossary of Islamic Terms*

abu (or abi)	ابو ، ابي	father (of)
alḥamdulillâh	الحمد لله	All praise is for Allah
âmeen	امين	O Allah, accept our invocation; amen
dhikr Allâh	ذكر الله	Remembrance of Allah; specifically, remembering Allah through praising and supplicating to Him
Hadith (ḥadeeth)	حديث	The collected statements and actions of Prophet Muhammad (ﷺ) that with the Qur'an form the basis of Islamic law
hadith (ḥadeeth)	حديث	A statement or action of Prophet Muhammad (ﷺ) that was remembered and recorded by his Companions and followers
halal (ḥalâl)	حلال	Permitted according to Islamic law

* The Arabic words are transliterated according to the conventions of the Transliteration Chart found in this book. If a word has become part of the English language (i.e., is found in a dictionary of Standard English), that spelling is used in this book and appears first in this Glossary, with the transliterated form in brackets after it.

Hijrah	هجرة	Migration: *esp*. the migration from Makkah to Madinah by Prophet Muhammad (ﷺ) and his Companions that marks the start of the Islamic calendar
inshallah	إن شاءالله	God willing
istikhârah	استخارة	A prayer by which one seeks guidance from Allah
jihad (jihâd)	جهاد	Struggle or striving (in Allah's cause)
jinn (plural of jinni)	جن	Non-human, rational beings created by Allah from fire, often referred to as 'demons' or 'devils'; They have free will like humans: some are Muslims, others disbelievers; some are obedient to Allah, others disobedient. Satan is a jinni. Some people try to 'foretell' the future by contacting a jinni. Some disobedient jinn mislead people into thinking that they can tell them what will happen in the future, near or far, or that the jinn can provide people with riches or some sort of power.
mujâhid (pl. mujâhideen)	مجاهد	One who strives in the way of Allah; a fighter in jihad
Quraysh	قريش	The dominant tribe in Makkah at the time of the Prophet's mission; their society was based on polytheism
subḥân Allâh	سبحان الله	Glory be to Allah

Sunnah	سنة	The practice and collected sayings of Prophet Muhammad (ﷺ) that together with the Qur'an forms the basis of Islamic law
Ummah	امة	Community or nation: *usu.* used to refer to the entire global community of Muslims
zakât (*or zakâh*)	زكاة	Obligatory charity: an 'alms tax' on wealth payable by Muslims and to be distributed to other Muslims who qualify as recipients

Notes